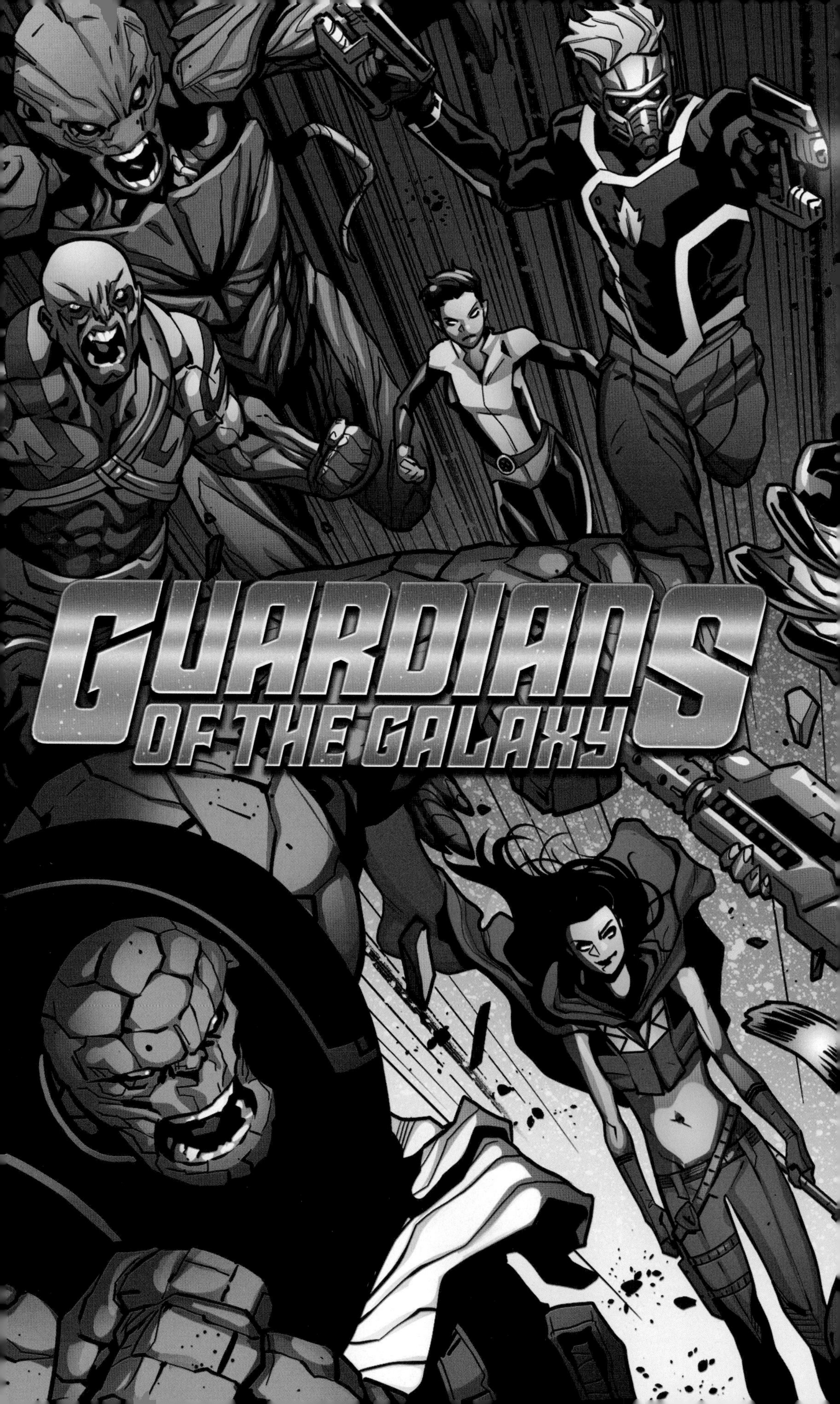
GUARDIANS
OF THE GALAXY

The entire galaxy is a mess. Warring empires and cosmic terrorists plague every corner. Someone has to rise above it all and fight for those who have no one to fight for them. A group of misfits – Drax the Destroyer, Gamora, Rocket Raccoon, Groot and Flash Thompson (a.k.a. Venom) – joined together under the leadership of Peter Quill (a.k.a. Star-Lord) to fight for those who have no one to fight for them. They serve a higher cause as the...

GUARDIANS OF THE GALAXY

In the midst of an all-out super hero battle, the Guardians lost their ship and were stranded on Earth. In the aftermath, Gamora discovered Peter had withheld the location of her enemy and estranged foster father, Thanos, who is imprisoned in the Triskelion. Enraged, the rest of the Guardians abandoned Peter...

GROUNDED

BRIAN MICHAEL BENDIS
WRITER

VALERIO SCHITI
ARTIST

RICHARD ISANOVE
COLOR ARTIST

ISSUE NO. 19 GUEST ARTISTS

PHIL NOTO
PP. 9-10

KEVIN MAGUIRE
PP. 25-26

ANDREA SORRENTINO
PP. 11-12

MARK BAGLEY & ANDREW HENNESSY
PP. 27-28

ED MCGUINNESS & MARK MORALES
PP. 17-18

SARA PICHELLI
PP. 29-30

ARTHUR ADAMS
PP. 23-24

FILIPE ANDRADE
PP. 31-32

VC's CORY PETIT
LETTERER

ARTHUR ADAMS & JASON KEITH
COVER ART

KATHLEEN WISNESKI
ASSISTANT EDITOR

DARREN SHAN
ASSOCIATE EDITOR

JORDAN D. WHITE
EDITOR

COLLECTION EDITOR: JENNIFER GRÜNWALD
ASSISTANT EDITOR: CAITLIN O'CONNELL
ASSOCIATE MANAGING EDITOR: KATERI WOODY
EDITOR, SPECIAL PROJECTS: MARK D. BEAZLEY

VP PRODUCTION & SPECIAL PROJECTS: JEFF YOUNGQUIST
SVP PRINT, SALES & MARKETING: DAVID GABRIEL
BOOK DESIGNER: ADAM DEL RE WITH JAY BOWEN

EDITOR IN CHIEF: AXEL ALONSO
CHIEF CREATIVE OFFICER: JOE QUESADA
PRESIDENT: DAN BUCKLEY
EXECUTIVE PRODUCER: ALAN FINE

GUARDIANS OF THE GALAXY: NEW GUARD VOL. 4 — GROUNDED PREMIERE. Contains material originally published in magazine form as GUARDIANS OF THE GALAXY #15-19. First printing 2017. ISBN# 978-1-302-90669-6. Publi by MARVEL WORLDWIDE, INC., a subsidiary of MARVEL ENTERTAINMENT, LLC. OFFICE OF PUBLICATION: 135 West 50th Street, New York, NY 10020. Copyright © 2017 MARVEL No similarity between any of the names, characters, per and/or institutions in this magazine with those of any living or dead person or institution is intended, and any such similarity which may exist is purely coincidental. Printed in the U.S.A. DAN BUCKLEY, President, Marvel Entertainment QUESADA, Chief Creative Officer; TOM BREVOORT, SVP of Publishing; DAVID BOGART, SVP of Business Affairs & Operations, Publishing & Partnership; C.B. CEBULSKI, VP of Brand Management & Development, Asia; DAVID GABRIEL, S Sales & Marketing, Publishing; JEFF YOUNGQUIST, VP of Production & Special Projects; DAN CARR, Executive Director of Publishing Technology; ALEX MORALES, Director of Publishing Operations; SUSAN CRESPI, Production Manager; LEE, Chairman Emeritus. For information regarding advertising in Marvel Comics or on Marvel.com, please contact Vit DeBellis, Integrated Sales Manager, at vdebellis@marvel.com. For Marvel subscription inquiries, please call 888-511- Manufactured between 4/28/2017 and 5/30/2017 by LSC COMMUNICATIONS INC., SALEM, VA, USA.

10 9 8 7 6 5 4 3 2 1

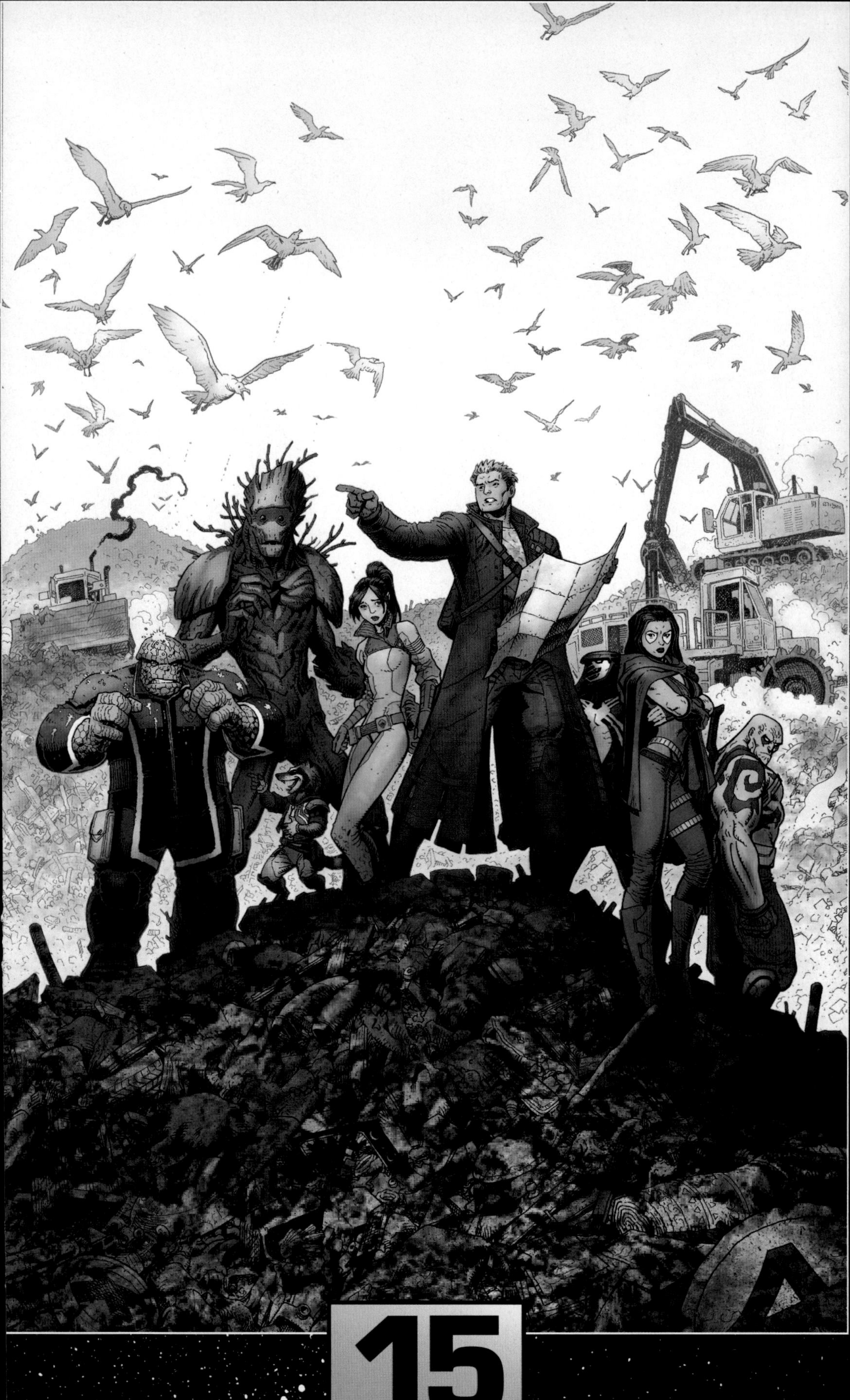

15

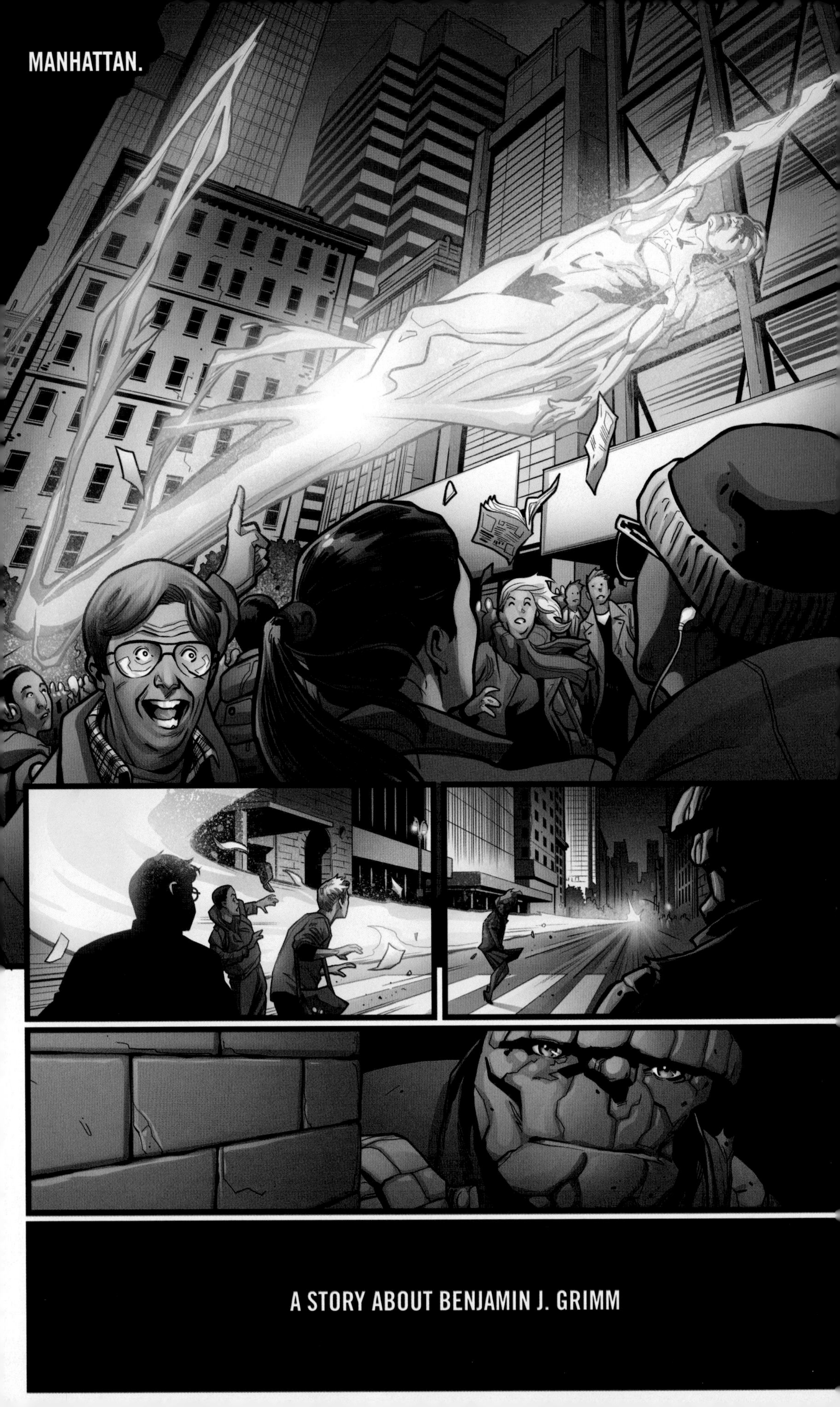
MANHATTAN.
A STORY ABOUT BENJAMIN J. GRIMM

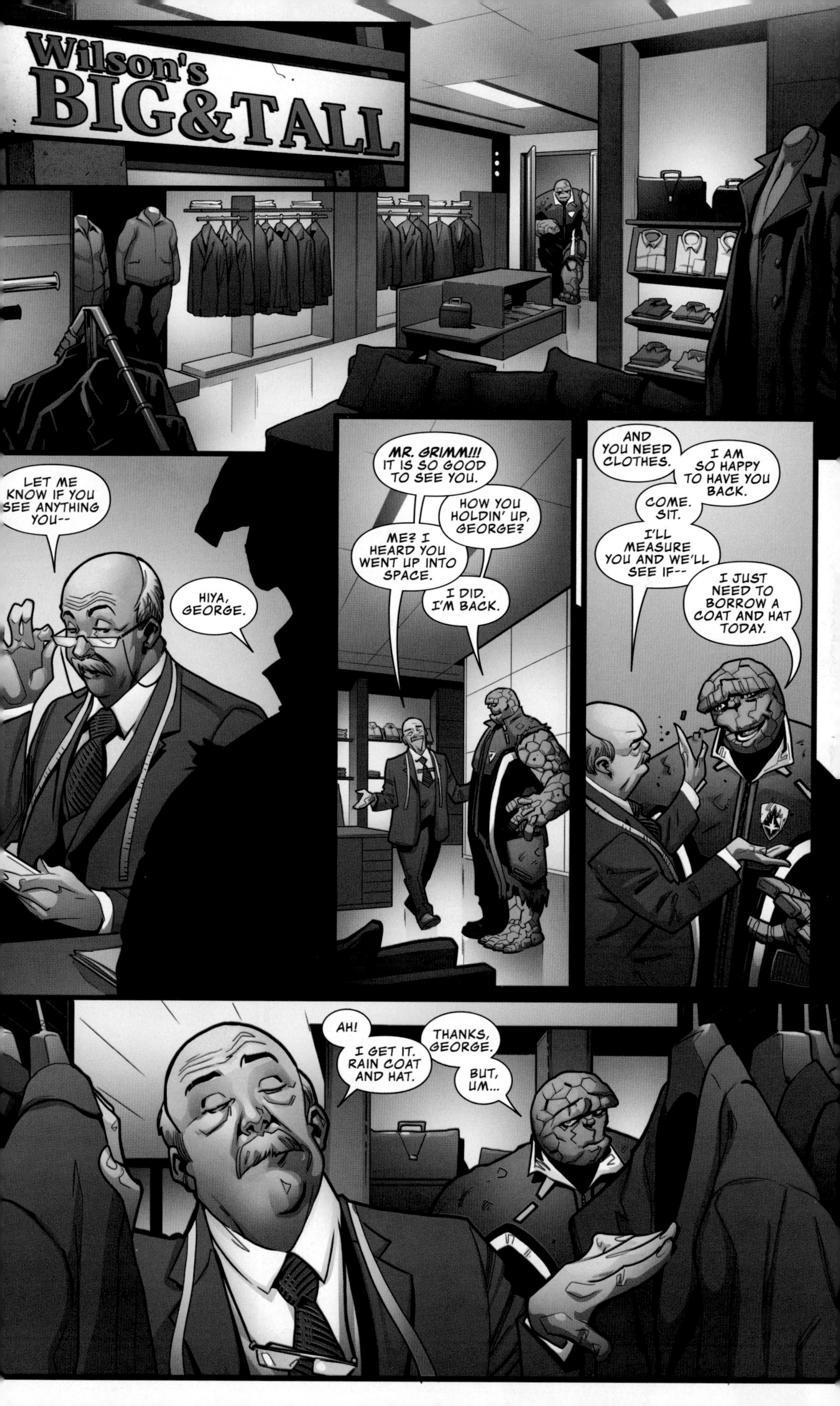

Wilson's BIG&TALL
LET ME KNOW IF YOU SEE ANYTHING YOU--
HIYA, GEORGE.
MR. GRIMM!!! IT IS SO GOOD TO SEE YOU.
HOW YOU HOLDIN' UP, GEORGE?
ME? I HEARD YOU WENT UP INTO SPACE.
I DID. I'M BACK.
AND YOU NEED CLOTHES.
I AM SO HAPPY TO HAVE YOU BACK.
COME. SIT.
I'LL MEASURE YOU AND WE'LL SEE IF--
I JUST NEED TO BORROW A COAT AND HAT TODAY.
AH!
I GET IT. RAIN COAT AND HAT.
THANKS, GEORGE.
BUT, UM...

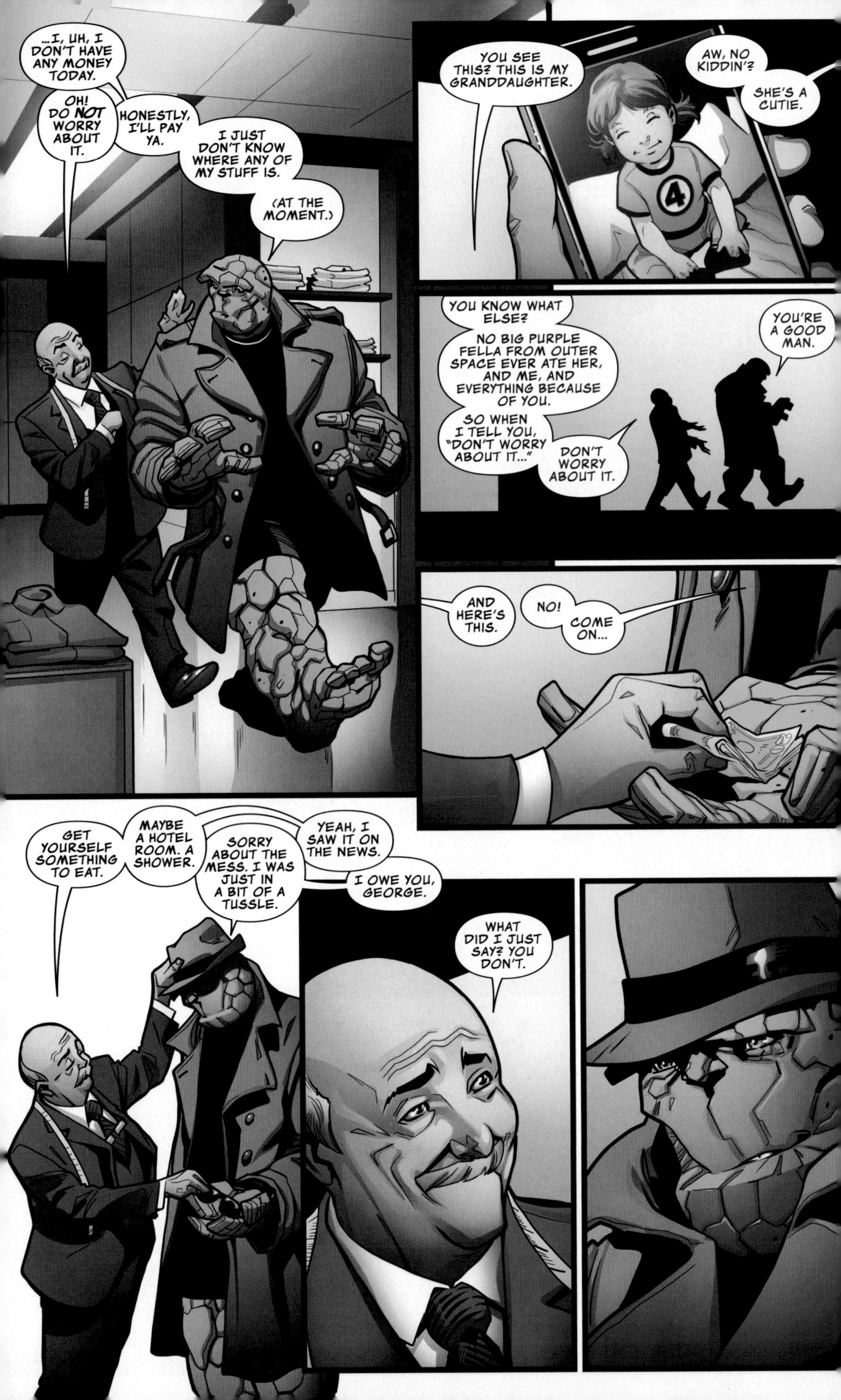
...I, UH, I DON'T HAVE ANY MONEY TODAY.
OH! DO NOT WORRY ABOUT IT.
HONESTLY, I'LL PAY YA.
I JUST DON'T KNOW WHERE ANY OF MY STUFF IS.
(AT THE MOMENT.)
YOU SEE THIS? THIS IS MY GRANDDAUGHTER.
AW, NO KIDDIN'?
SHE'S A CUTIE.
YOU KNOW WHAT ELSE?
NO BIG PURPLE FELLA FROM OUTER SPACE EVER ATE HER, AND ME, AND EVERYTHING BECAUSE OF YOU.
SO WHEN I TELL YOU, "DON'T WORRY ABOUT IT..."
DON'T WORRY ABOUT IT.
YOU'RE A GOOD MAN.
AND HERE'S THIS.
NO!
COME ON...
GET YOURSELF SOMETHING TO EAT.
MAYBE A HOTEL ROOM. A SHOWER.
SORRY ABOUT THE MESS. I WAS JUST IN A BIT OF A TUSSLE.
YEAH, I SAW IT ON THE NEWS.
I OWE YOU, GEORGE.
WHAT DID I JUST SAY? YOU DON'T.

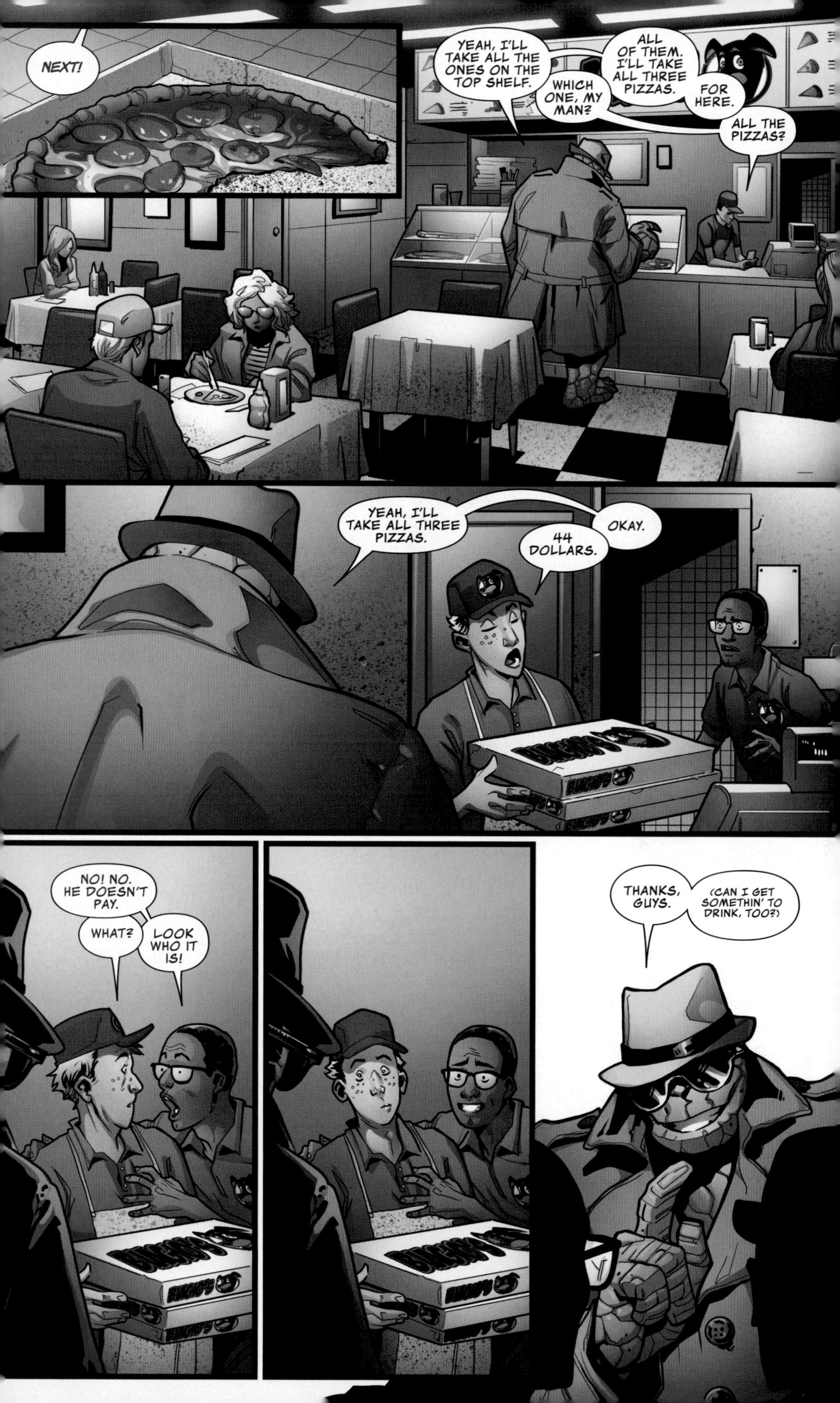
NEXT!
YEAH, I'LL TAKE ALL THE ONES ON THE TOP SHELF.
WHICH ONE, MY MAN?
ALL OF THEM. I'LL TAKE ALL THREE PIZZAS.
FOR HERE.
ALL THE PIZZAS?
YEAH, I'LL TAKE ALL THREE PIZZAS.
OKAY.
44 DOLLARS.
NO! NO. HE DOESN'T PAY.
WHAT?
LOOK WHO IT IS!
THANKS, GUYS.
(CAN I GET SOMETHIN' TO DRINK, TOO?)

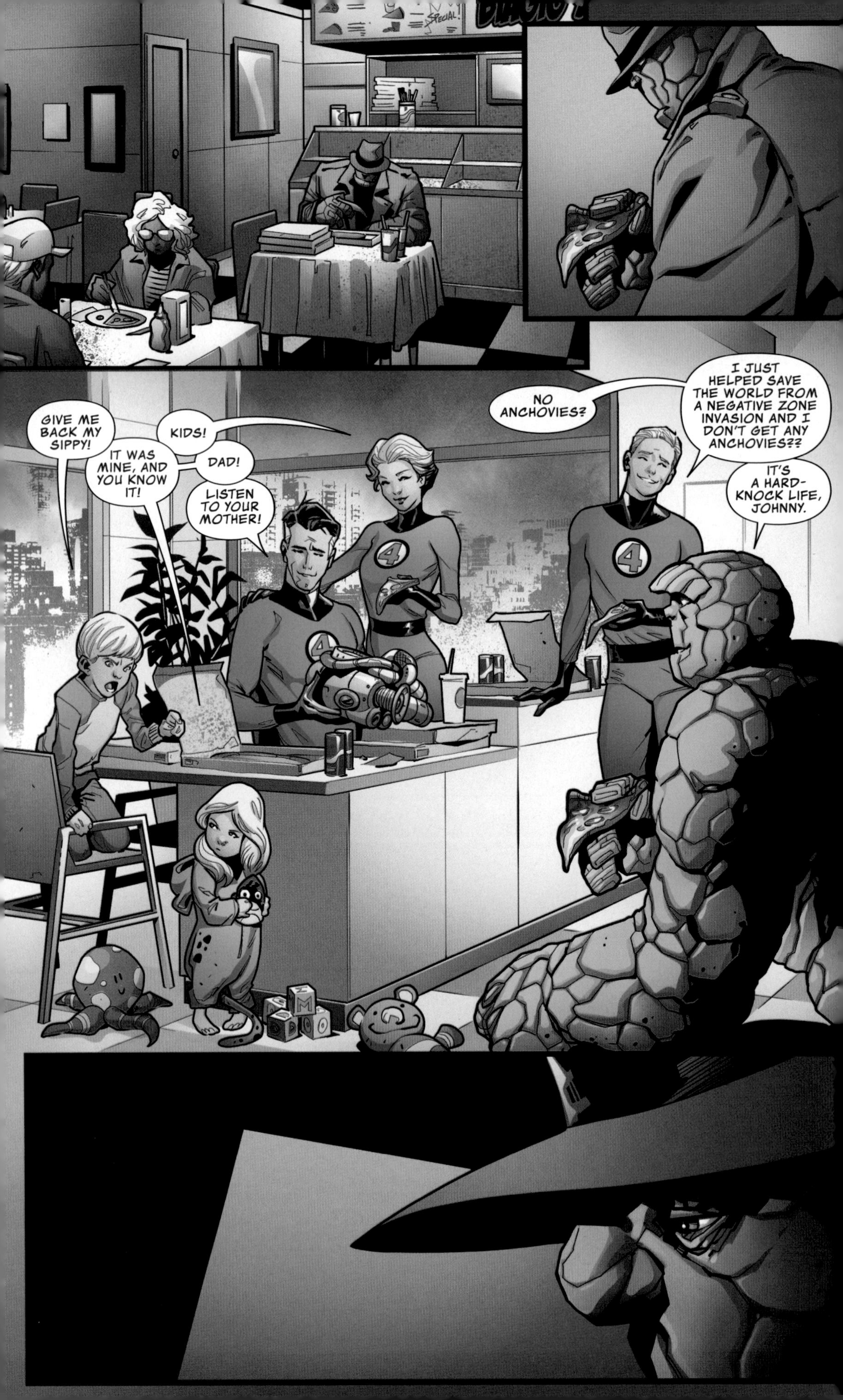

SPECIAL!
GIVE ME BACK MY SIPPY!
IT WAS MINE, AND YOU KNOW IT!
KIDS!
DAD!
LISTEN TO YOUR MOTHER!
NO ANCHOVIES?
I JUST HELPED SAVE THE WORLD FROM A NEGATIVE ZONE INVASION AND I DON'T GET ANY ANCHOVIES??
IT'S A HARD-KNOCK LIFE, JOHNNY.

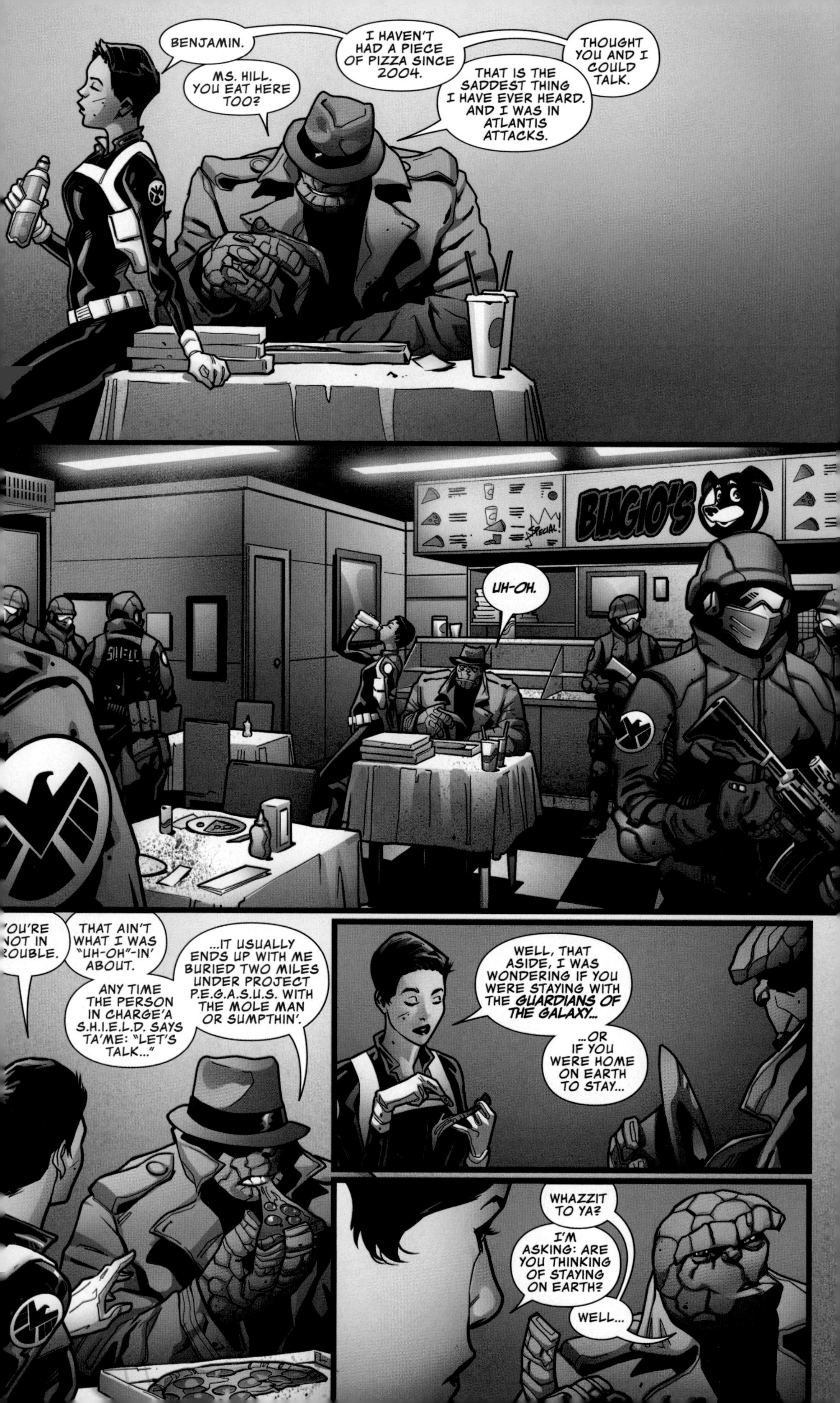
BENJAMIN.
MS. HILL. YOU EAT HERE TOO?
I HAVEN'T HAD A PIECE OF PIZZA SINCE 2004.
THAT IS THE SADDEST THING I HAVE EVER HEARD. AND I WAS IN ATLANTIS ATTACKS.
THOUGHT YOU AND I COULD TALK.
BIAGIO'S
SPECIAL!
UH-OH.
OU'RE NOT IN ROUBLE.
THAT AIN'T WHAT I WAS "UH-OH"-IN' ABOUT.
ANY TIME THE PERSON IN CHARGE'A S.H.I.E.L.D. SAYS TA'ME: "LET'S TALK..."
...IT USUALLY ENDS UP WITH ME BURIED TWO MILES UNDER PROJECT P.E.G.A.S.U.S. WITH THE MOLE MAN OR SUMPTHIN'.
WELL, THAT ASIDE, I WAS WONDERING IF YOU WERE STAYING WITH THE GUARDIANS OF THE GALAXY...
...OR IF YOU WERE HOME ON EARTH TO STAY...
WHAZZIT TO YA?
I'M ASKING: ARE YOU THINKING OF STAYING ON EARTH?
WELL...

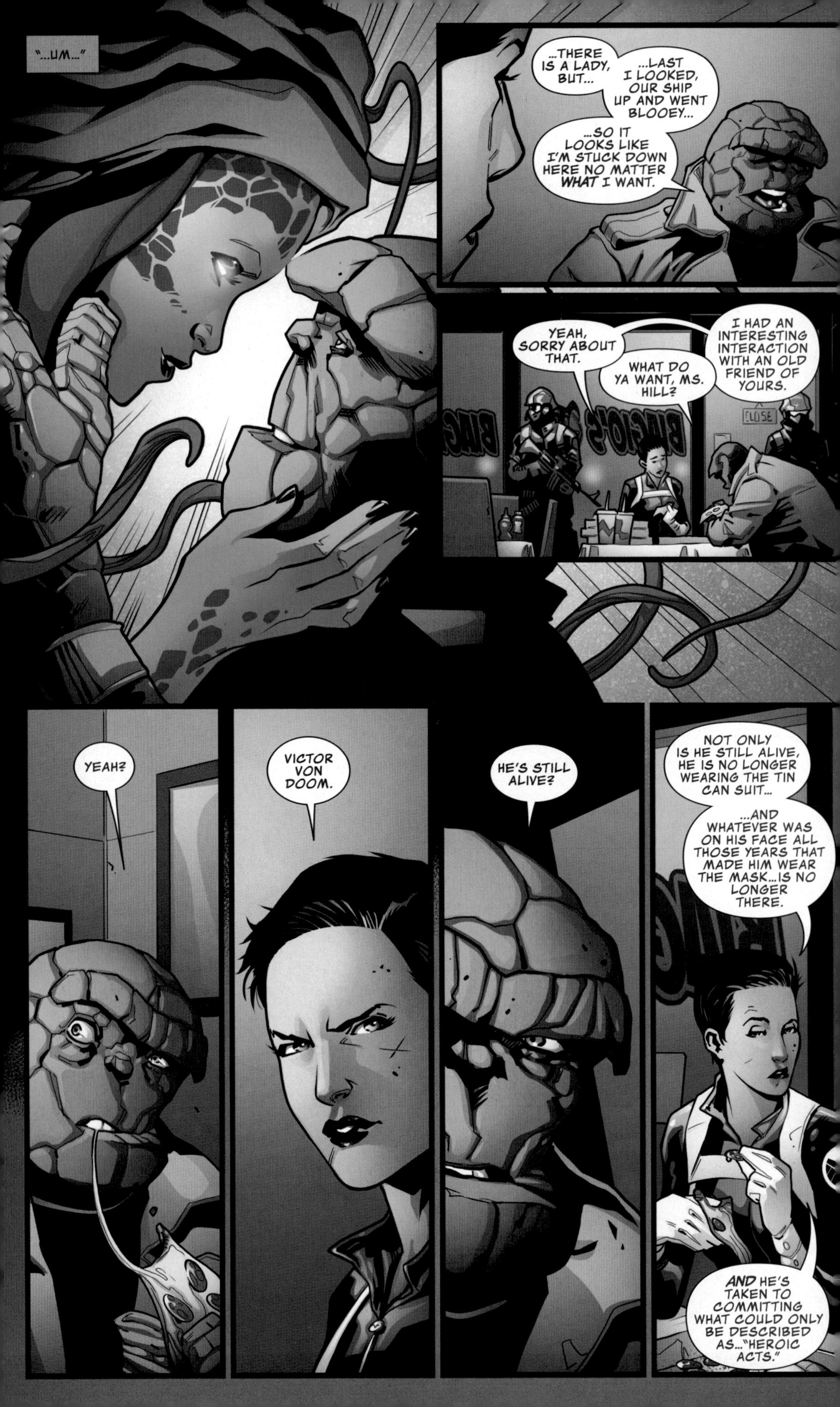
"...UM..."
...THERE IS A LADY, BUT...
...LAST I LOOKED, OUR SHIP UP AND WENT BLOOEY...
...SO IT LOOKS LIKE I'M STUCK DOWN HERE NO MATTER *WHAT* I WANT.
YEAH, SORRY ABOUT THAT.
WHAT DO YA WANT, MS. HILL?
I HAD AN INTERESTING INTERACTION WITH AN OLD FRIEND OF YOURS.
CLOSE
YEAH?
VICTOR VON DOOM.
HE'S STILL ALIVE?
NOT ONLY IS HE STILL ALIVE, HE IS NO LONGER WEARING THE TIN CAN SUIT...
...AND WHATEVER WAS ON HIS FACE ALL THOSE YEARS THAT MADE HIM WEAR THE MASK...IS NO LONGER THERE.
AND HE'S TAKEN TO COMMITTING WHAT COULD ONLY BE DESCRIBED AS..."HEROIC ACTS."

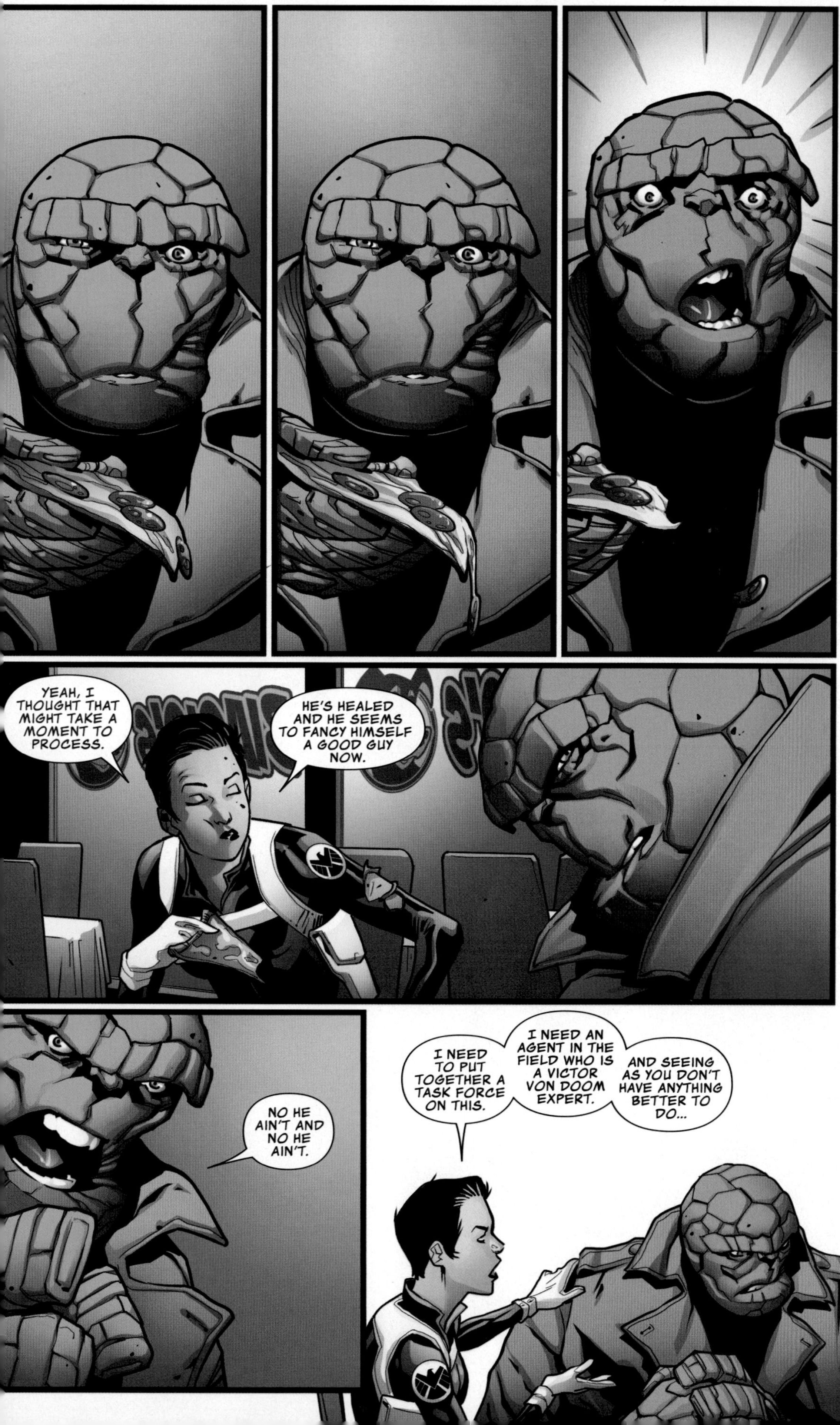
YEAH, I THOUGHT THAT MIGHT TAKE A MOMENT TO PROCESS.
HE'S HEALED AND HE SEEMS TO FANCY HIMSELF A GOOD GUY NOW.
NO HE AIN'T AND NO HE AIN'T.
I NEED TO PUT TOGETHER A TASK FORCE ON THIS.
I NEED AN AGENT IN THE FIELD WHO IS A VICTOR VON DOOM EXPERT.
AND SEEING AS YOU DON'T HAVE ANYTHING BETTER TO DO...

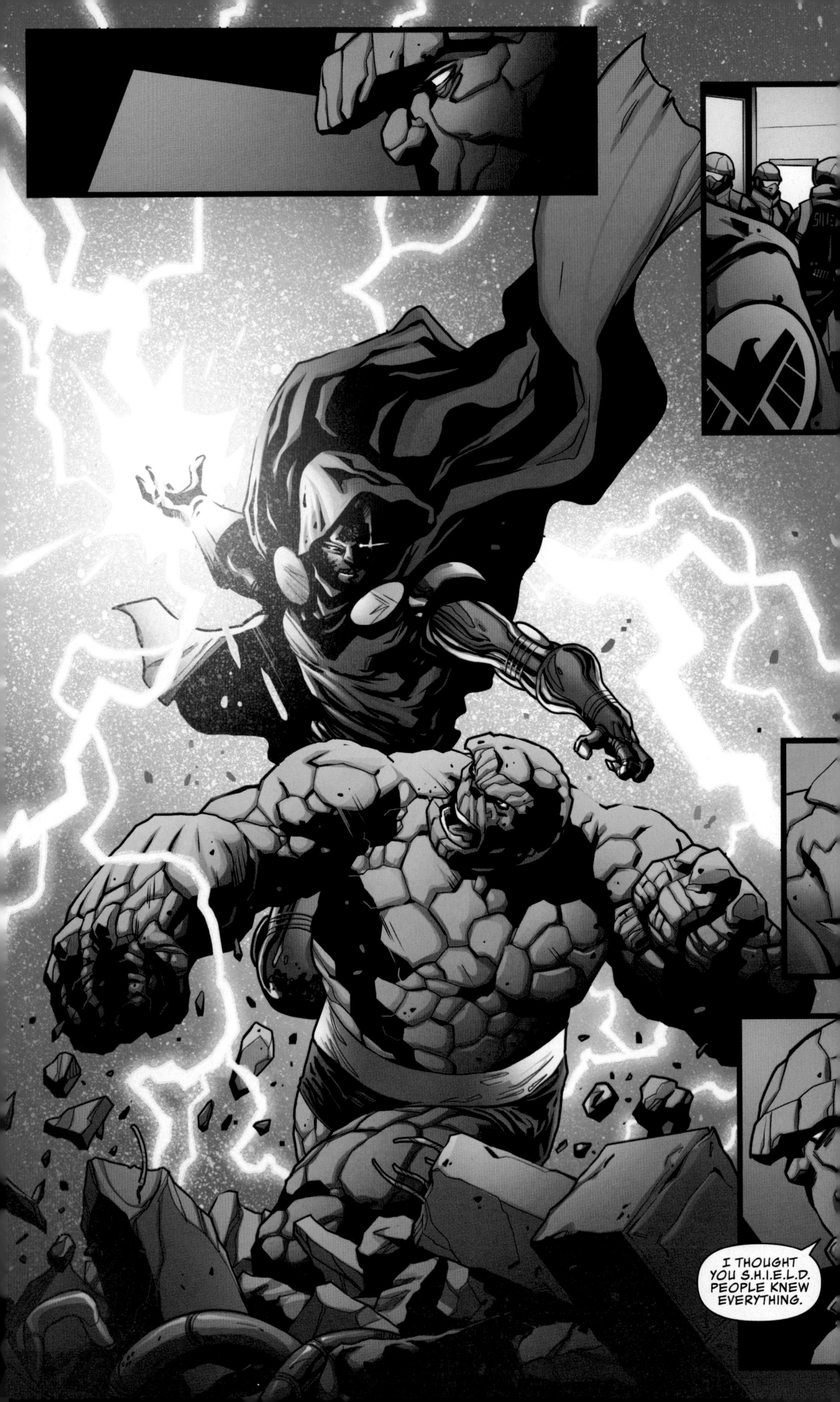
I THOUGHT YOU S.H.I.E.L.D. PEOPLE KNEW EVERYTHING.

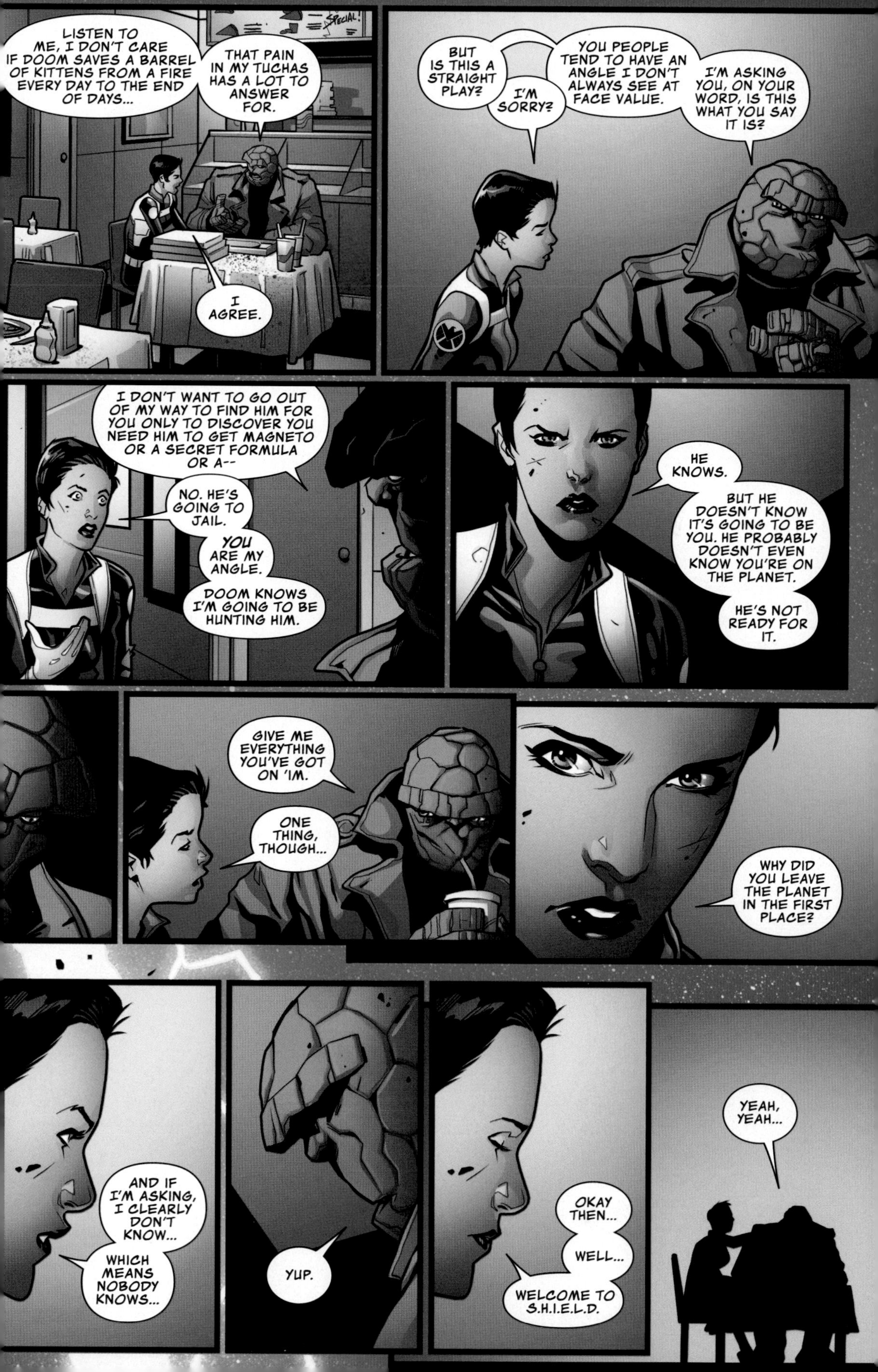
SPECIAL!
LISTEN TO ME, I DON'T CARE IF DOOM SAVES A BARREL OF KITTENS FROM A FIRE EVERY DAY TO THE END OF DAYS...
THAT PAIN IN MY TUCHAS HAS A LOT TO ANSWER FOR.
I AGREE.
BUT IS THIS A STRAIGHT PLAY?
I'M SORRY?
YOU PEOPLE TEND TO HAVE AN ANGLE I DON'T ALWAYS SEE AT FACE VALUE.
I'M ASKING YOU, ON YOUR WORD, IS THIS WHAT YOU SAY IT IS?
I DON'T WANT TO GO OUT OF MY WAY TO FIND HIM FOR YOU ONLY TO DISCOVER YOU NEED HIM TO GET MAGNETO OR A SECRET FORMULA OR A--
NO. HE'S GOING TO JAIL.
YOU ARE MY ANGLE.
DOOM KNOWS I'M GOING TO BE HUNTING HIM.
HE KNOWS.
BUT HE DOESN'T KNOW IT'S GOING TO BE YOU. HE PROBABLY DOESN'T EVEN KNOW YOU'RE ON THE PLANET.
HE'S NOT READY FOR IT.
GIVE ME EVERYTHING YOU'VE GOT ON 'IM.
ONE THING, THOUGH...
WHY DID YOU LEAVE THE PLANET IN THE FIRST PLACE?
AND IF I'M ASKING, I CLEARLY DON'T KNOW...
WHICH MEANS NOBODY KNOWS...
YUP.
OKAY THEN...
WELL...
WELCOME TO S.H.I.E.L.D.
YEAH, YEAH...

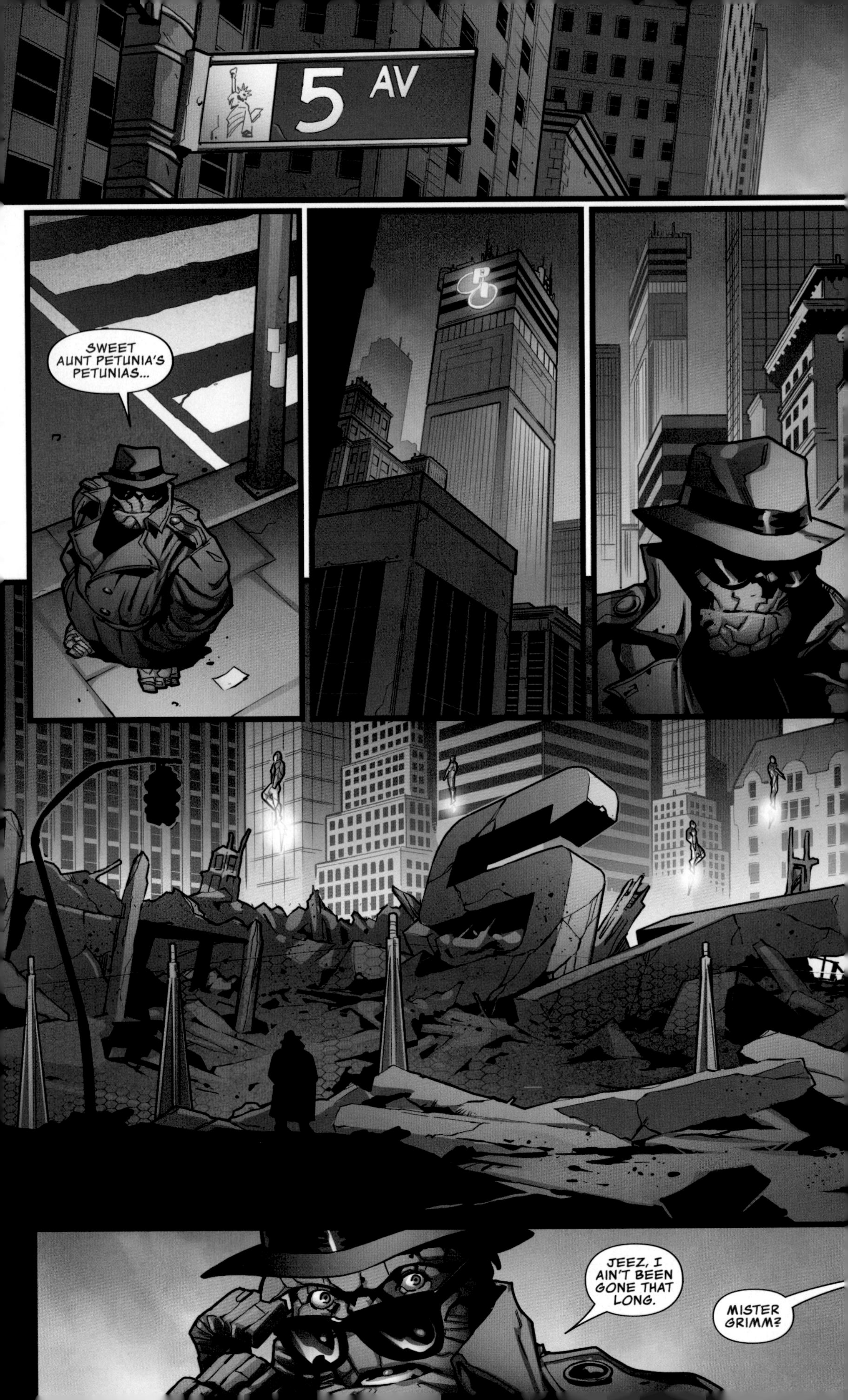
5 AV
SWEET AUNT PETUNIA'S PETUNIAS...
JEEZ, I AIN'T BEEN GONE THAT LONG.
MISTER GRIMM?

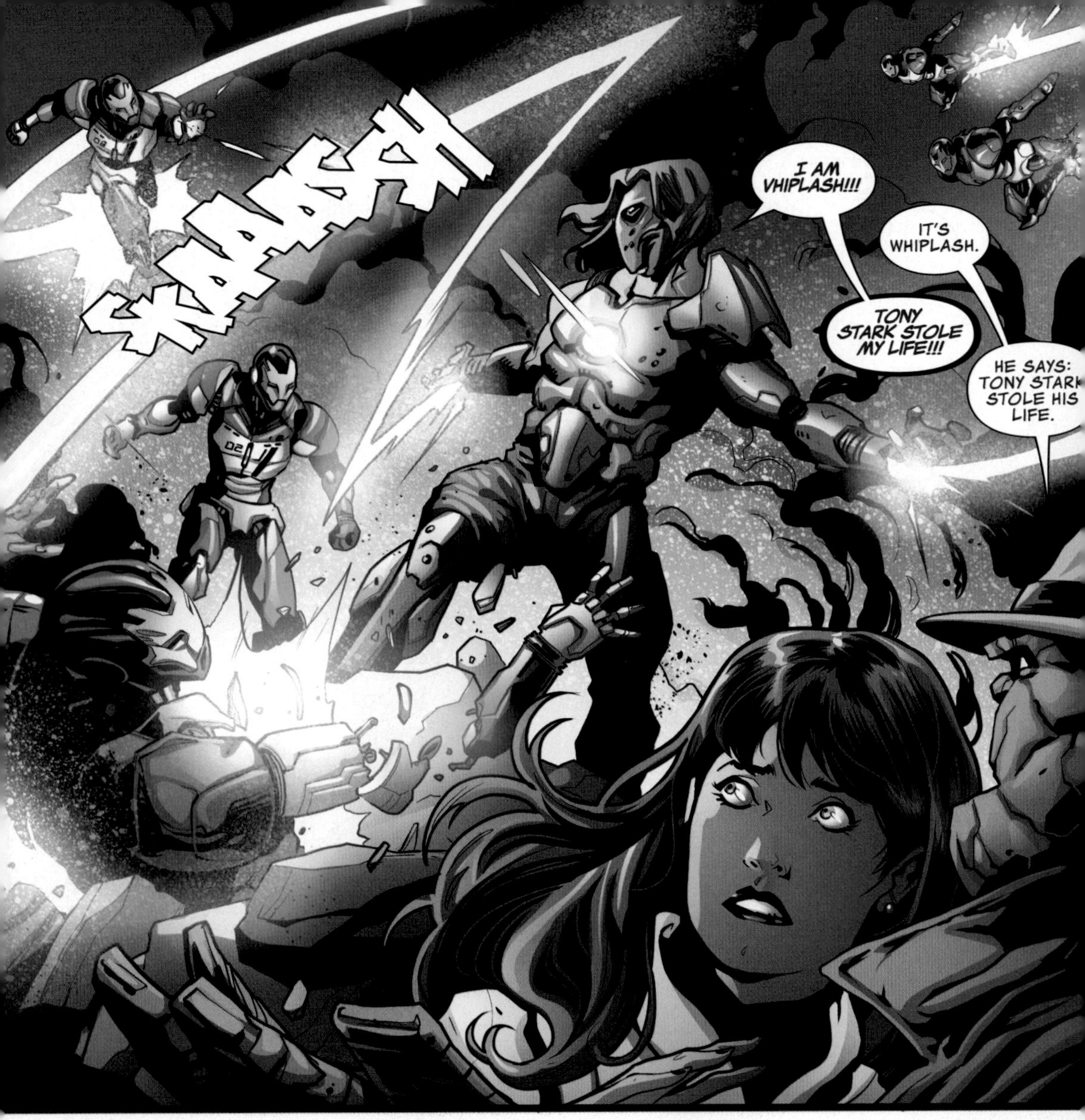
KRAAKSH
I AM VHIPLASH!!!
IT'S WHIPLASH.
TONY STARK STOLE MY LIFE!!!
HE SAYS: TONY STARK STOLE HIS LIFE.

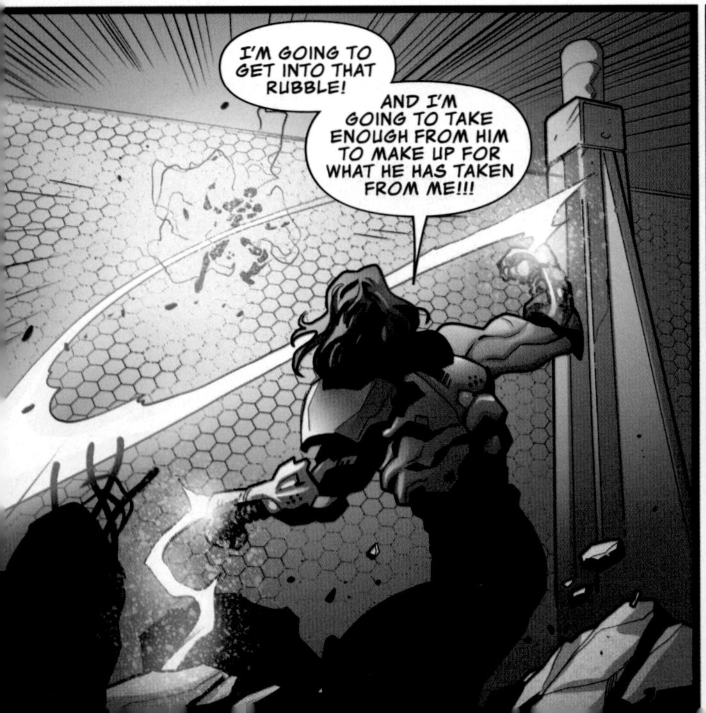
I'M GOING TO GET INTO THAT RUBBLE!
AND I'M GOING TO TAKE ENOUGH FROM HIM TO MAKE UP FOR WHAT HE HAS TAKEN FROM ME!!!

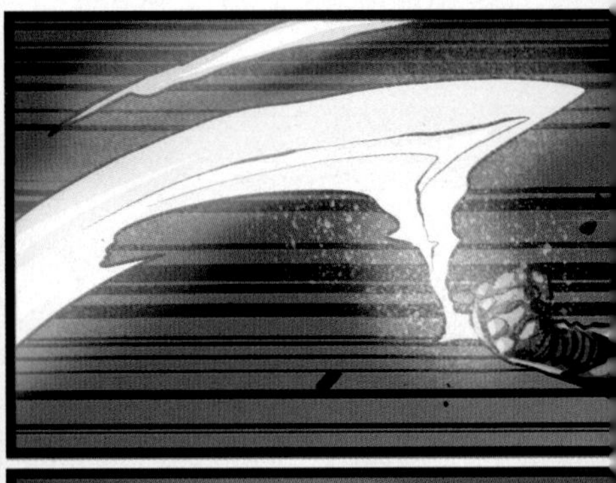

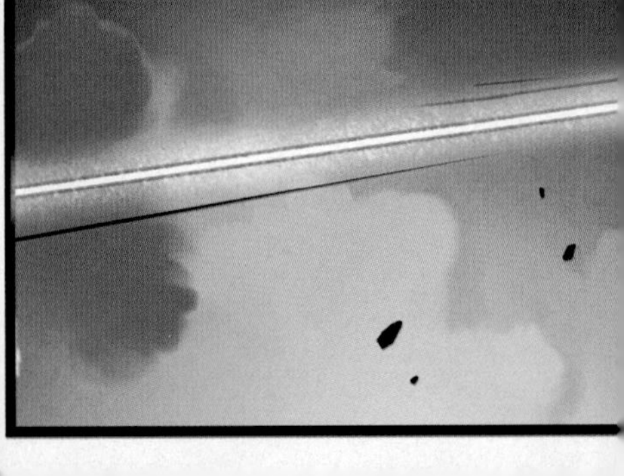

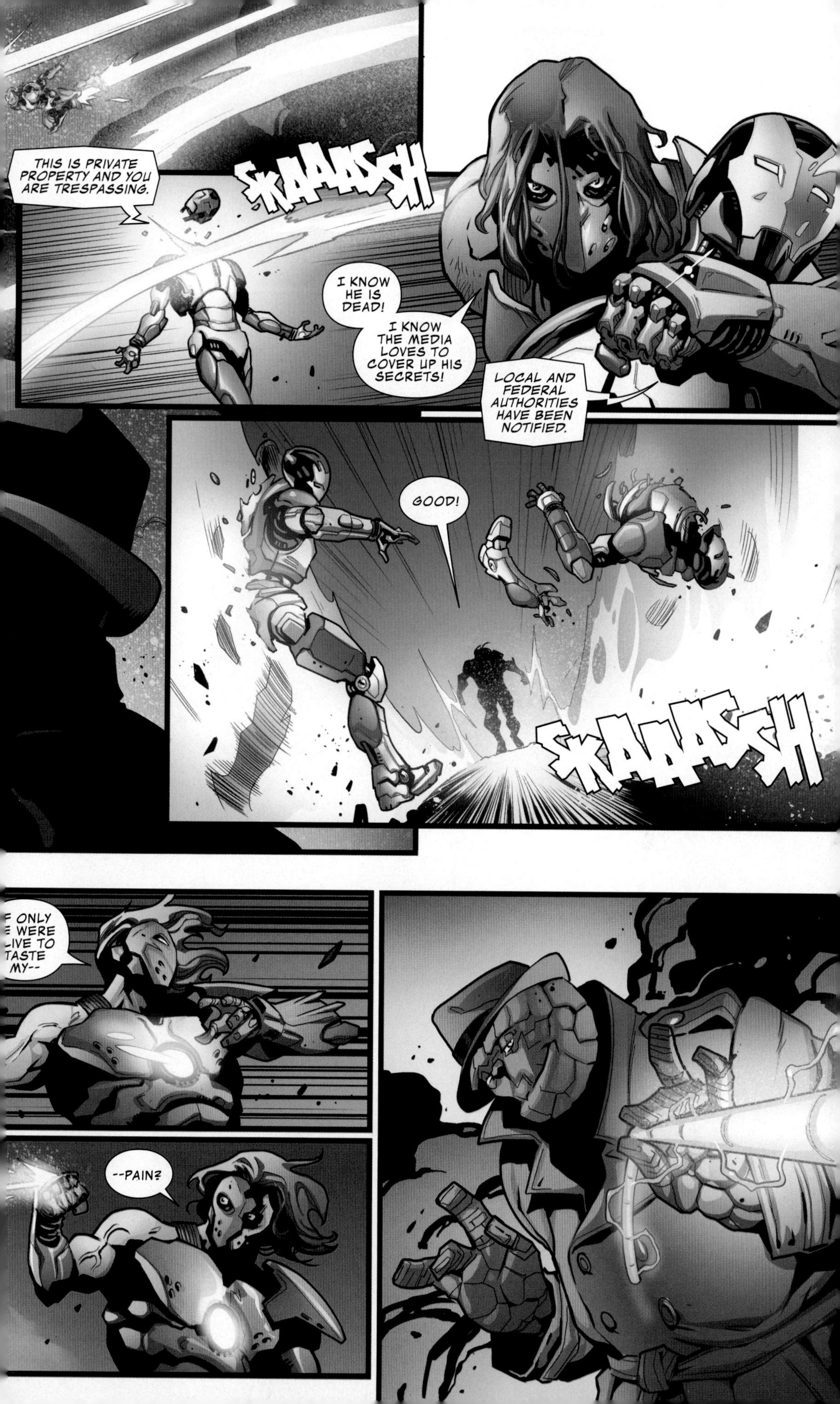
THIS IS PRIVATE PROPERTY AND YOU ARE TRESPASSING.
SKAAASSH
I KNOW HE IS DEAD!
I KNOW THE MEDIA LOVES TO COVER UP HIS SECRETS!
LOCAL AND FEDERAL AUTHORITIES HAVE BEEN NOTIFIED.
GOOD!
SKAAASSH
F ONLY E WERE LIVE TO TASTE MY--
--PAIN?

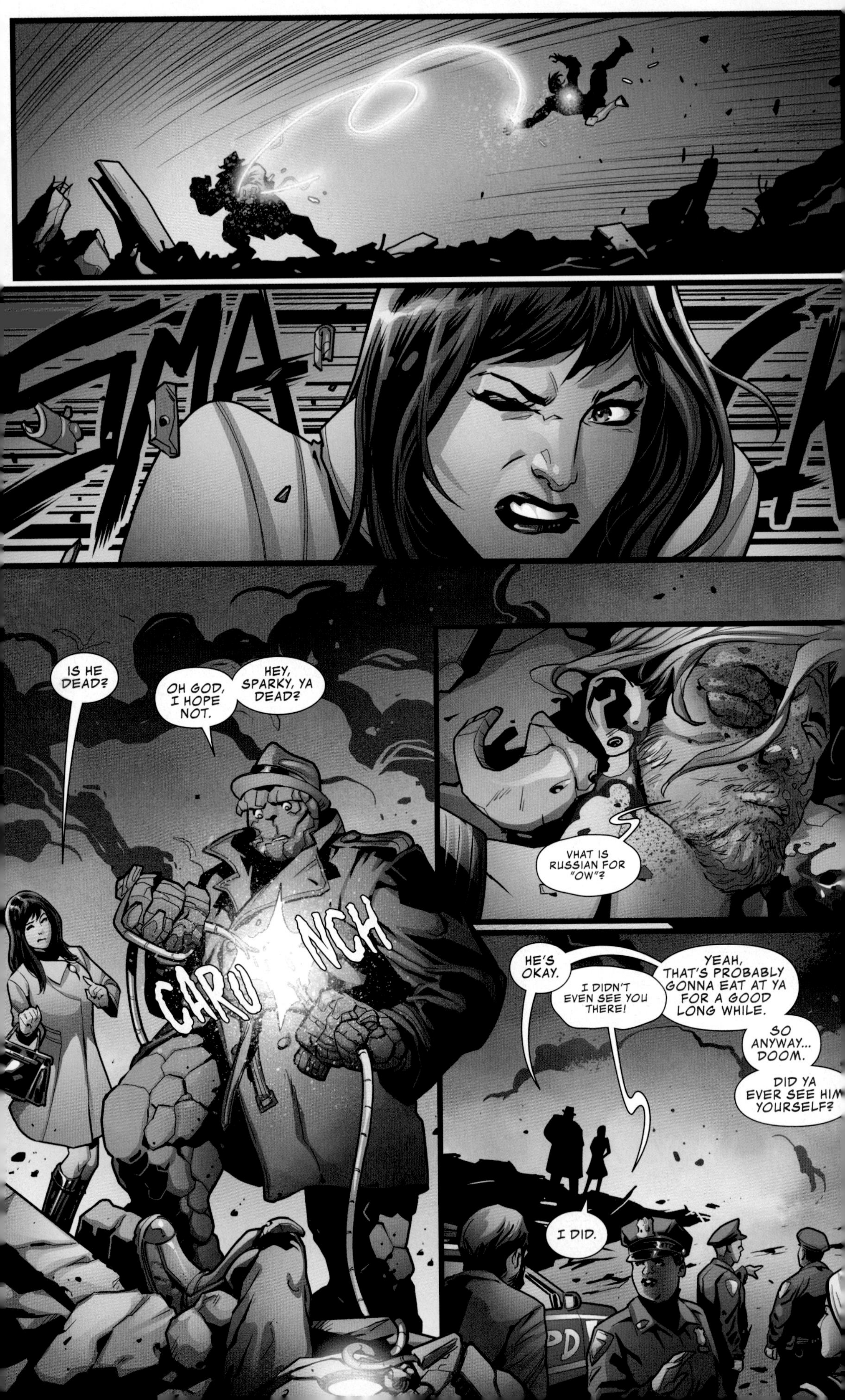

SMACK
IS HE DEAD?
OH GOD, I HOPE NOT.
HEY, SPARKY, YA DEAD?
VHAT IS RUSSIAN FOR "OW"?
CRRUNCH
HE'S OKAY.
I DIDN'T EVEN SEE YOU THERE!
YEAH, THAT'S PROBABLY GONNA EAT AT YA FOR A GOOD LONG WHILE.
SO ANYWAY... DOOM.
DID YA EVER SEE HIM YOURSELF?
I DID.

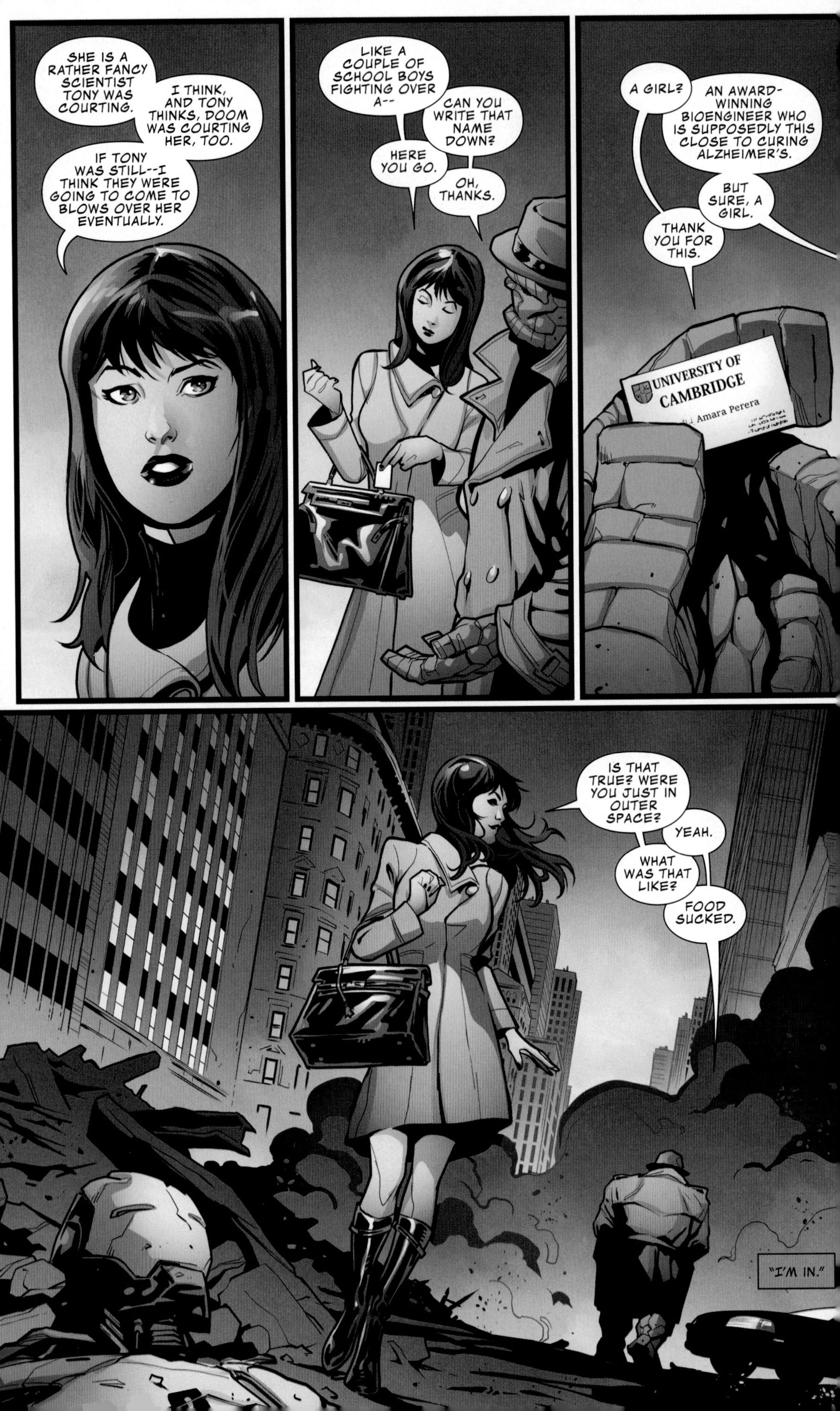

SHE IS A RATHER FANCY SCIENTIST TONY WAS COURTING.
I THINK, AND TONY THINKS, DOOM WAS COURTING HER, TOO.
IF TONY WAS STILL--I THINK THEY WERE GOING TO COME TO BLOWS OVER HER EVENTUALLY.
LIKE A COUPLE OF SCHOOL BOYS FIGHTING OVER A--
CAN YOU WRITE THAT NAME DOWN?
HERE YOU GO.
OH, THANKS.
A GIRL?
AN AWARD-WINNING BIOENGINEER WHO IS SUPPOSEDLY THIS CLOSE TO CURING ALZHEIMER'S.
BUT SURE, A GIRL.
THANK YOU FOR THIS.
UNIVERSITY OF CAMBRIDGE
Amara Perera
IS THAT TRUE? WERE YOU JUST IN OUTER SPACE?
YEAH.
WHAT WAS THAT LIKE?
FOOD SUCKED.
"I'M IN."

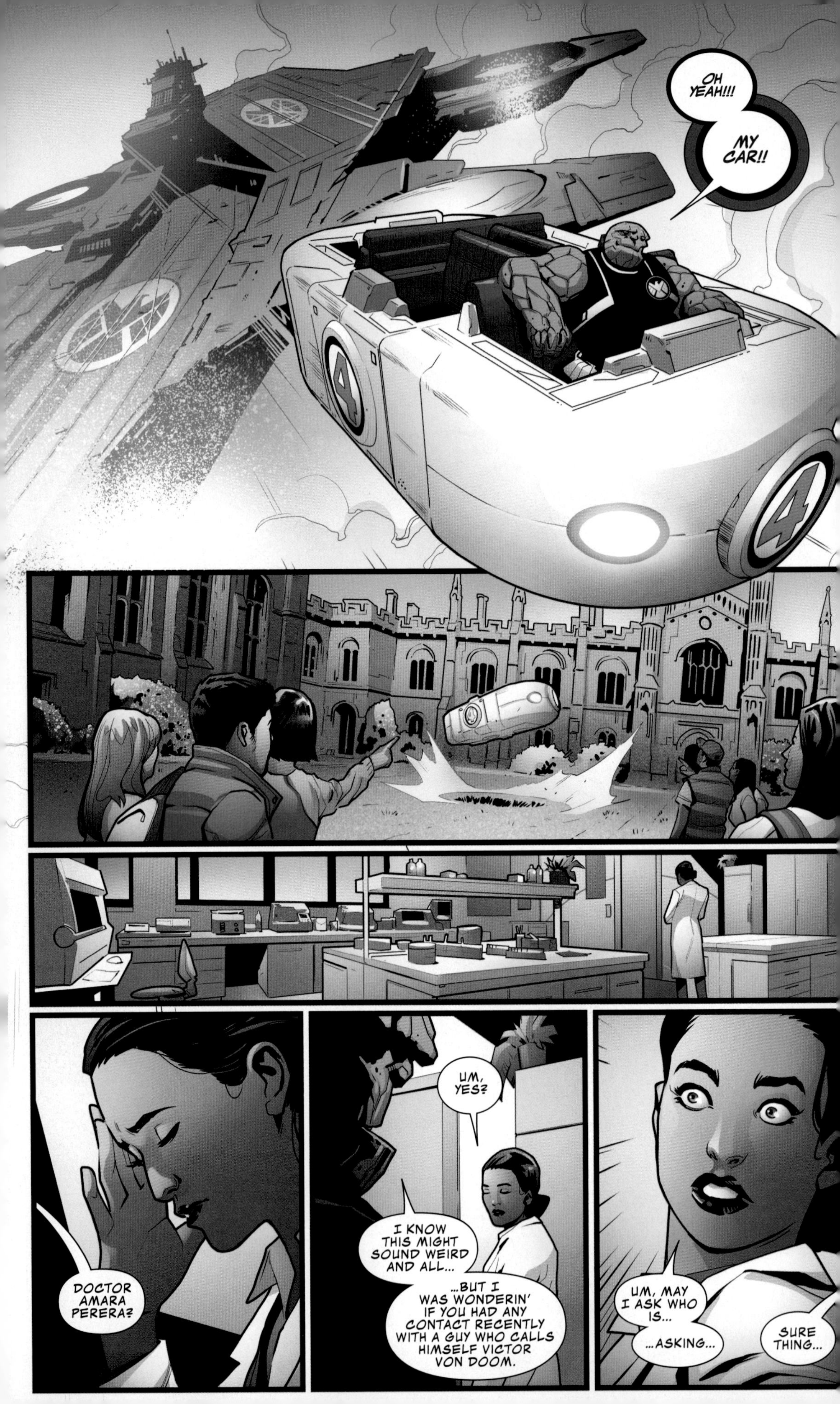
OH YEAH!!!
MY CAR!!
UM, YES?
DOCTOR AMARA PERERA?
I KNOW THIS MIGHT SOUND WEIRD AND ALL...
...BUT I WAS WONDERIN' IF YOU HAD ANY CONTACT RECENTLY WITH A GUY WHO CALLS HIMSELF VICTOR VON DOOM.
UM, MAY I ASK WHO IS...
...ASKING...
SURE THING...

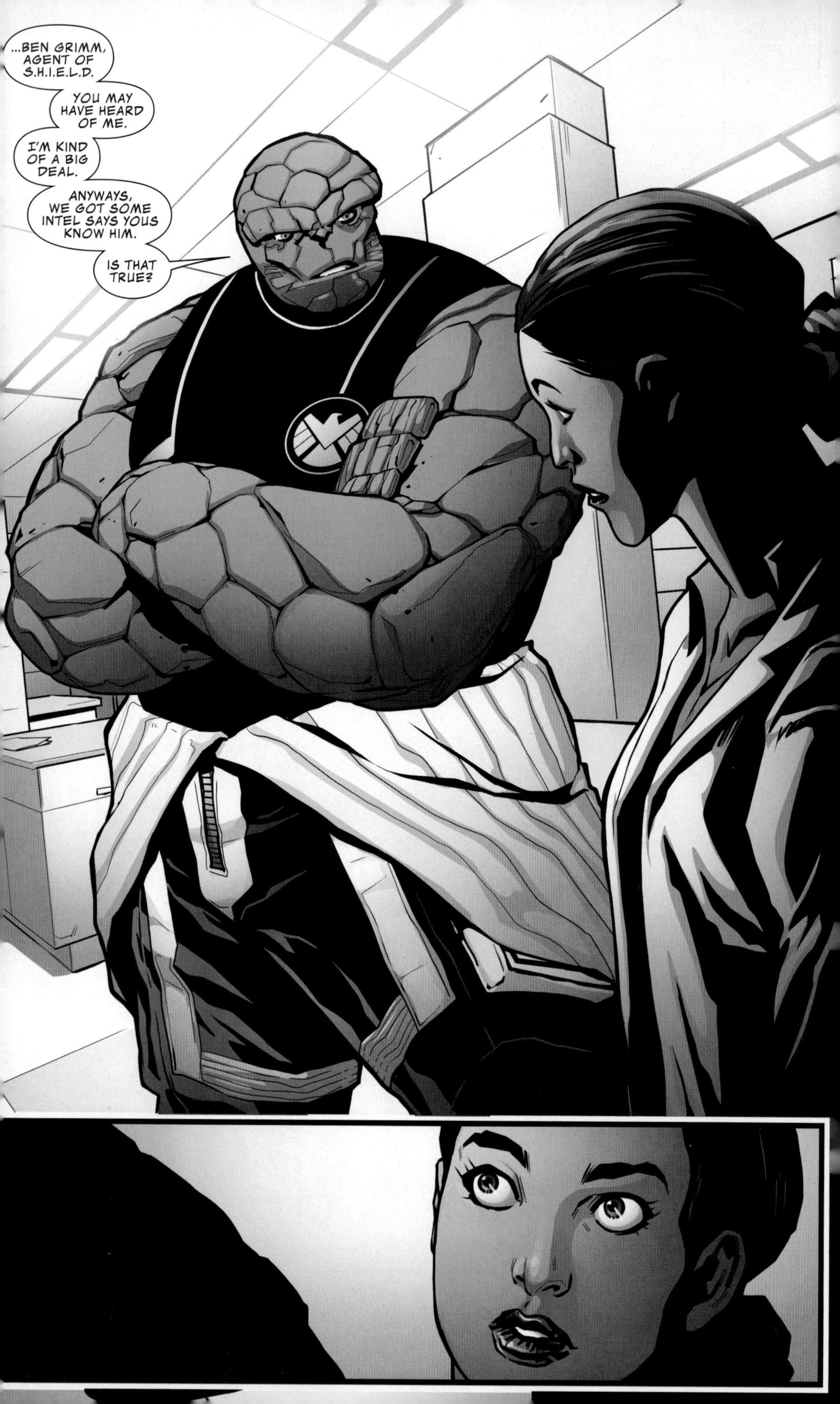
...BEN GRIMM, AGENT OF S.H.I.E.L.D.
YOU MAY HAVE HEARD OF ME.
I'M KIND OF A BIG DEAL.
ANYWAYS, WE GOT SOME INTEL SAYS YOUS KNOW HIM.
IS THAT TRUE?

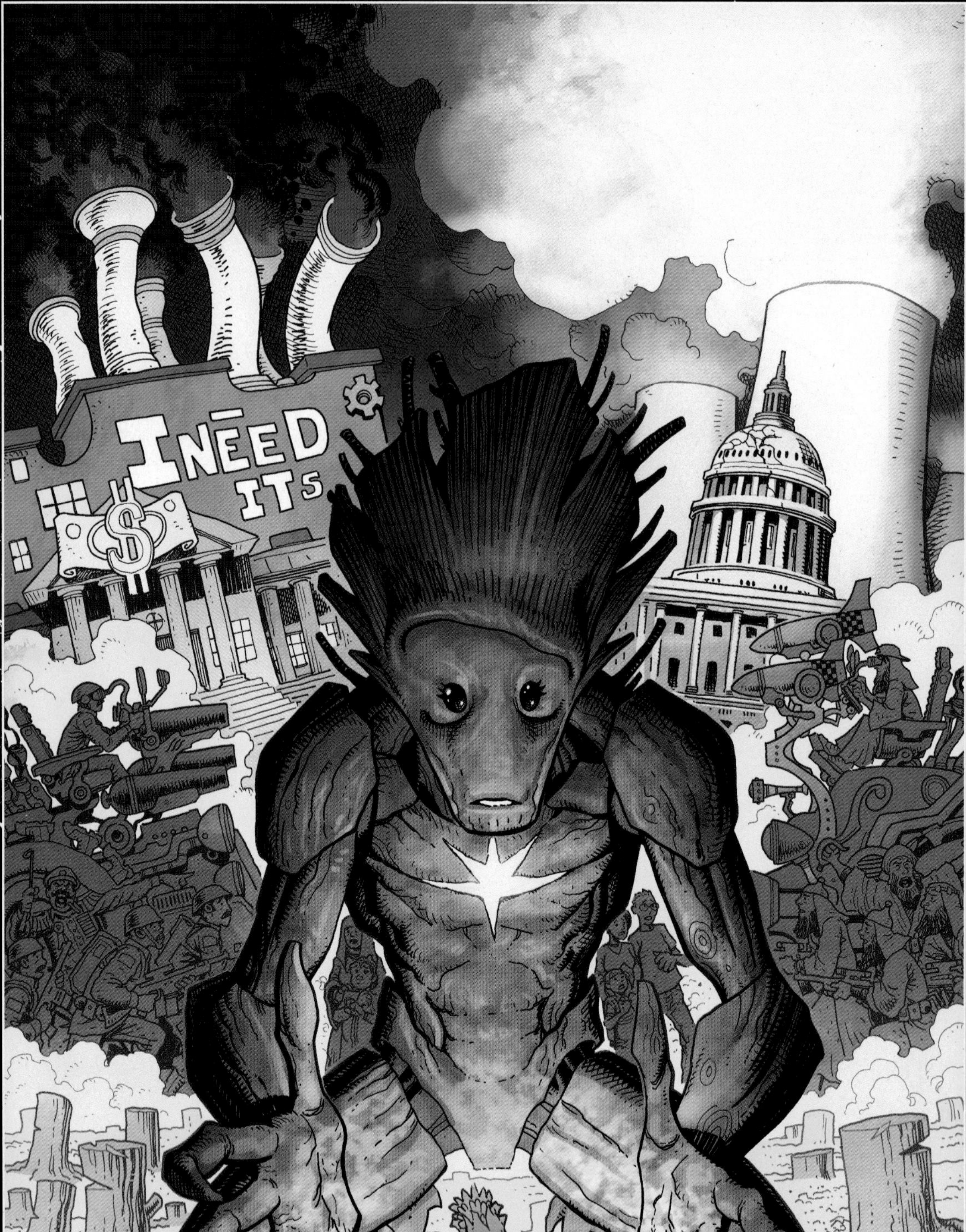
INEED
ITS
ARTHUR ADAMS
JASON!
9-20-2016

16

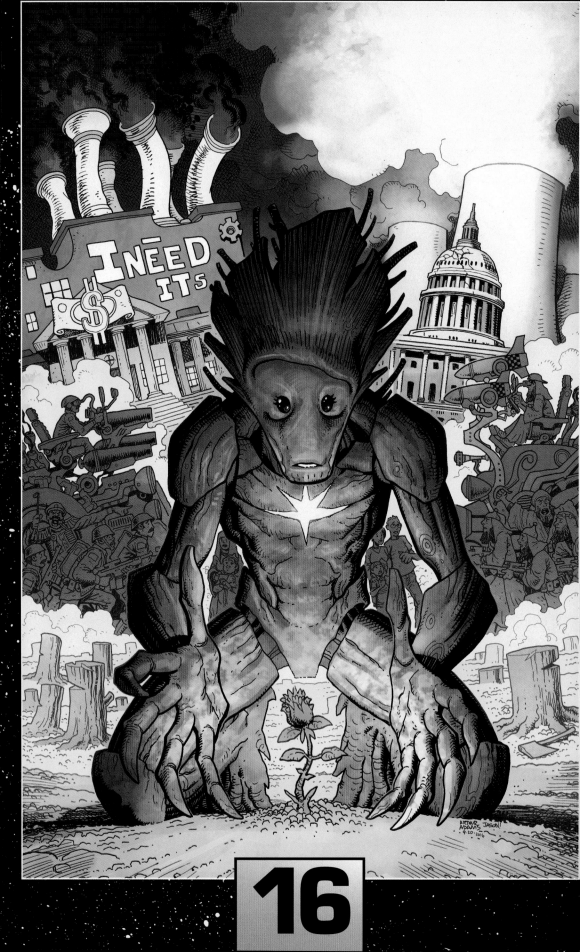

In this galaxy filled with creatures
of all shapes and sizes...

With Infinity Stones, Tesseracts,
and all kinds of prizes...

With beings as big as the massive Galactus...

And as small as a fleeb on the tip of a tiny Scarlakus...

There are millions and bazillions of creatures on one planet or another.

Some causing all kinds of trouble and some just looking for their mother.

Some look like an eyeball, and some look like a foot.

But there is only one you...

And there is only one...

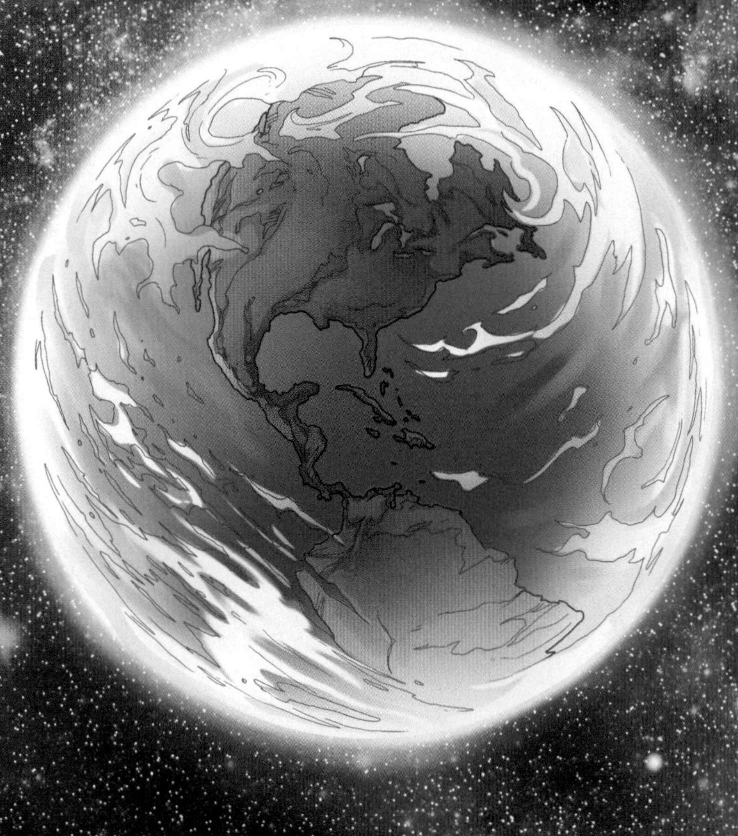

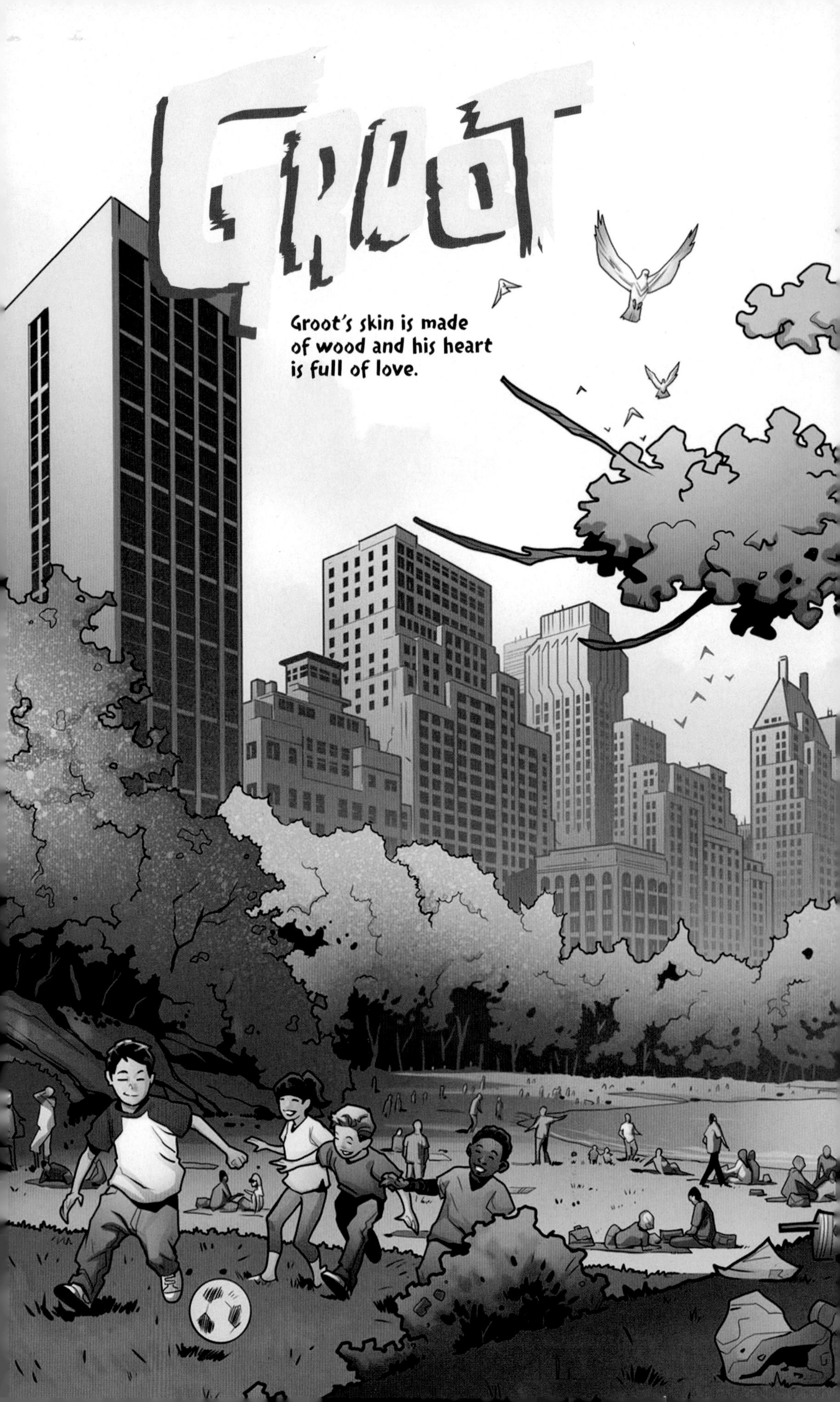
GROOT
Groot's skin is made of wood and his heart is full of love.

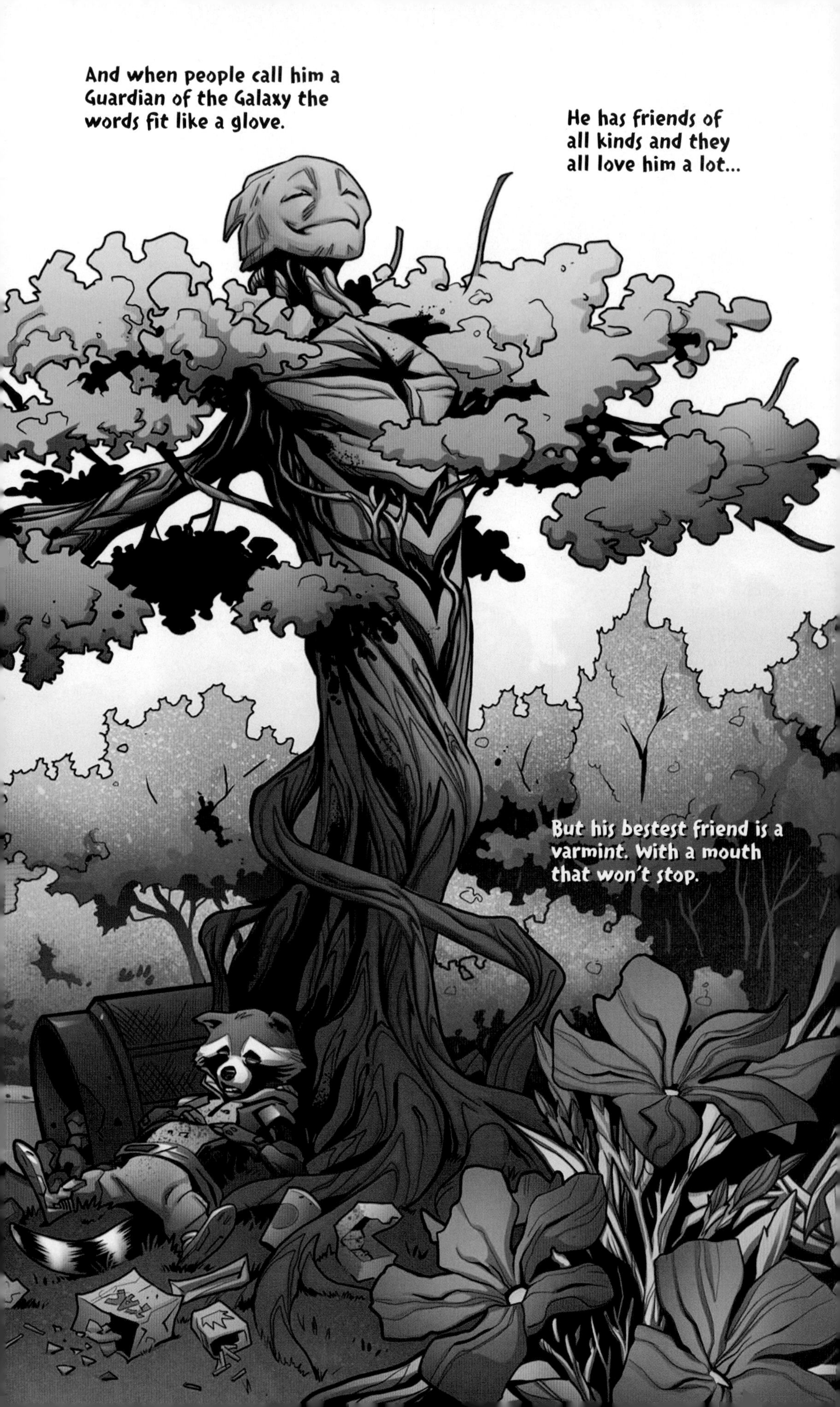
And when people call him a Guardian of the Galaxy the words fit like a glove.
He has friends of all kinds and they all love him a lot...
But his bestest friend is a varmint. With a mouth that won't stop.

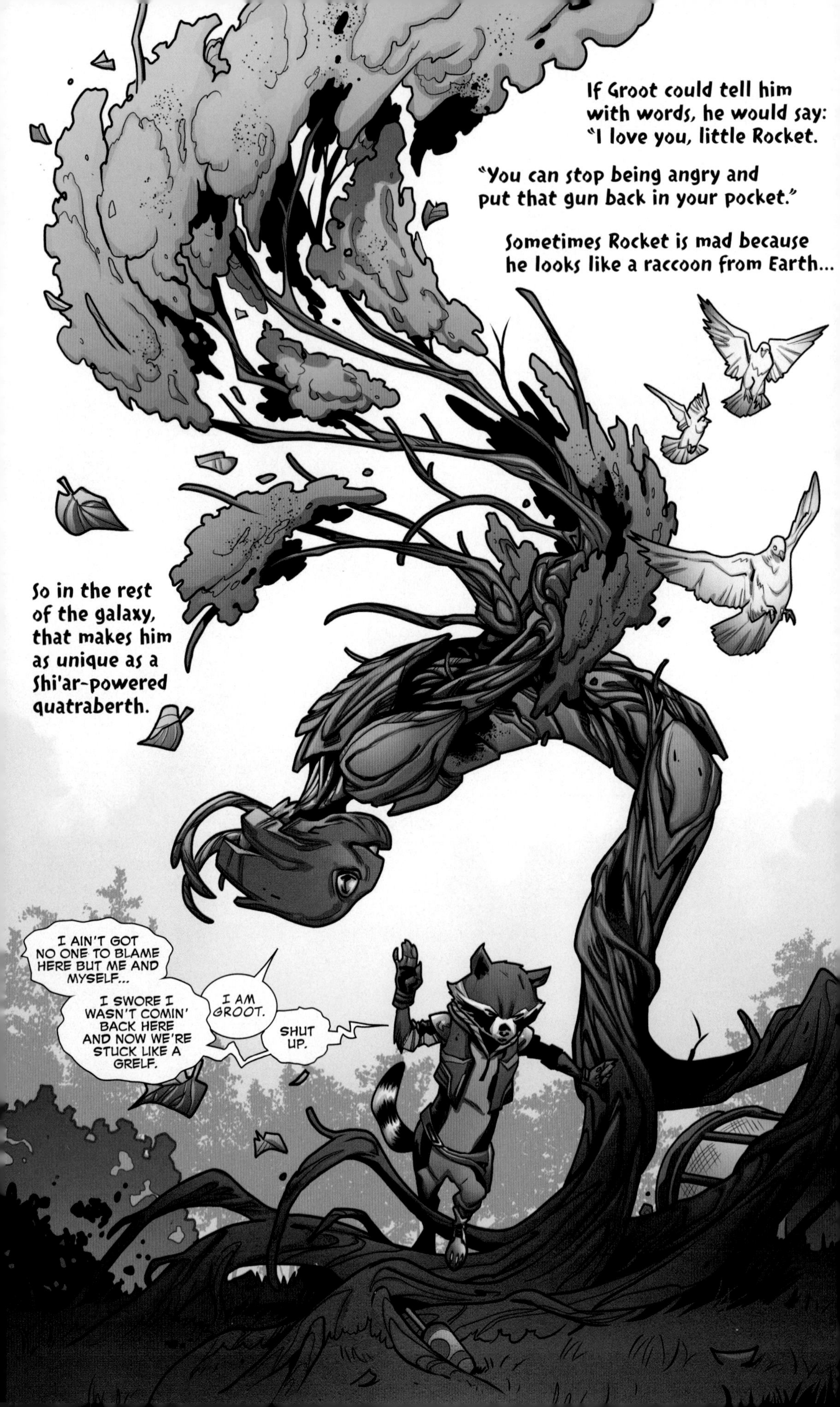

If Groot could tell him with words, he would say: "I love you, little Rocket.
"You can stop being angry and put that gun back in your pocket."
Sometimes Rocket is mad because he looks like a raccoon from Earth...
So in the rest of the galaxy, that makes him as unique as a Shi'ar-powered quatraberth.
I AIN'T GOT NO ONE TO BLAME HERE BUT ME AND MYSELF...
I SWORE I WASN'T COMIN' BACK HERE AND NOW WE'RE STUCK LIKE A GRELF.
I AM GROOT.
SHUT UP.

Groot's travels have taken him from over there to over here.
He has met and he has loved and there are many he holds dear.
There are Gamora, Drax, and the Star-Lord Peter Quill...

And sometimes Iron Man, Ben Grimm, and Venom come by with time to kill...

There are Kitty Pryde and Bug and Mantis and Moondragon.

And even Nova and Captain Marvel have hooked up to Guardians' space-bound wagon.

Now stuck here on Earth, Groot is making as much out of it as he can.

But he knows he sticks out in a world run by hu-man.

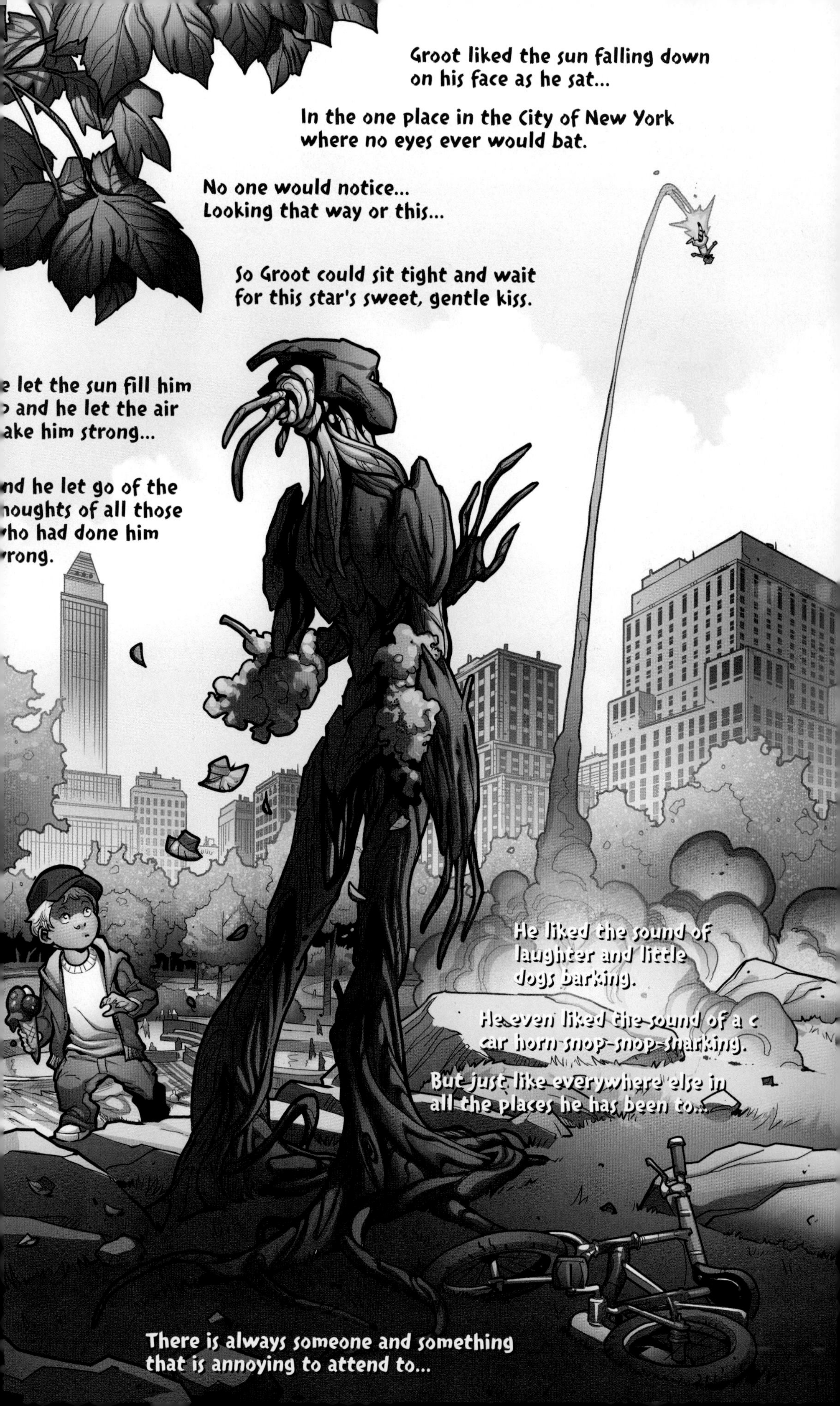

Groot liked the sun falling down on his face as he sat...
In the one place in the City of New York where no eyes ever would bat.
No one would notice... Looking that way or this...
So Groot could sit tight and wait for this star's sweet, gentle kiss.
e let the sun fill him
and he let the air
ake him strong...
nd he let go of the
houghts of all those
ho had done him
rong.
He liked the sound of laughter and little dogs barking.
He even liked the sound of a c car horn snop-snop-sharking.
But just like everywhere else in all the places he has been to...
There is always someone and something that is annoying to attend to...

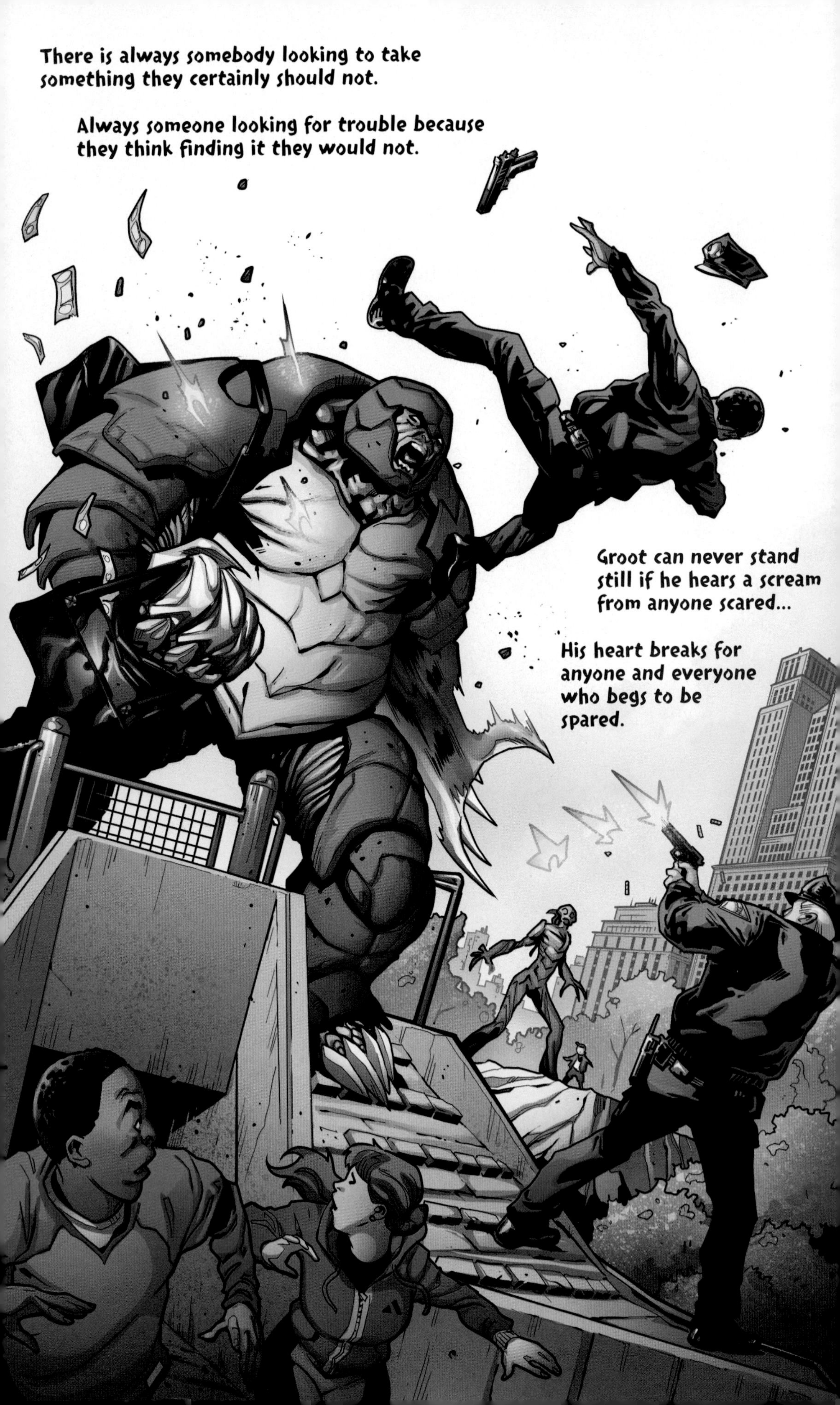
There is always somebody looking to take something they certainly should not.
Always someone looking for trouble because they think finding it they would not.
Groot can never stand still if he hears a scream from anyone scared...
His heart breaks for anyone and everyone who begs to be spared.

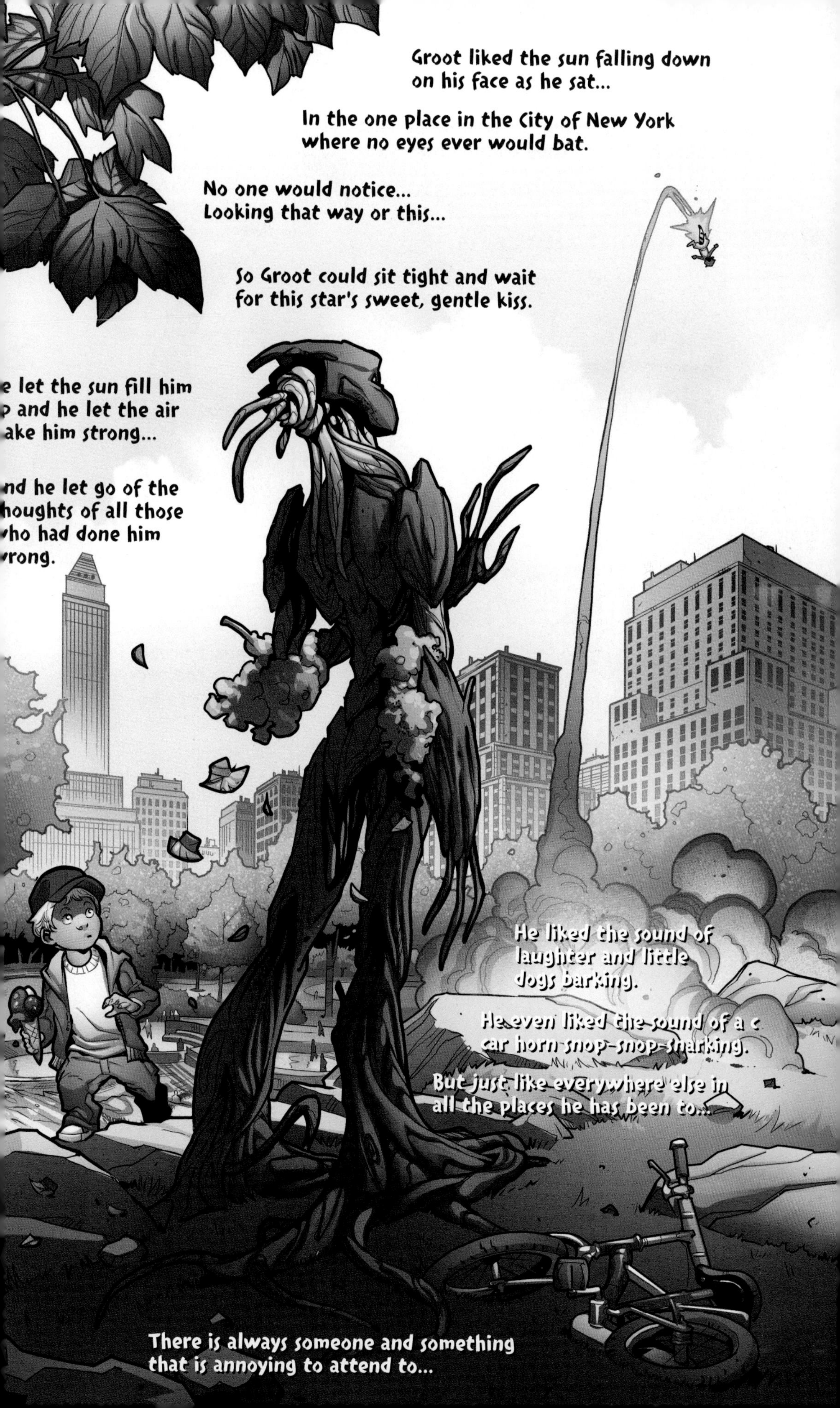
Groot liked the sun falling down on his face as he sat...
In the one place in the City of New York where no eyes ever would bat.
No one would notice... Looking that way or this...
So Groot could sit tight and wait for this star's sweet, gentle kiss.
e let the sun fill him p and he let the air ake him strong...
nd he let go of the houghts of all those ho had done him rong.
He liked the sound of laughter and little dogs barking.
He even liked the sound of a c car horn snop-snop-snarking.
But just like everywhere else in all the places he has been to...
There is always someone and something that is annoying to attend to...

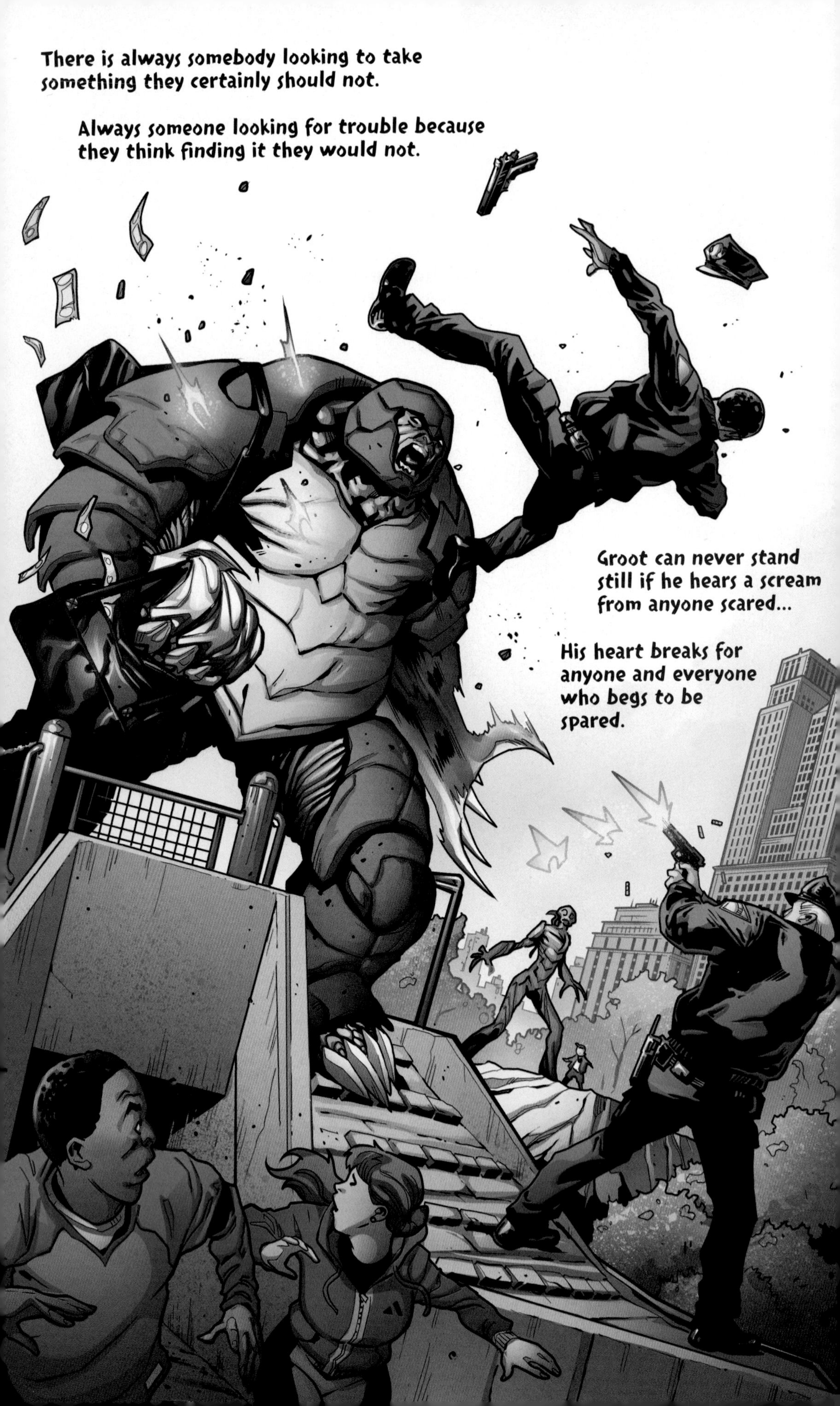
There is always somebody looking to take something they certainly should not.
Always someone looking for trouble because they think finding it they would not.
Groot can never stand still if he hears a scream from anyone scared...
His heart breaks for anyone and everyone who begs to be spared.

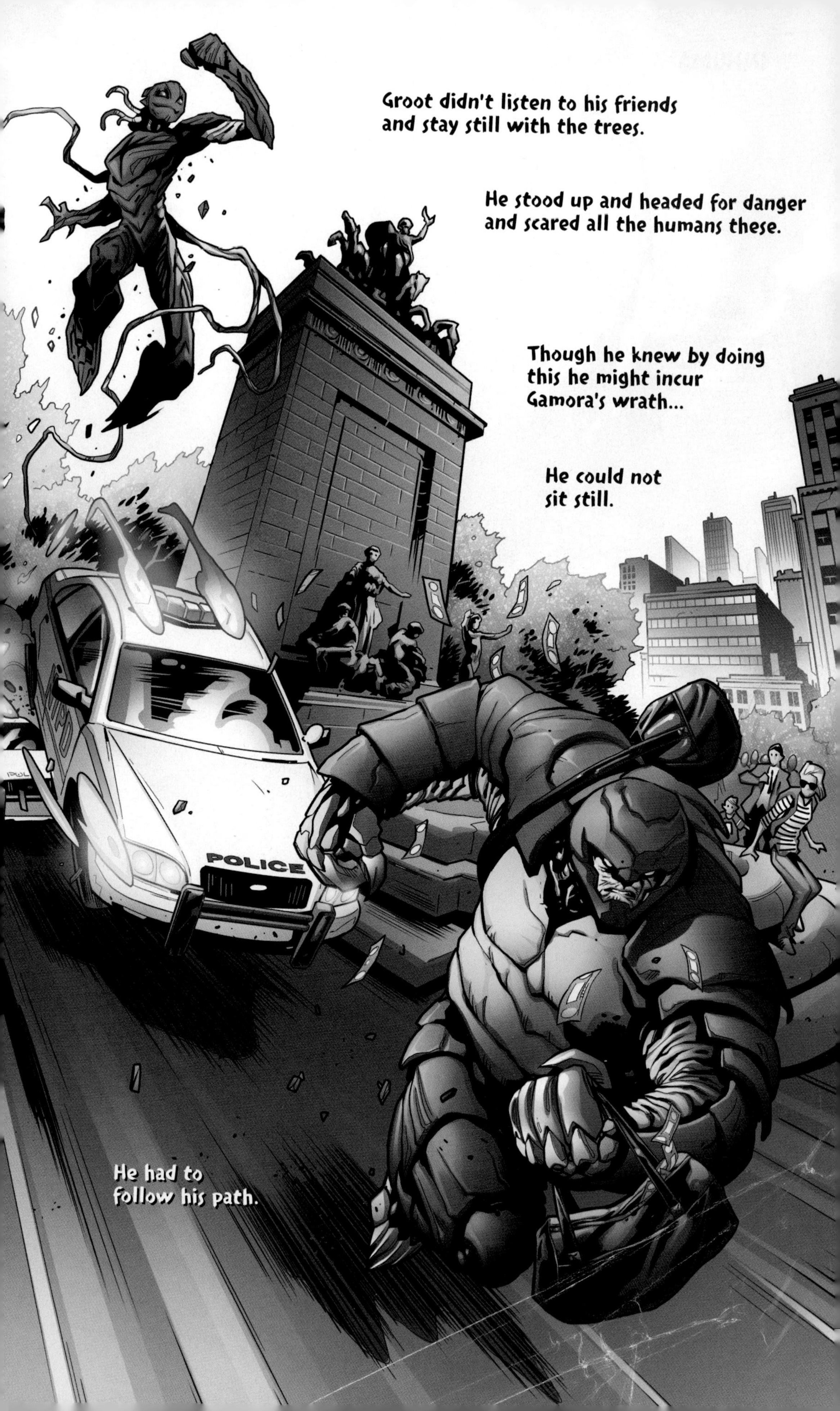
Groot didn't listen to his friends and stay still with the trees.
He stood up and headed for danger and scared all the humans these.
Though he knew by doing this he might incur Gamora's wrath...
He could not sit still.
NYPD
POLICE
He had to follow his path.

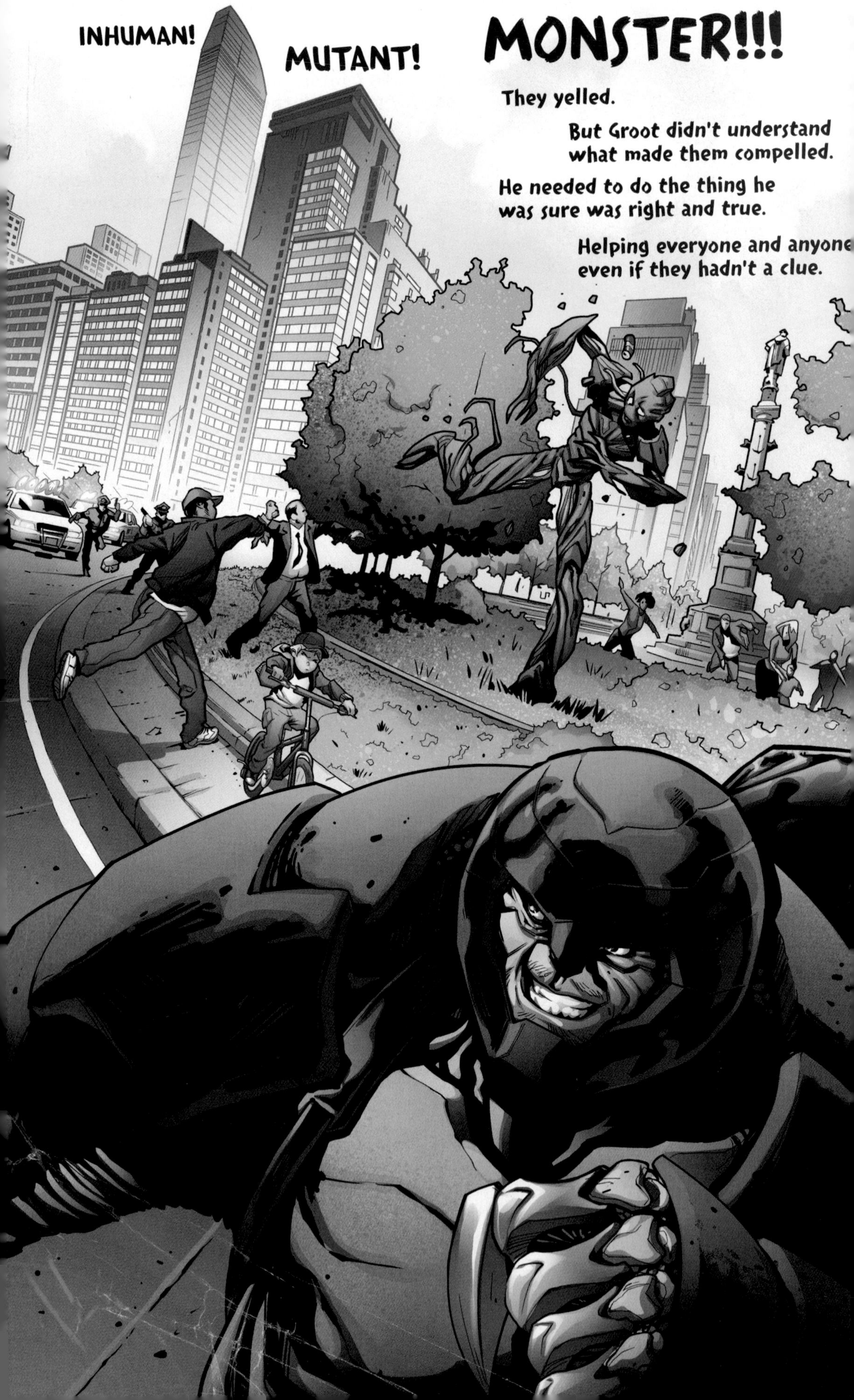
INHUMAN!
MUTANT!
MONSTER!!!
They yelled.
But Groot didn't understand
what made them compelled.
He needed to do the thing he
was sure was right and true.
Helping everyone and anyone
even if they hadn't a clue.

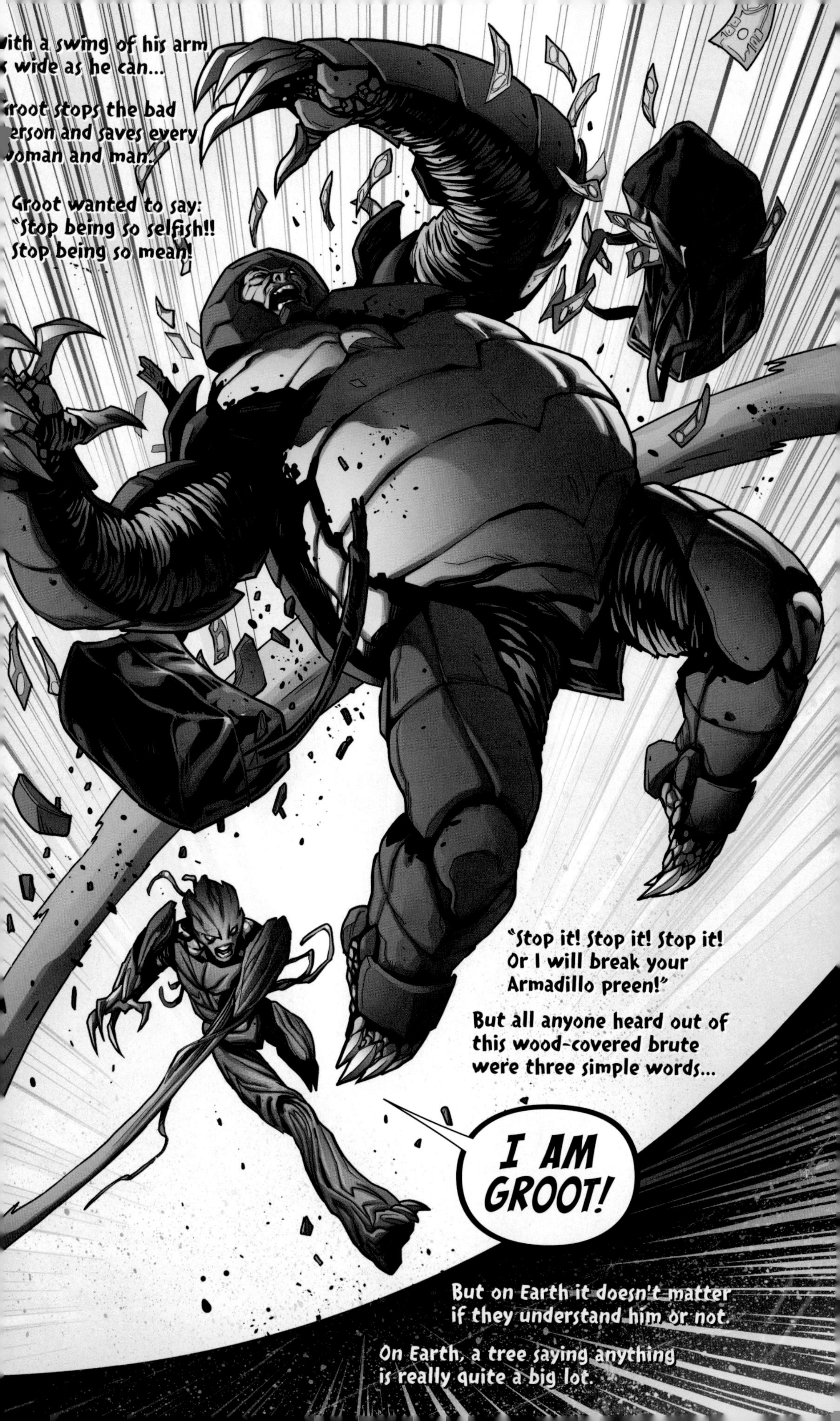
ith a swing of his arm
wide as he can...
roost stops the bad
erson and saves every
oman and man.
Groot wanted to say:
"Stop being so selfish!!
Stop being so mean!
"Stop it! Stop it! Stop it!
Or I will break your
Armadillo preen!"
But all anyone heard out of
this wood-covered brute
were three simple words...
I AM
GROOT!
But on Earth it doesn't matter
if they understand him or not.
On Earth, a tree saying anything
is really quite a big lot.

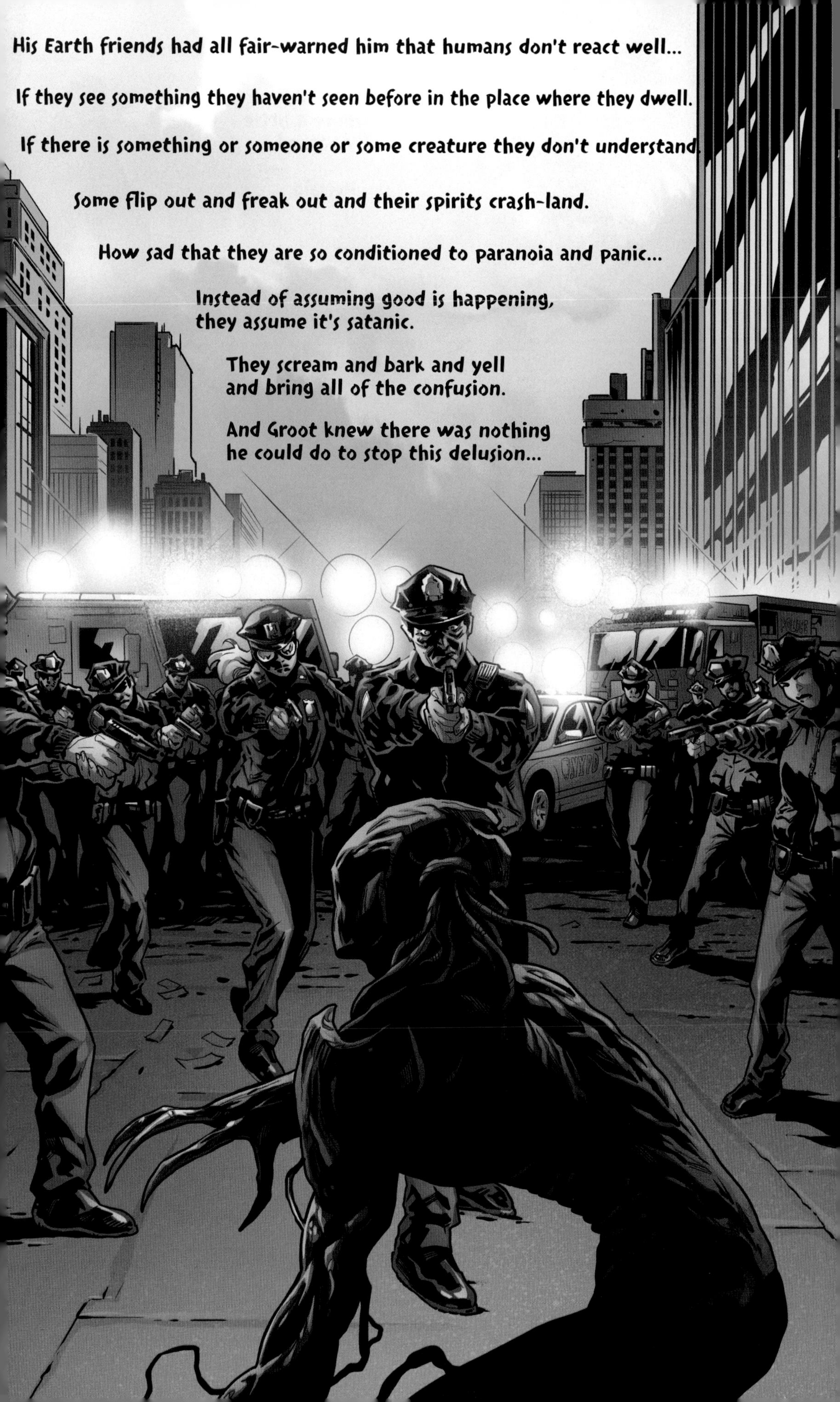
His Earth friends had all fair-warned him that humans don't react well...
If they see something they haven't seen before in the place where they dwell.
If there is something or someone or some creature they don't understand,
Some flip out and freak out and their spirits crash-land.
How sad that they are so conditioned to paranoia and panic...
Instead of assuming good is happening, they assume it's satanic.
They scream and bark and yell and bring all of the confusion.
And Groot knew there was nothing he could do to stop this delusion...
NYPD

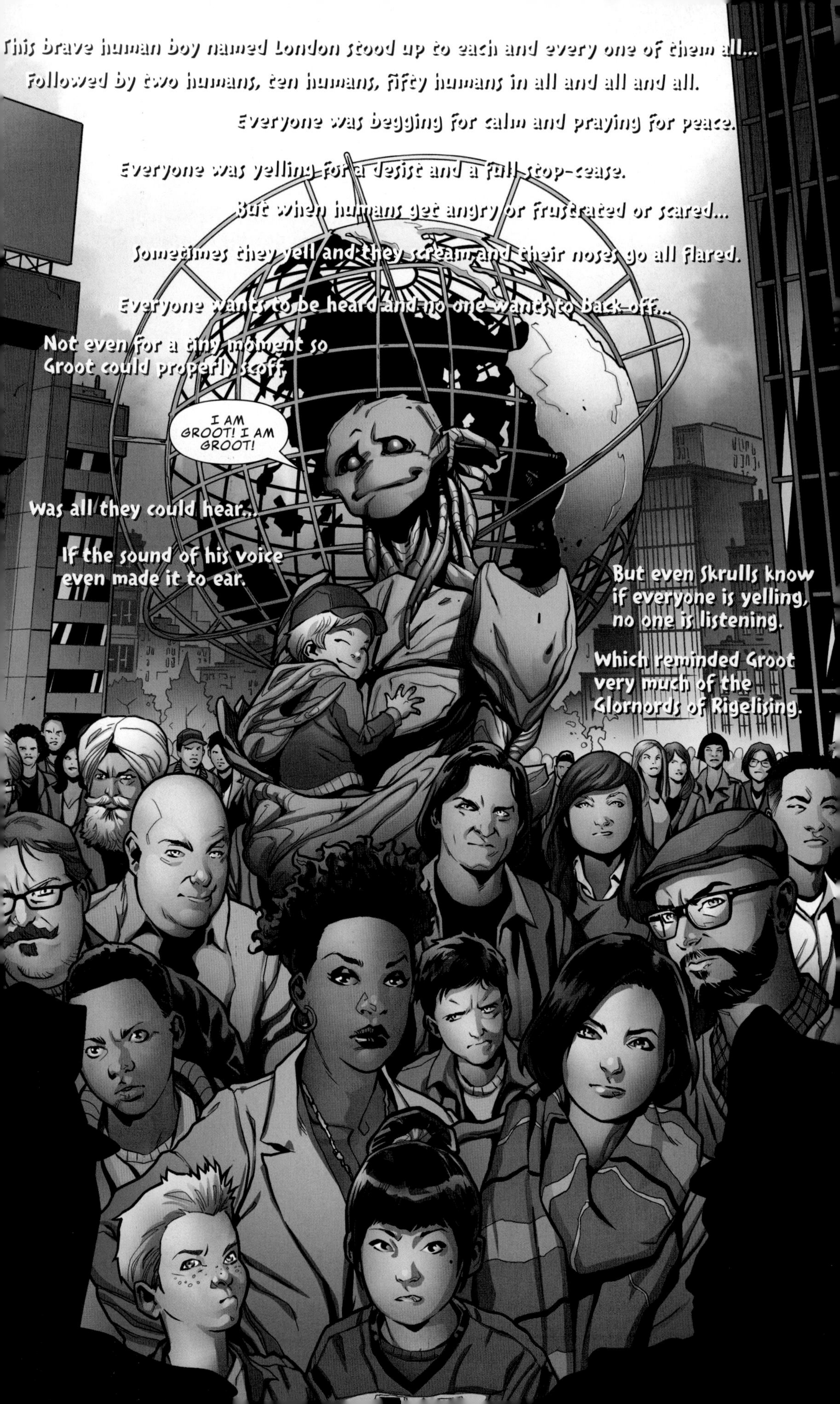
This brave human boy named London stood up to each and every one of them all...
Followed by two humans, ten humans, fifty humans in all and all and all.
Everyone was begging for calm and praying for peace.
Everyone was yelling for a desist and a full stop-cease.
But when humans get angry or frustrated or scared...
Sometimes they yell and they scream and their noses go all flared.
Everyone wants to be heard and no one wants to back off...
Not even for a tiny moment so Groot could properly scoff.
I AM GROOT! I AM GROOT!
Was all they could hear...
If the sound of his voice even made it to ear.
But even Skrulls know if everyone is yelling, no one is listening.
Which reminded Groot very much of the Glornords of Rigelising.

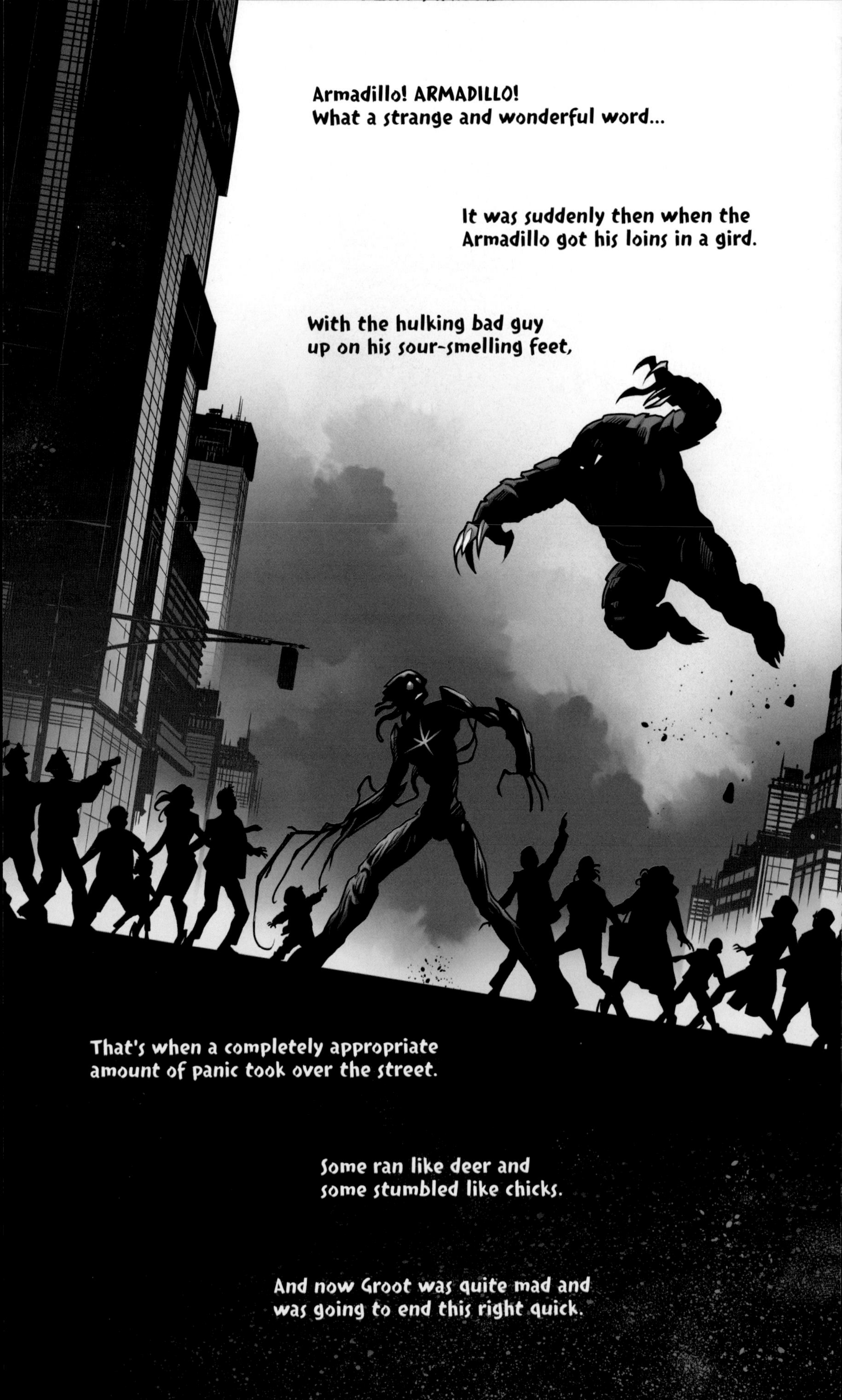
Armadillo! ARMADILLO!
What a strange and wonderful word...
It was suddenly then when the
Armadillo got his loins in a gird.
With the hulking bad guy
up on his sour-smelling feet,
That's when a completely appropriate
amount of panic took over the street.
Some ran like deer and
some stumbled like chicks.
And now Groot was quite mad and
was going to end this right quick.

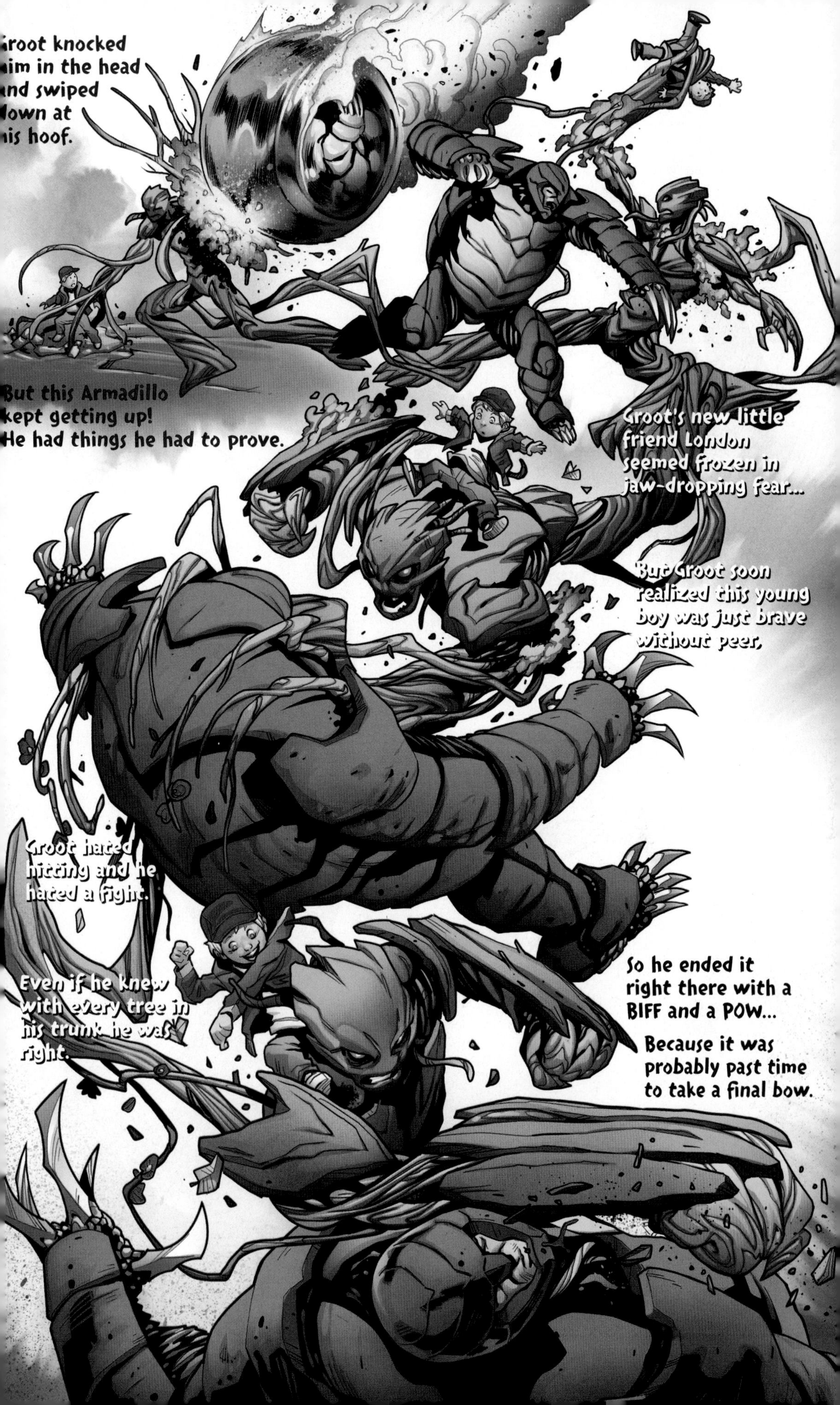

root knocked
im in the head
nd swiped
own at
is hoof.
But this Armadillo
kept getting up!
He had things he had to prove.
Groot's new little
friend London
seemed frozen in
jaw-dropping fear...
But Groot soon
realized this young
boy was just brave
without peer.
Groot hated
hitting and he
hated a fight.
Even if he knew
with every tree in
his trunk he was
right.
So he ended it
right there with a
BIFF and a POW...
Because it was
probably past time
to take a final bow.

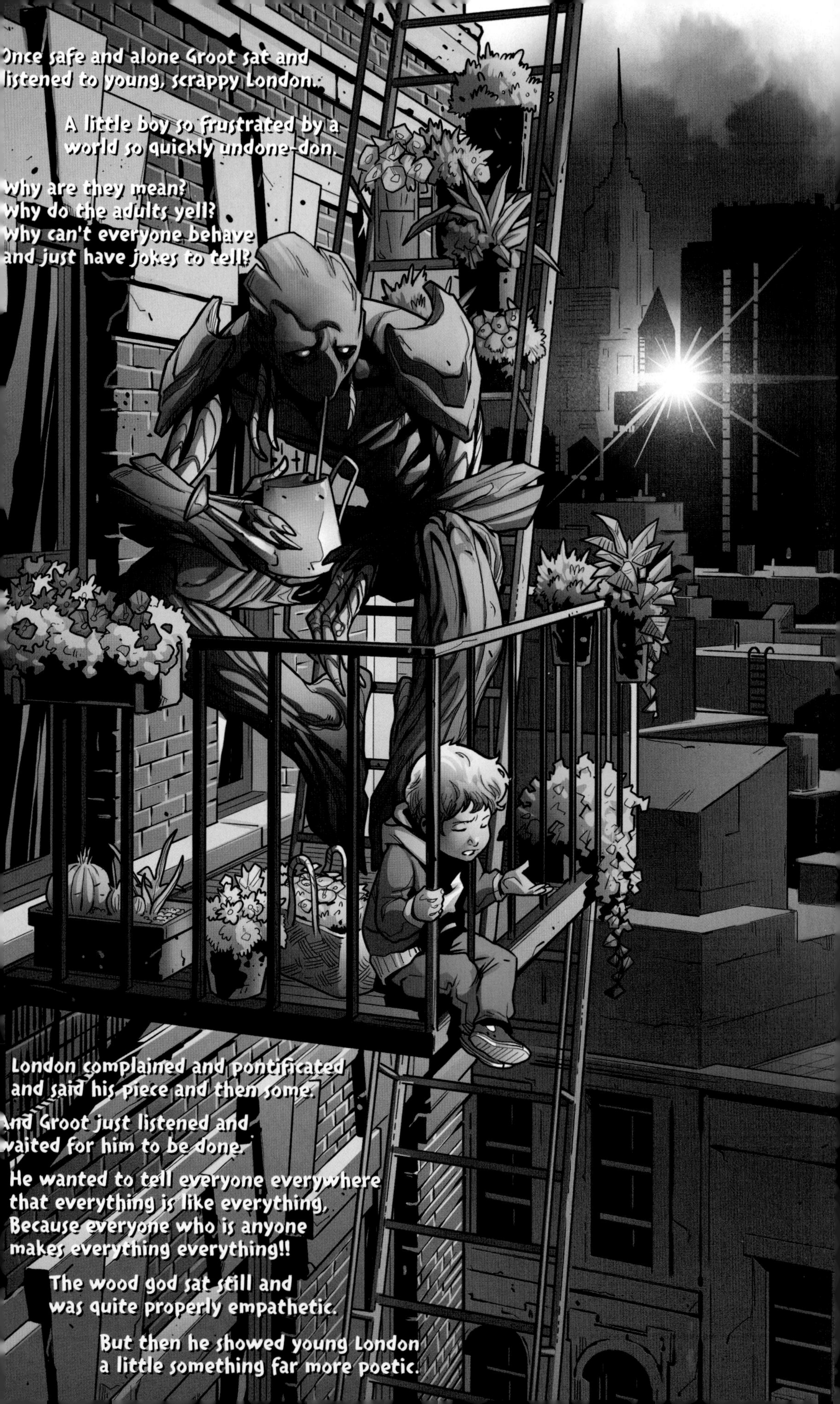
Once safe and alone Groot sat and listened to young, scrappy London.
A little boy so frustrated by a world so quickly undone-don.
Why are they mean?
Why do the adults yell?
Why can't everyone behave and just have jokes to tell?
London complained and pontificated and said his piece and then some.
And Groot just listened and waited for him to be done.
He wanted to tell everyone everywhere that everything is like everything,
Because everyone who is anyone makes everything everything!!
The wood god sat still and was quite properly empathetic.
But then he showed young London a little something far more poetic.

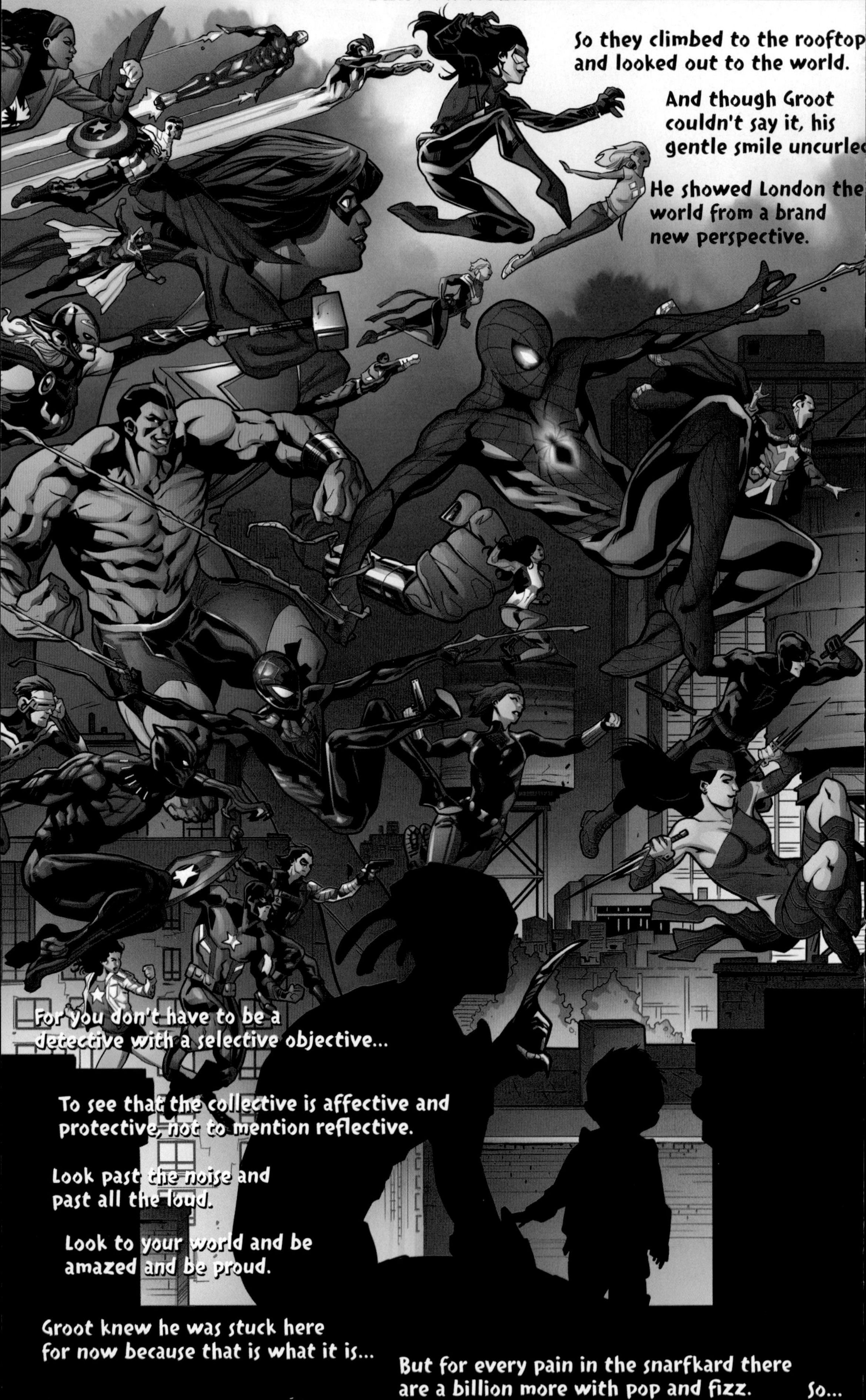
So they climbed to the rooftop
and looked out to the world.
And though Groot
couldn't say it, his
gentle smile uncurle
He showed London the
world from a brand
new perspective.
For you don't have to be a
detective with a selective objective...
To see that the collective is affective and
protective, not to mention reflective.
Look past the noise and
past all the loud.
Look to your world and be
amazed and be proud.
Groot knew he was stuck here
for now because that is what it is...
But for every pain in the snarfkard there
are a billion more with pop and fizz.
So...

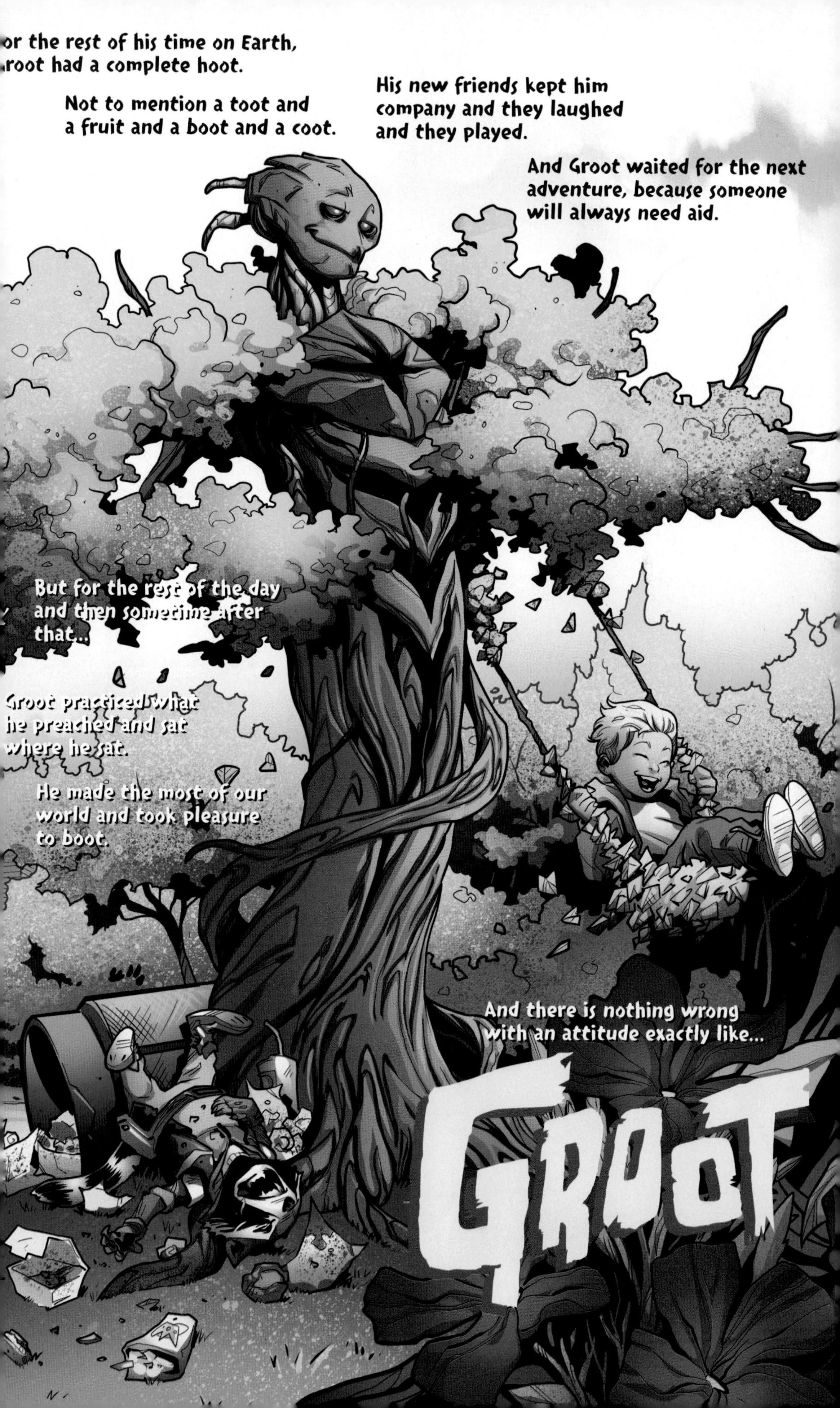
or the rest of his time on Earth,
root had a complete hoot.
Not to mention a toot and
a fruit and a boot and a coot.
His new friends kept him
company and they laughed
and they played.
And Groot waited for the next
adventure, because someone
will always need aid.
But for the rest of the day
and then sometime after
that...
Groot practiced what
he preached and sat
where he sat.
He made the most of our
world and took pleasure
to boot.
And there is nothing wrong
with an attitude exactly like...
GROOT

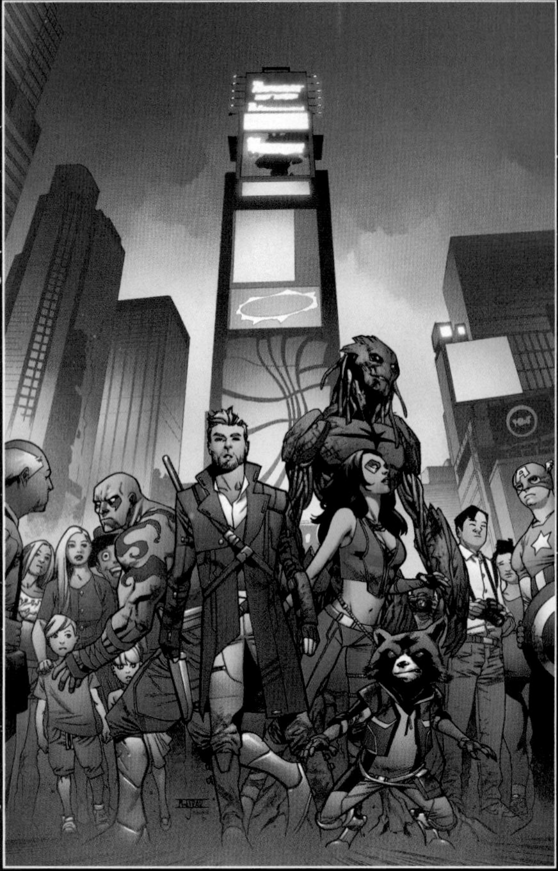

#15 SDCC VARIANT BY
MAHMUD ASRAR & RICHARD ISANOVE

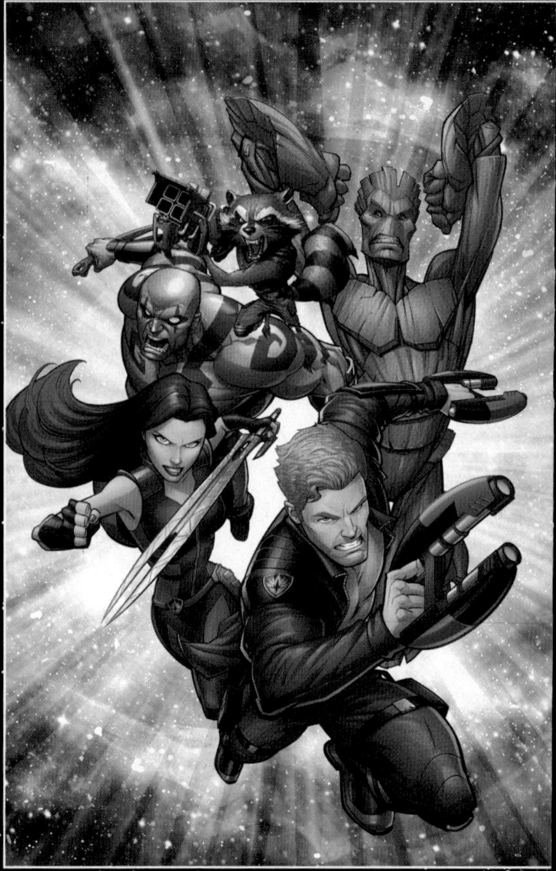

#15 ANIMATION VARIANT

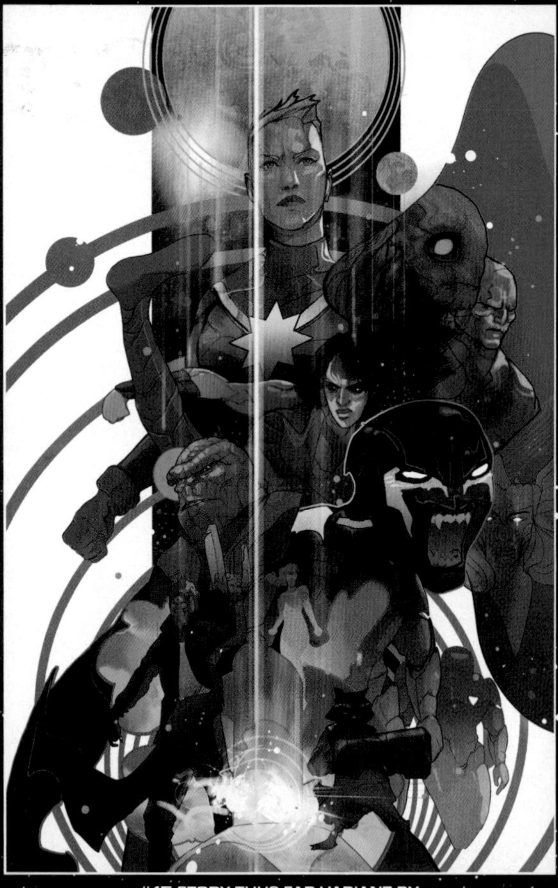

#15 STORY THUS FAR VARIANT BY
CHRISTIAN WARD

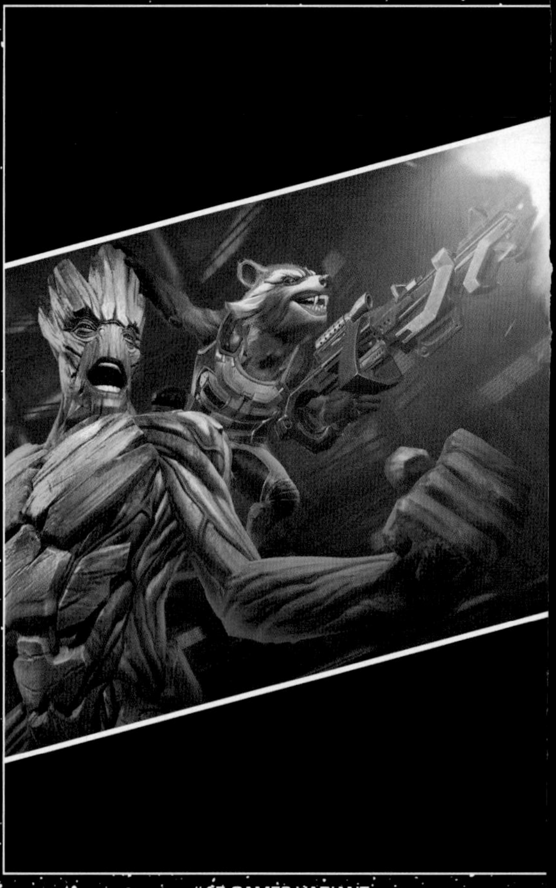

#15 GAMES VARIANT

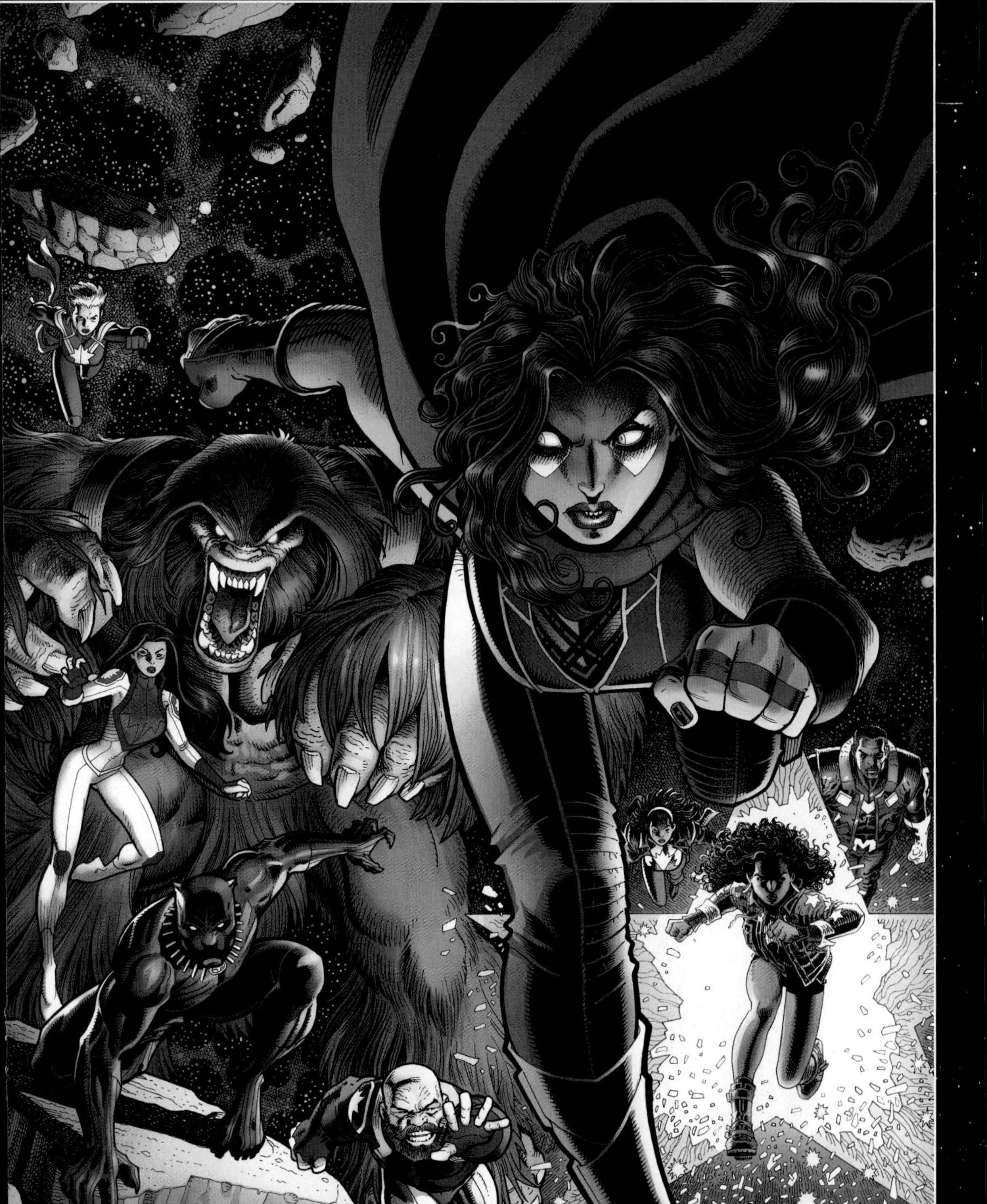
ARTHUR ADAMS
12-5-2016

17

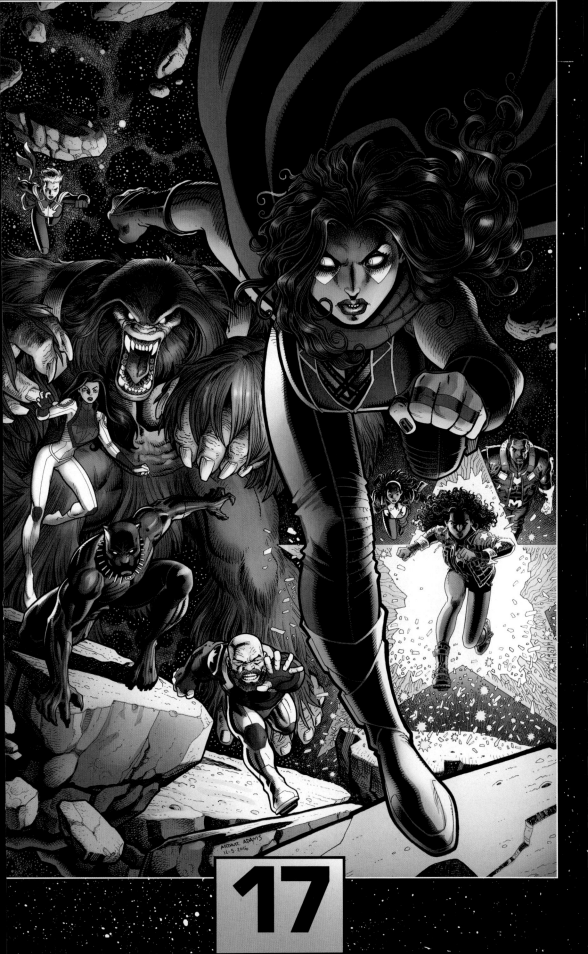

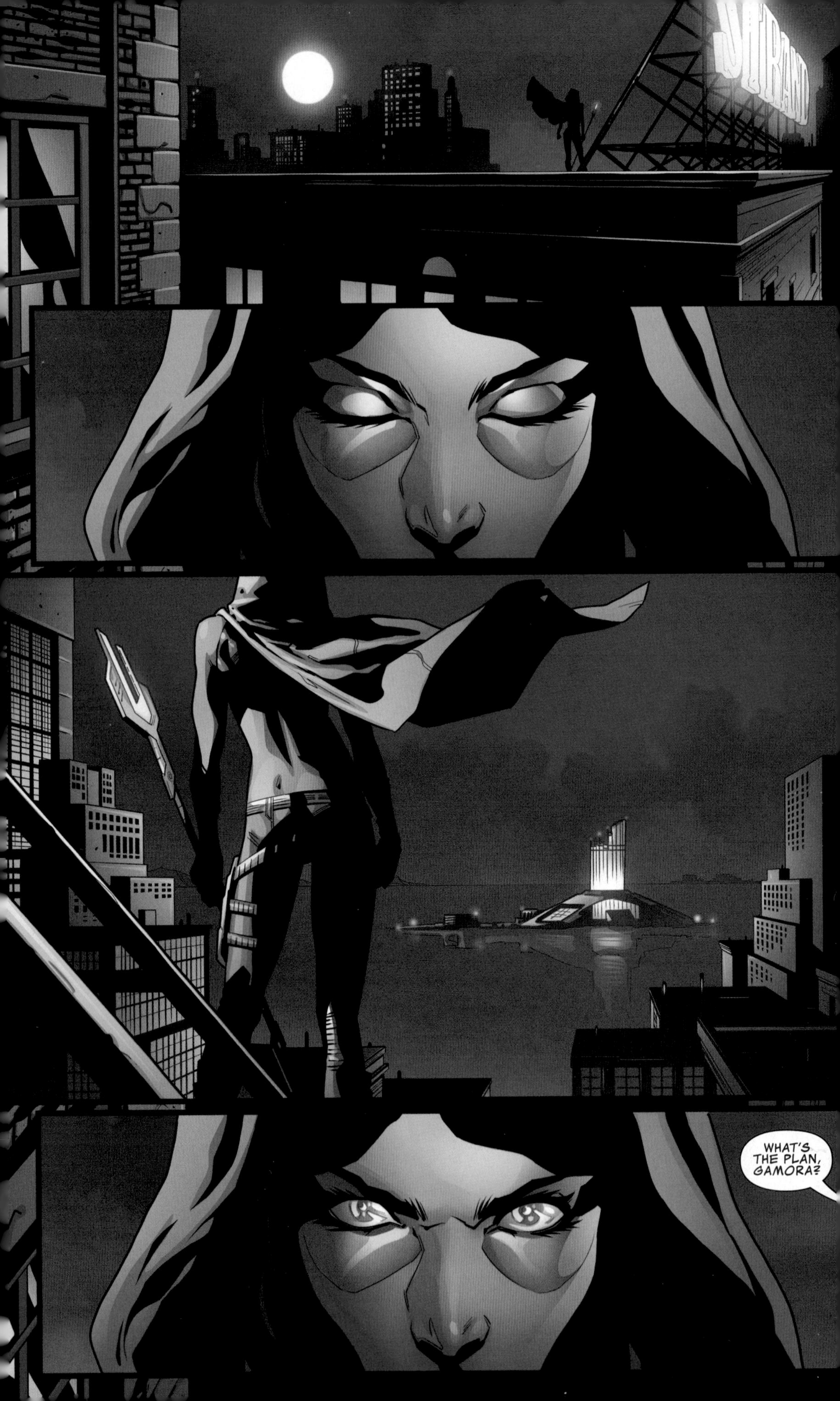

WHAT'S THE PLAN, GAMORA?

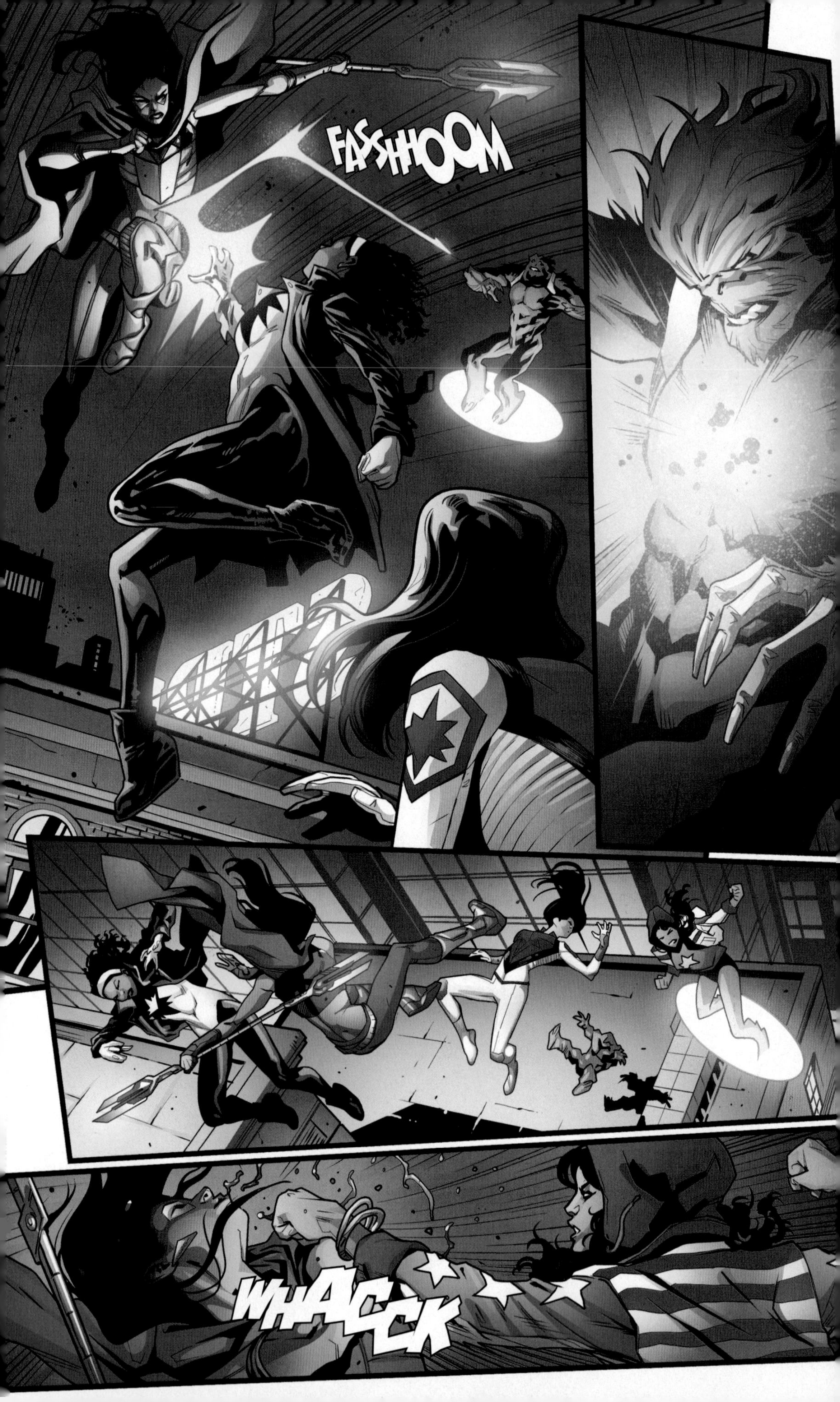
FASHHOOM
WHACCK

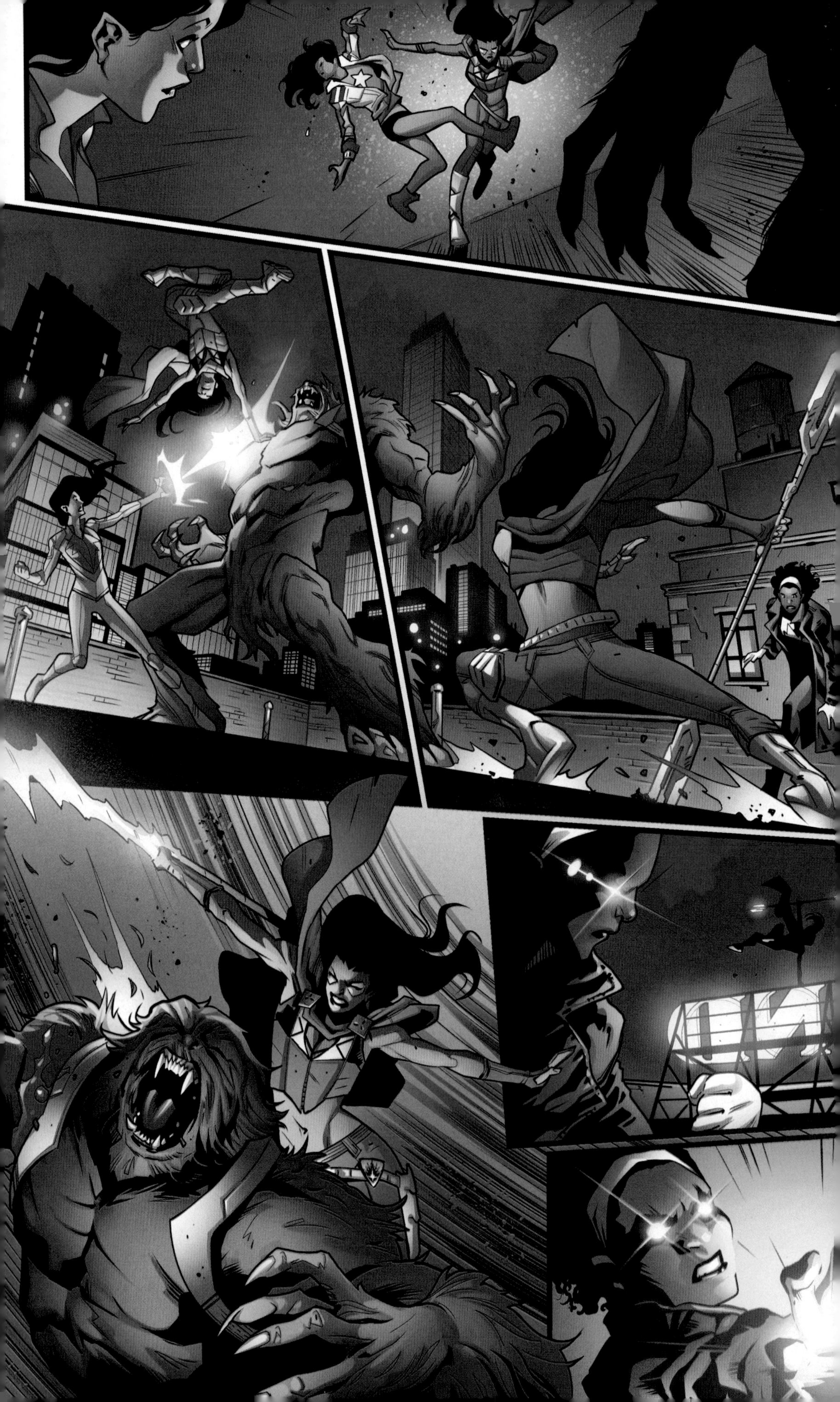

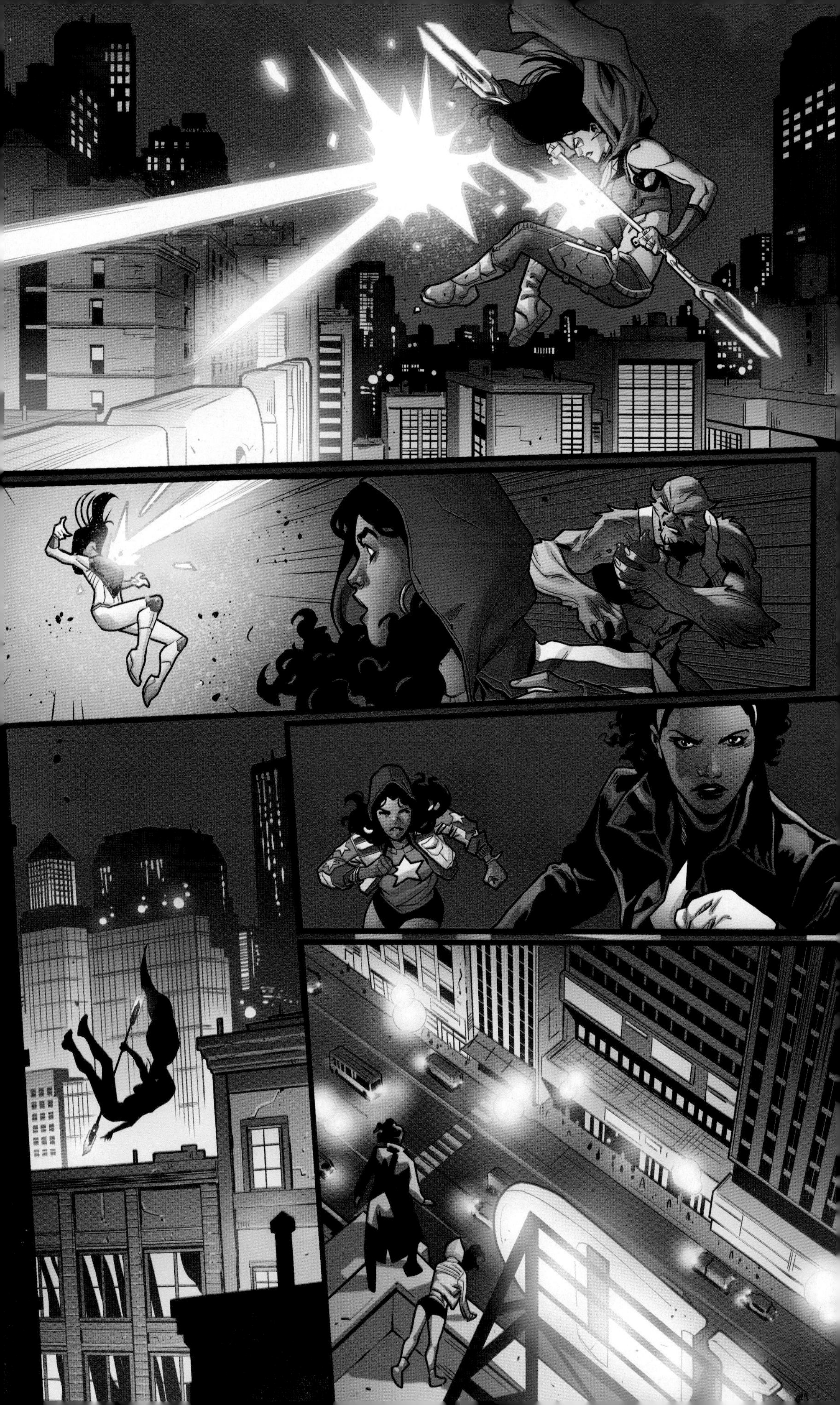

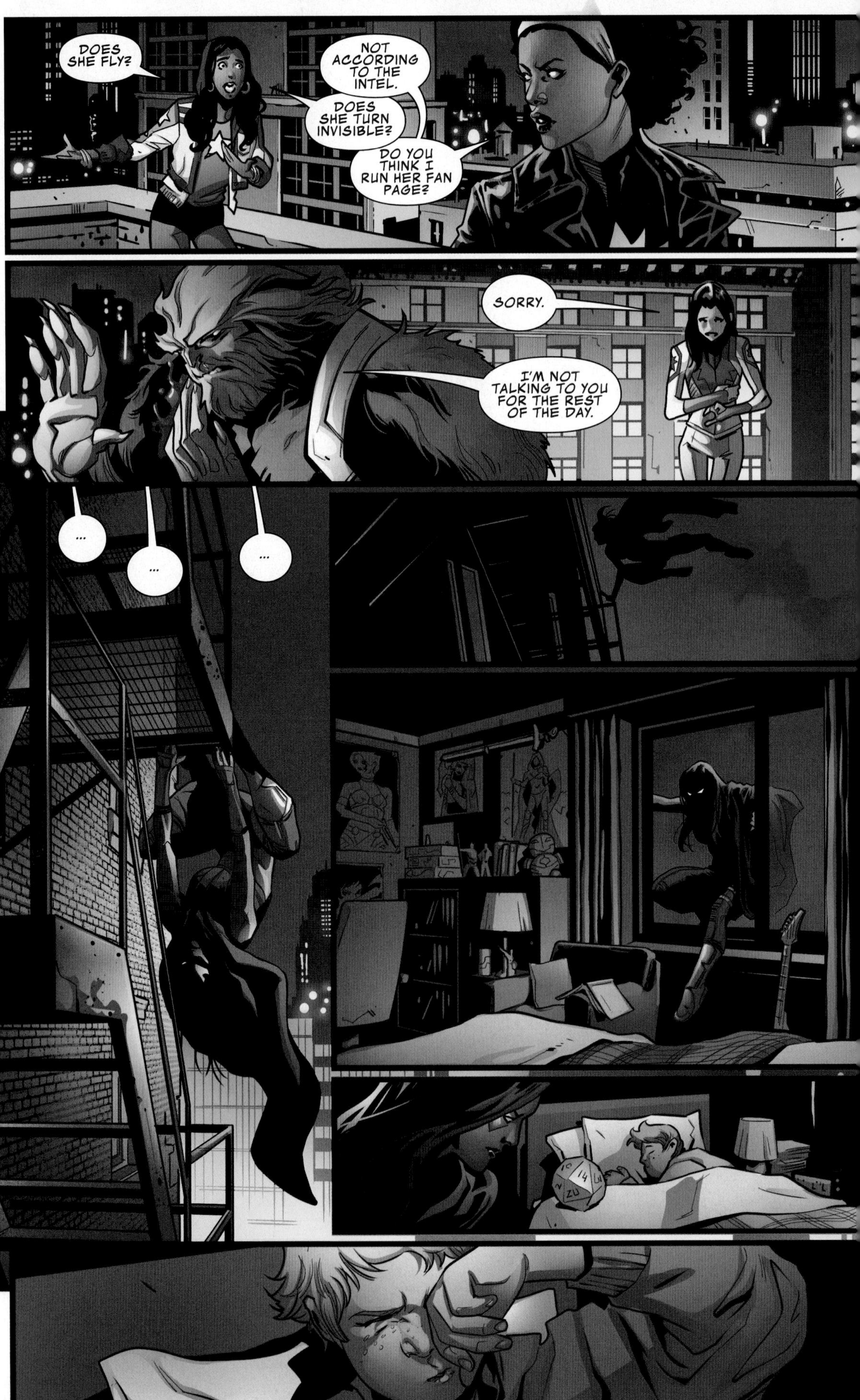
DOES SHE FLY?
NOT ACCORDING TO THE INTEL.
DOES SHE TURN INVISIBLE?
DO YOU THINK I RUN HER FAN PAGE?
SORRY.
I'M NOT TALKING TO YOU FOR THE REST OF THE DAY.
...
...
...

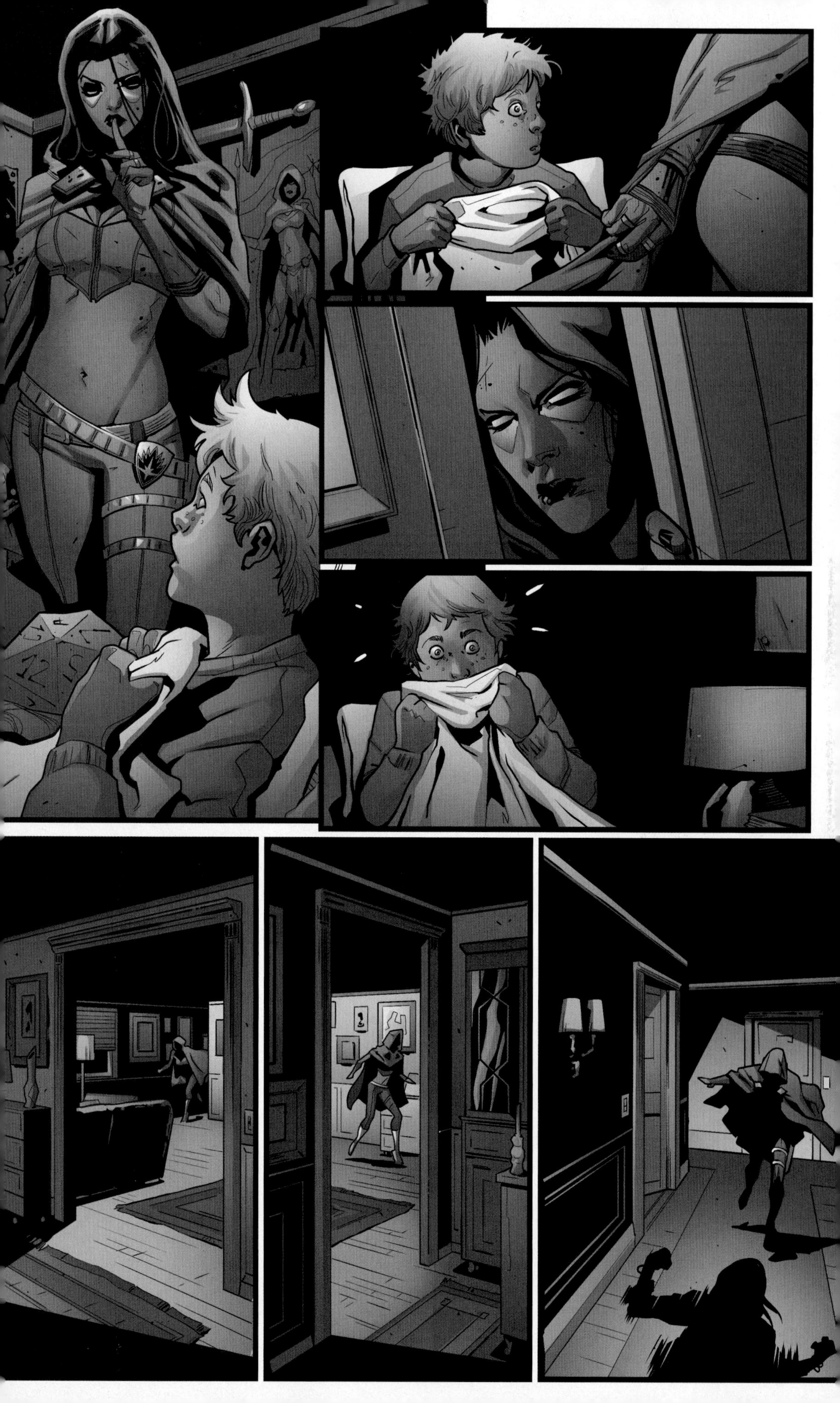

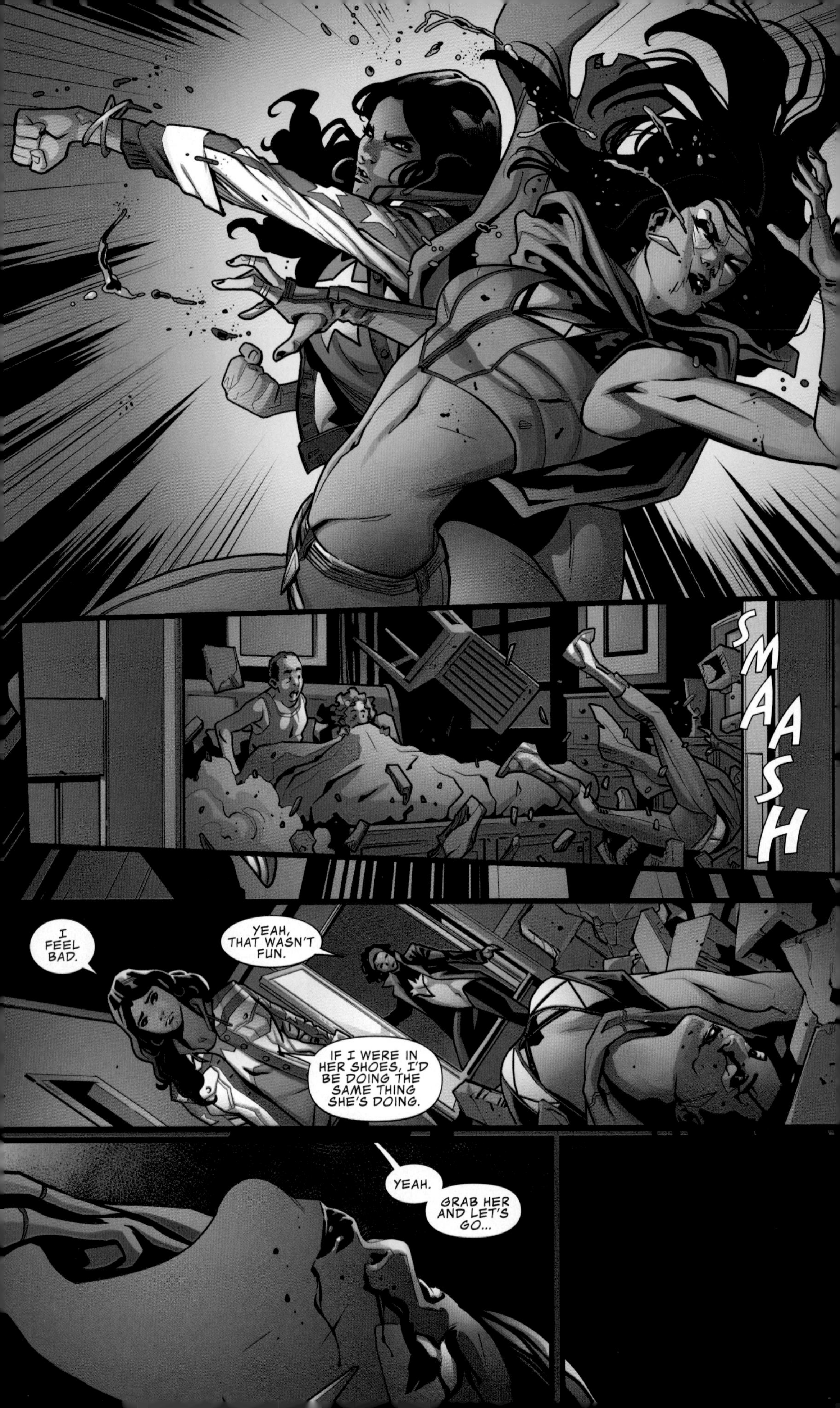
SMAASH
I FEEL BAD.
YEAH, THAT WASN'T FUN.
IF I WERE IN HER SHOES, I'D BE DOING THE SAME THING SHE'S DOING.
YEAH.
GRAB HER AND LET'S GO...

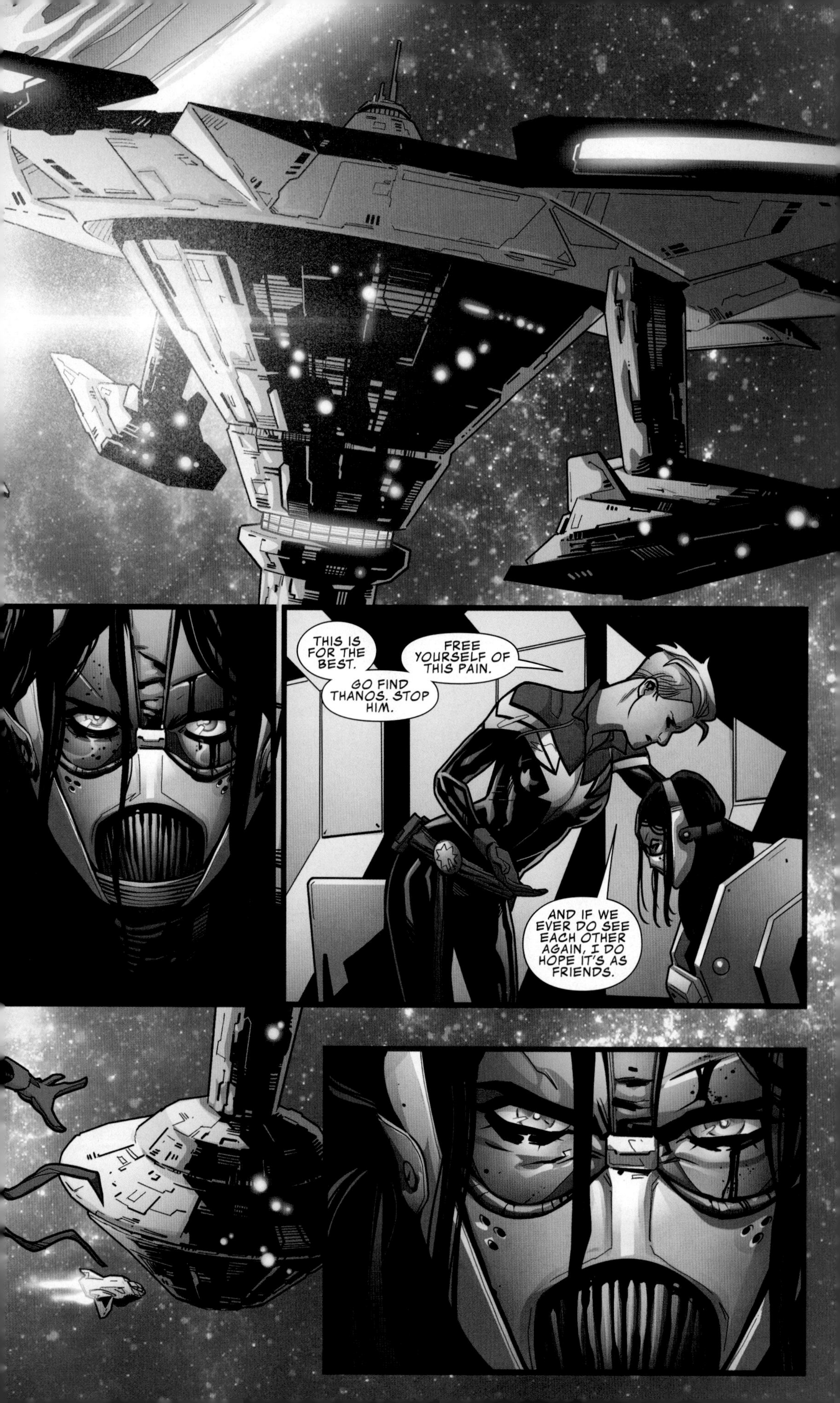
THIS IS FOR THE BEST.
GO FIND THANOS. STOP HIM.
FREE YOURSELF OF THIS PAIN.
AND IF WE EVER DO SEE EACH OTHER AGAIN, I DO HOPE IT'S AS FRIENDS.

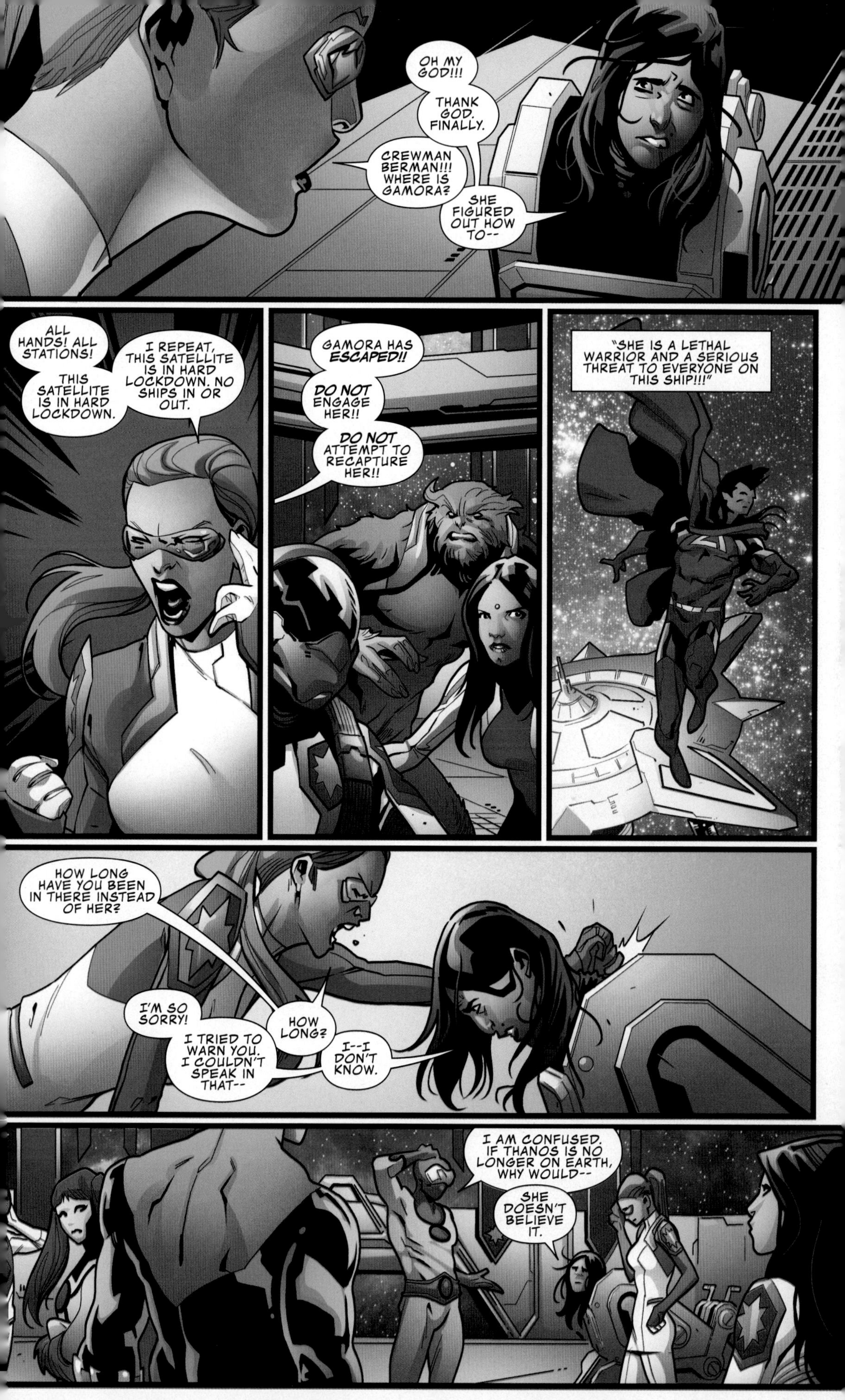
OH MY GOD!!!
THANK GOD. FINALLY.
CREWMAN BERMAN!!! WHERE IS GAMORA?
SHE FIGURED OUT HOW TO--
ALL HANDS! ALL STATIONS!
THIS SATELLITE IS IN HARD LOCKDOWN.
I REPEAT, THIS SATELLITE IS IN HARD LOCKDOWN. NO SHIPS IN OR OUT.
GAMORA HAS ESCAPED!!
DO NOT ENGAGE HER!!
DO NOT ATTEMPT TO RECAPTURE HER!!
"SHE IS A LETHAL WARRIOR AND A SERIOUS THREAT TO EVERYONE ON THIS SHIP!!!"
HOW LONG HAVE YOU BEEN IN THERE INSTEAD OF HER?
I'M SO SORRY!
I TRIED TO WARN YOU. I COULDN'T SPEAK IN THAT--
HOW LONG?
I--I DON'T KNOW.
I AM CONFUSED. IF THANOS IS NO LONGER ON EARTH, WHY WOULD--
SHE DOESN'T BELIEVE IT.

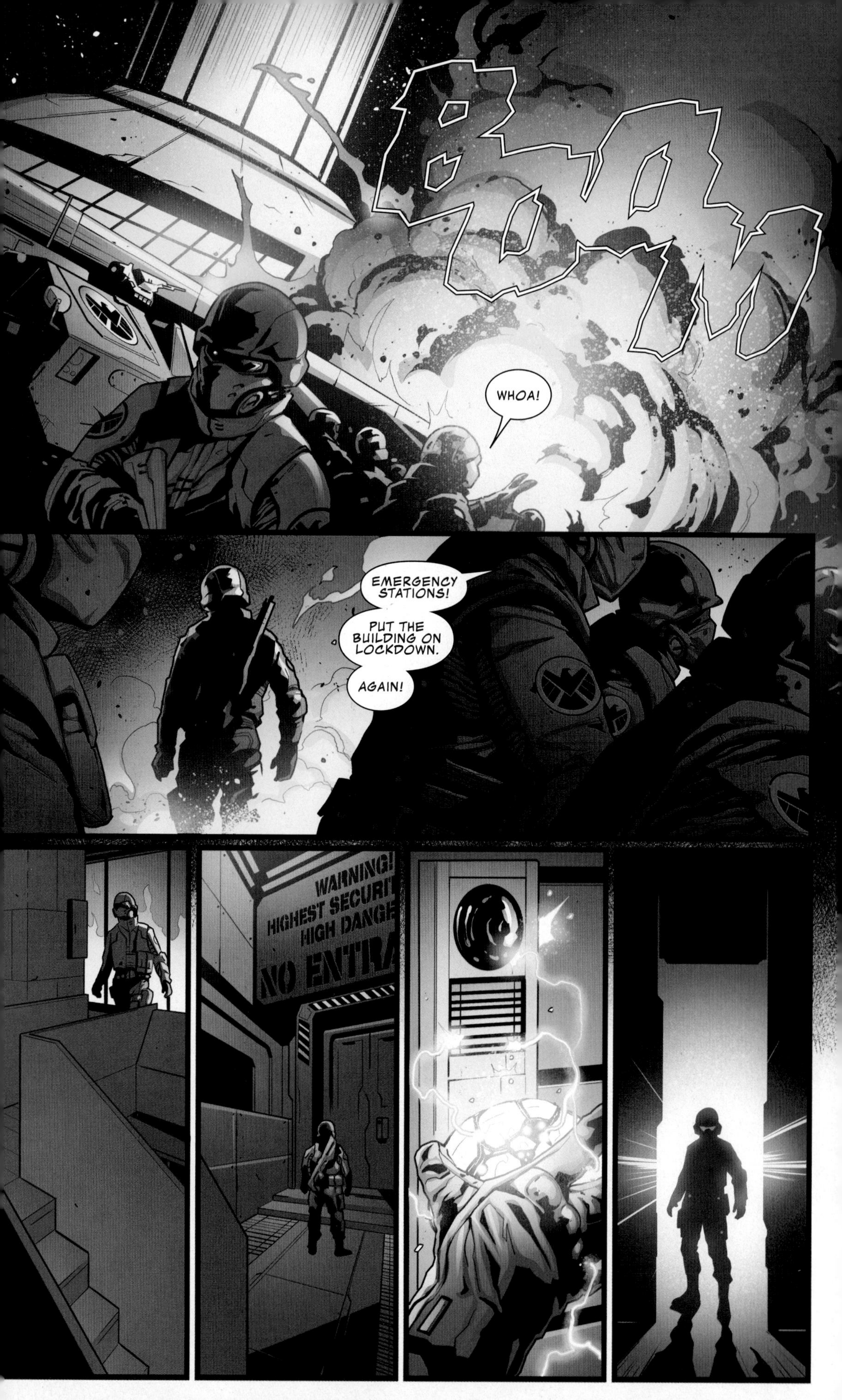
BOOM
WHOA!
EMERGENCY STATIONS!
PUT THE BUILDING ON LOCKDOWN.
AGAIN!
WARNING!
HIGHEST SECURIT
HIGH DANGE
NO ENTRA

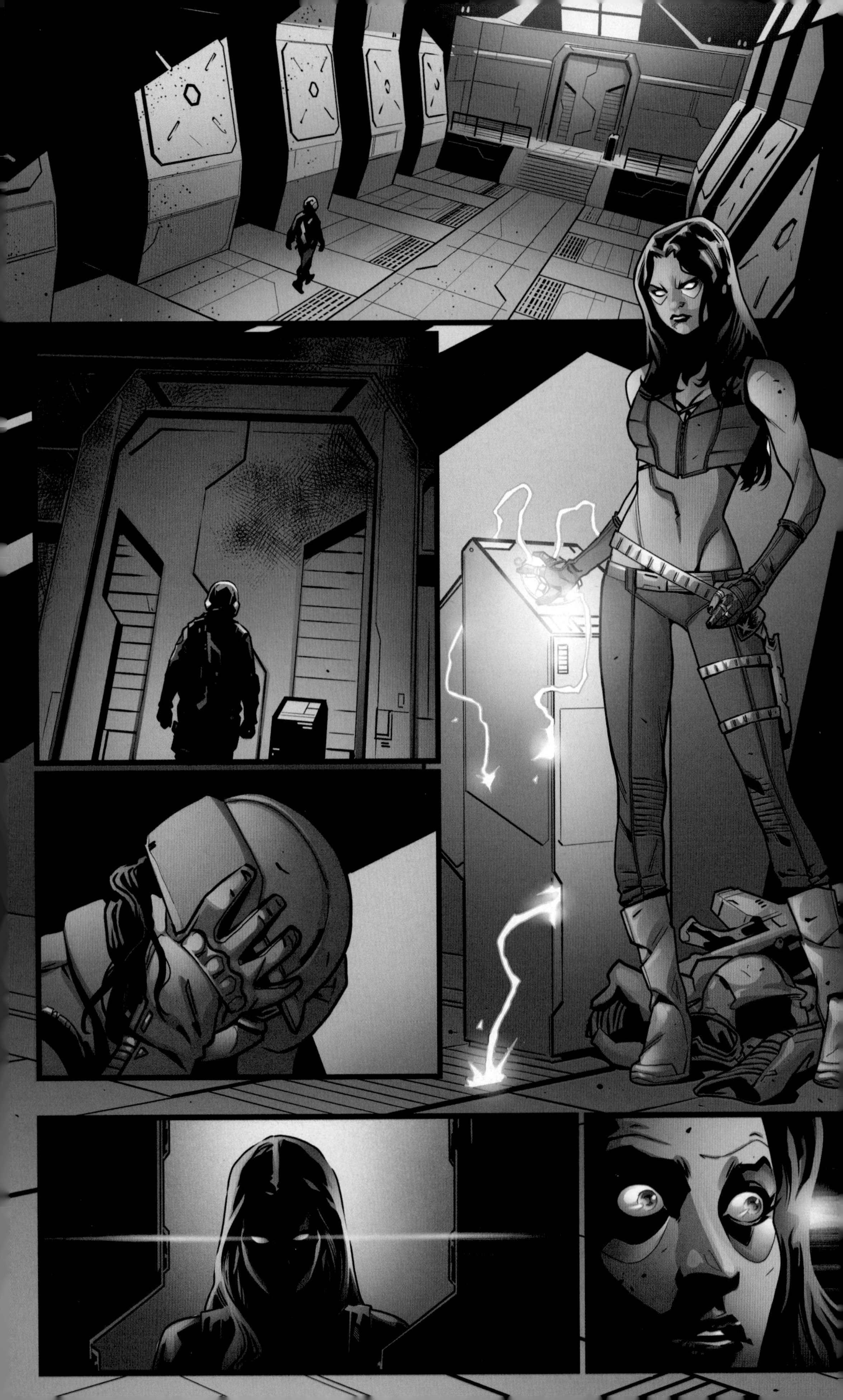

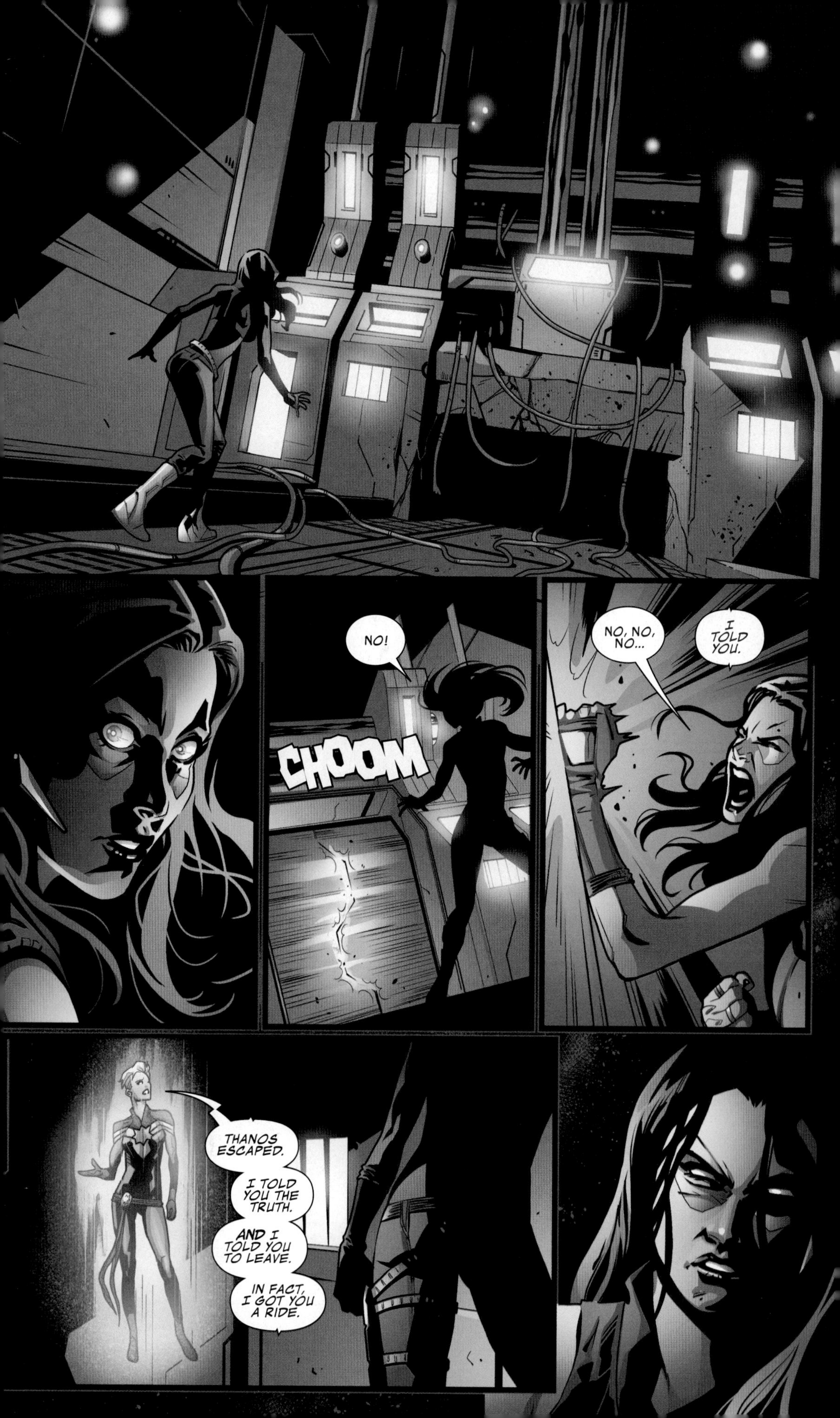
NO!
CHOOM
NO, NO, NO...
I TOLD YOU.
THANOS ESCAPED.
I TOLD YOU THE TRUTH.
AND I TOLD YOU TO LEAVE.
IN FACT, I GOT YOU A RIDE.

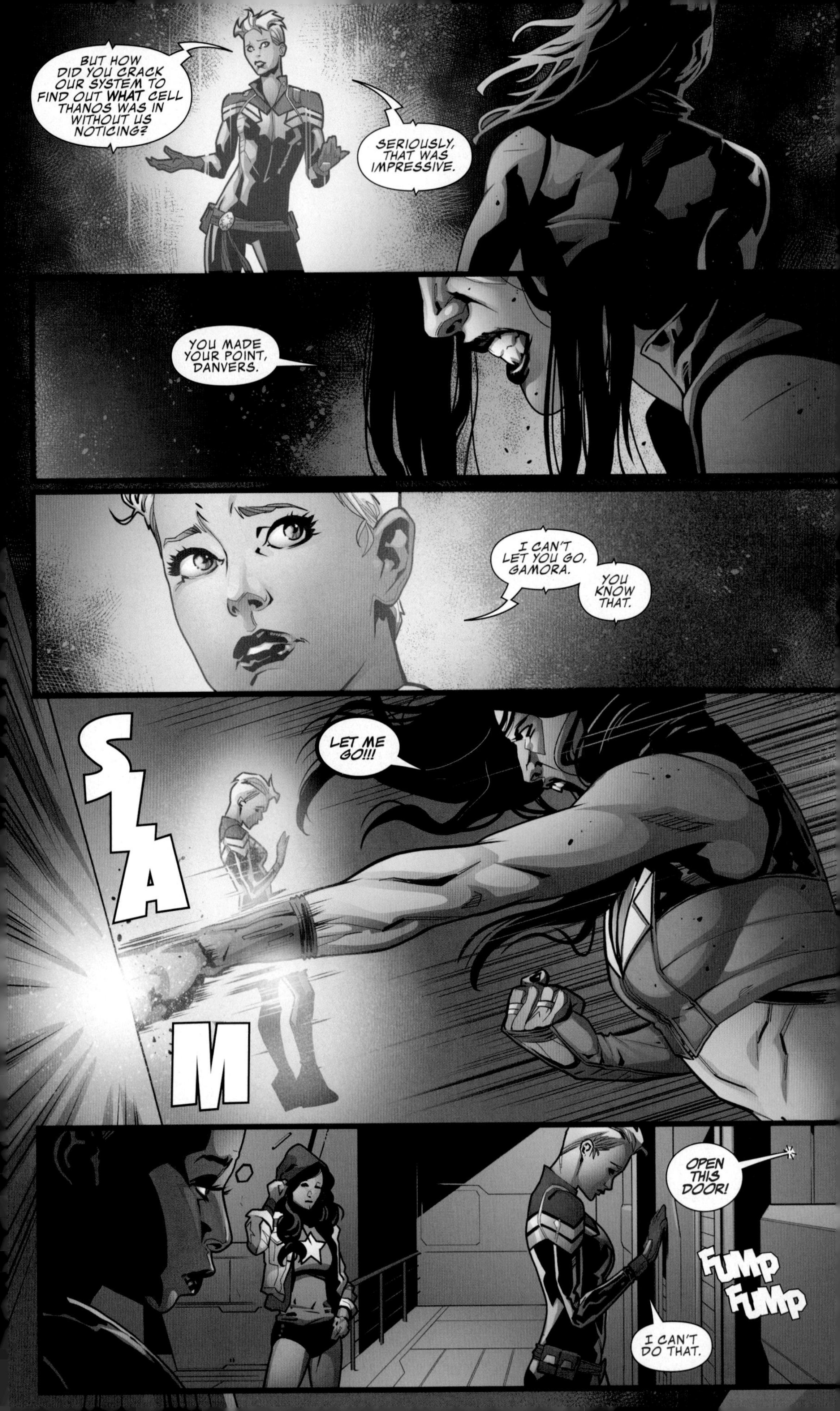

BUT HOW DID YOU CRACK OUR SYSTEM TO FIND OUT WHAT CELL THANOS WAS IN WITHOUT US NOTICING?
SERIOUSLY, THAT WAS IMPRESSIVE.
YOU MADE YOUR POINT, DANVERS.
I CAN'T LET YOU GO, GAMORA.
YOU KNOW THAT.
SLAM
LET ME GO!!!
OPEN THIS DOOR!
FUMP FUMP
I CAN'T DO THAT.

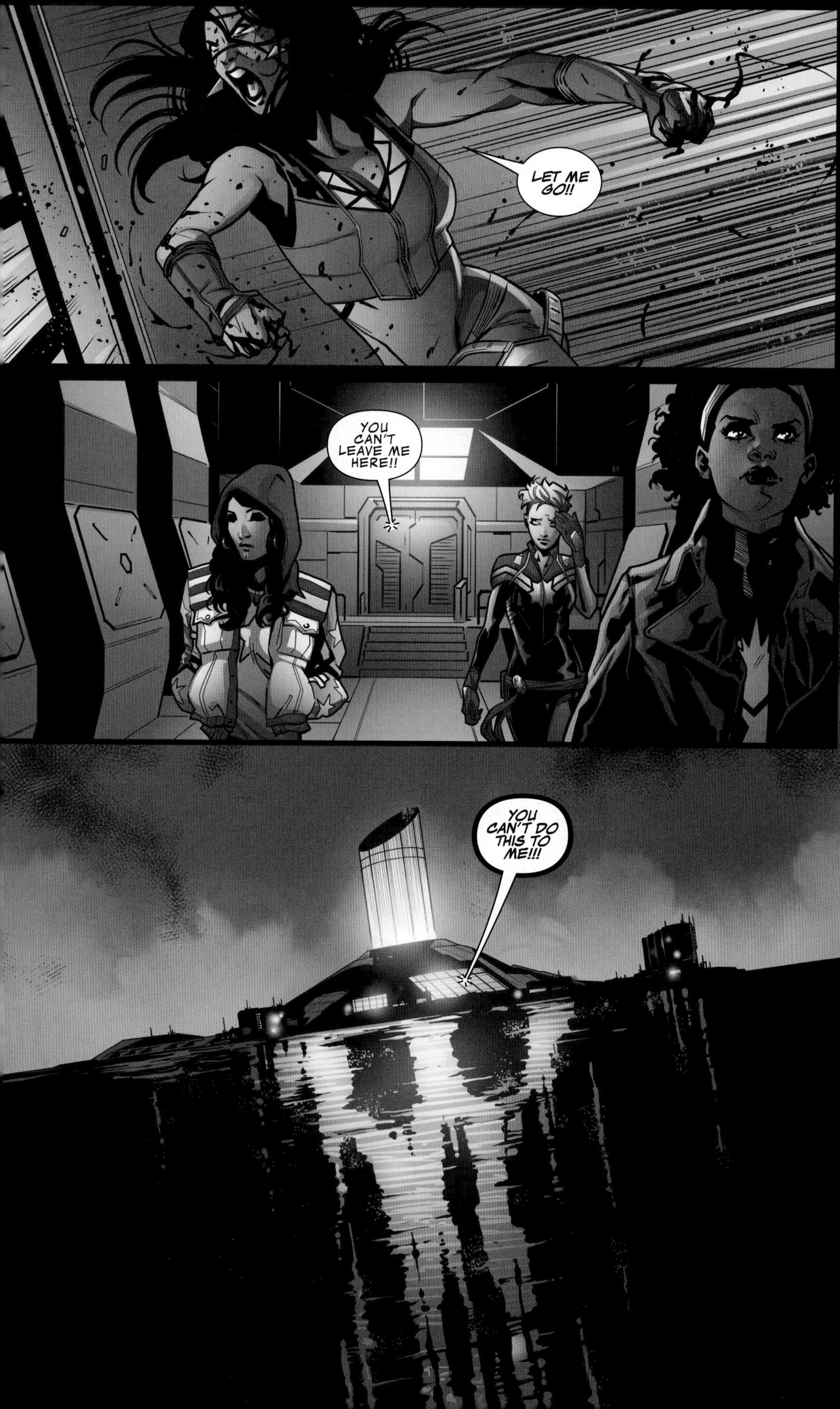
LET ME GO!!
YOU CAN'T LEAVE ME HERE!!
YOU CAN'T DO THIS TO ME!!!

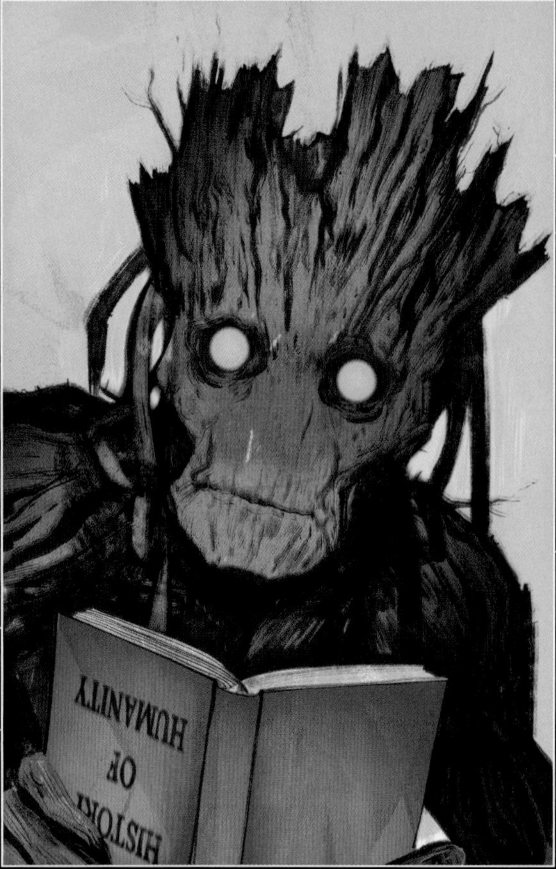
OF
HUMANITY

#16 VARIANT BY
TULA LOTAY

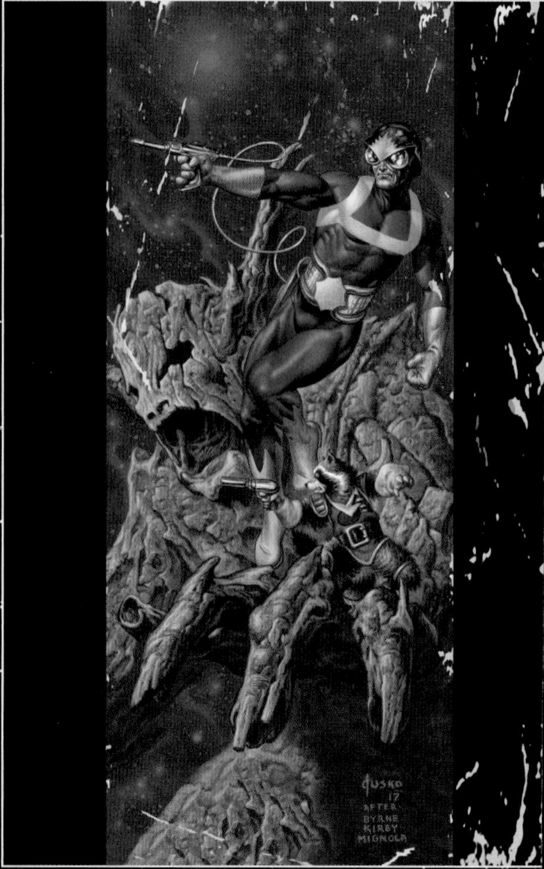
JUSKO
17
AFTER
BYRNE
KIRBY
MIGNOLA

#17 CORNER BOX VARIANT BY
JOE JUSKO

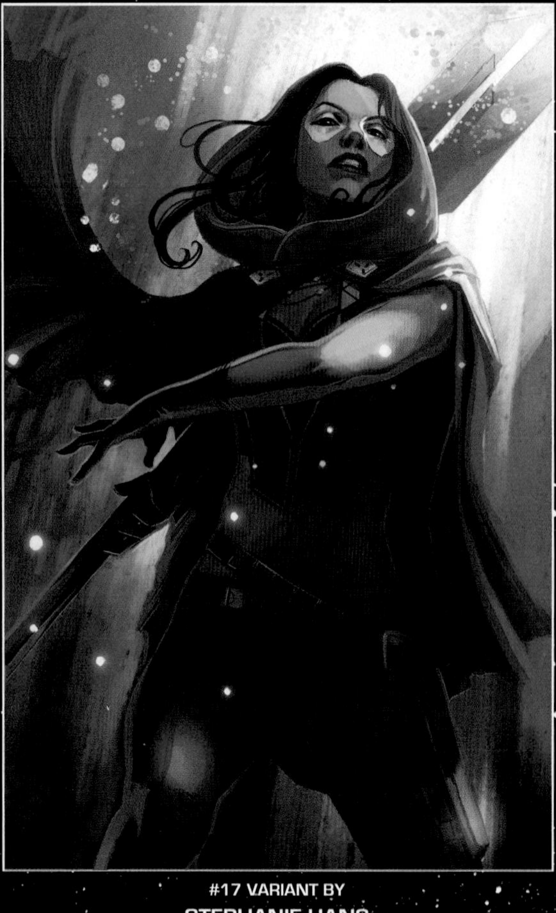

#17 VARIANT BY
STEPHANIE HANS

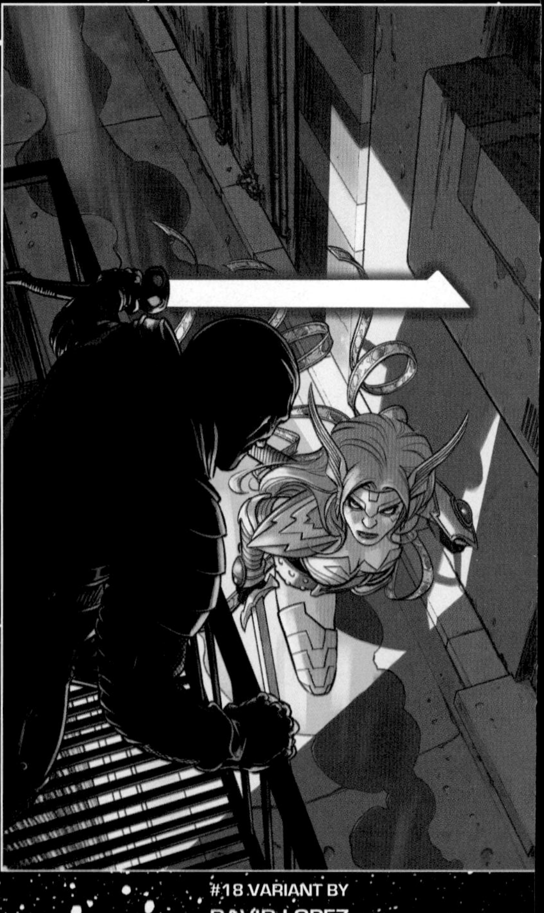

#18 VARIANT BY
DAVID LOPEZ

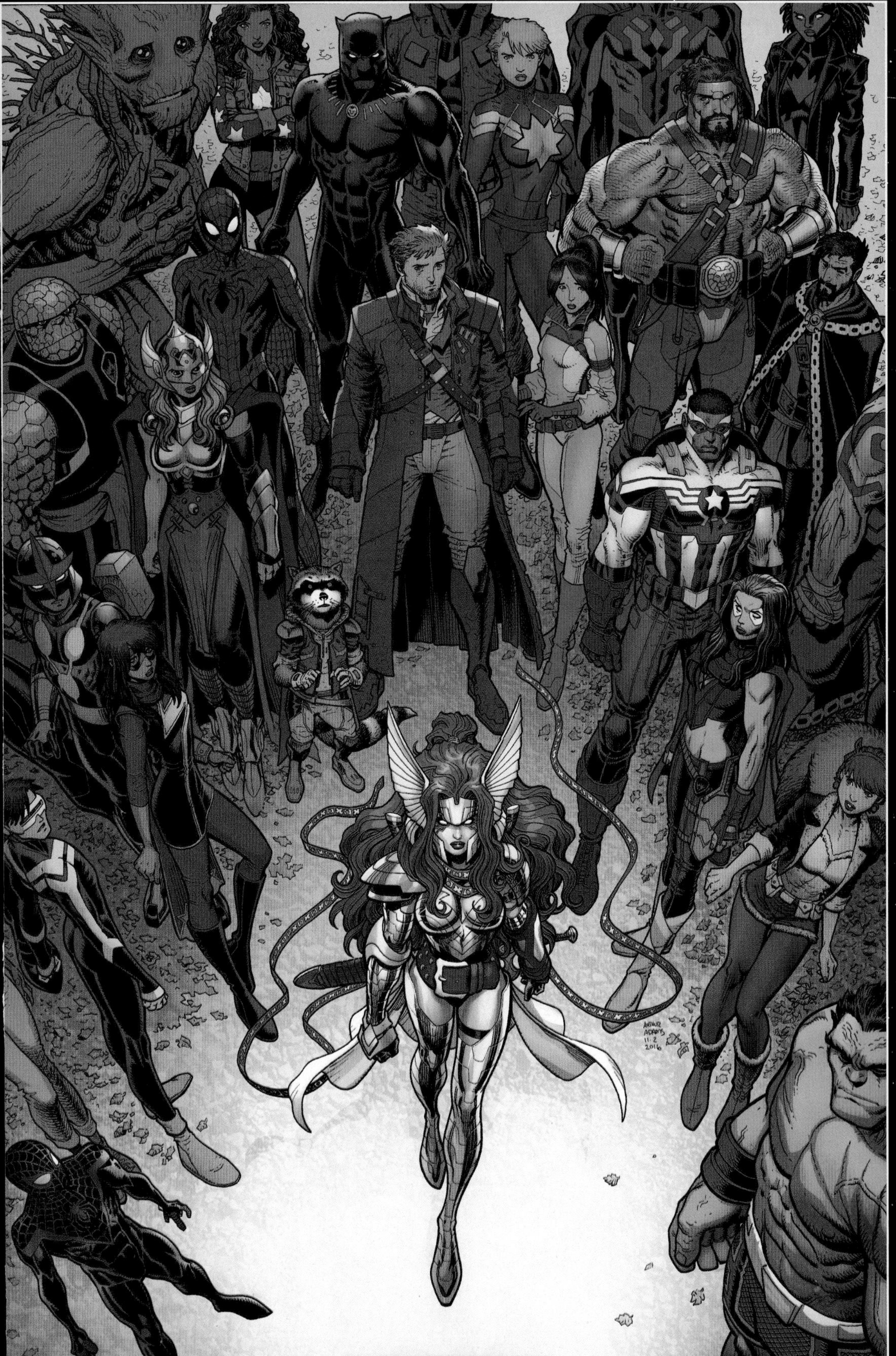
ARTHUR ADAMS 11.2 2016

18

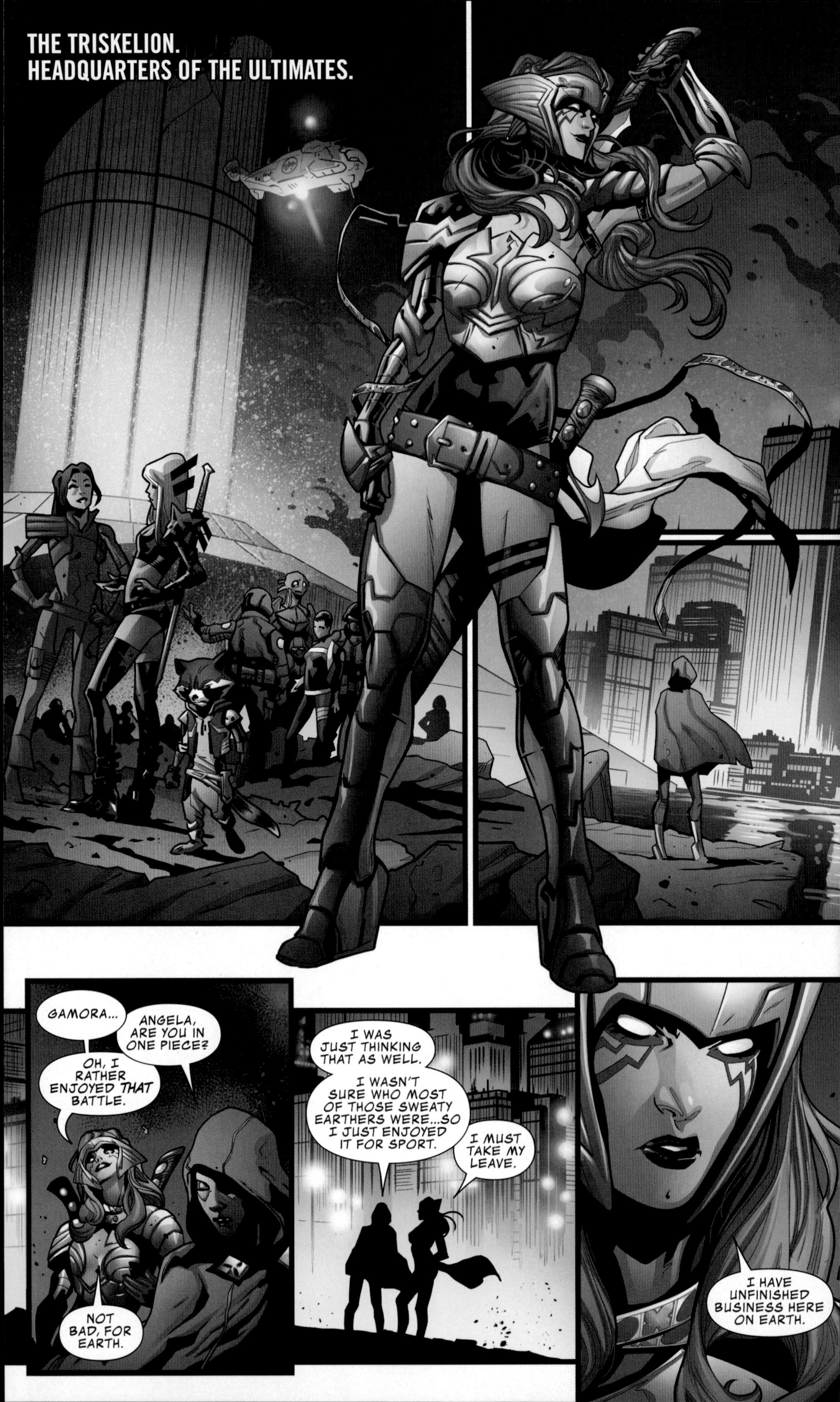
THE TRISKELION.
HEADQUARTERS OF THE ULTIMATES.
GAMORA...
ANGELA, ARE YOU IN ONE PIECE?
OH, I RATHER ENJOYED THAT BATTLE.
NOT BAD, FOR EARTH.
I WAS JUST THINKING THAT AS WELL.
I WASN'T SURE WHO MOST OF THOSE SWEATY EARTHERS WERE...SO I JUST ENJOYED IT FOR SPORT.
I MUST TAKE MY LEAVE.
I HAVE UNFINISHED BUSINESS HERE ON EARTH.

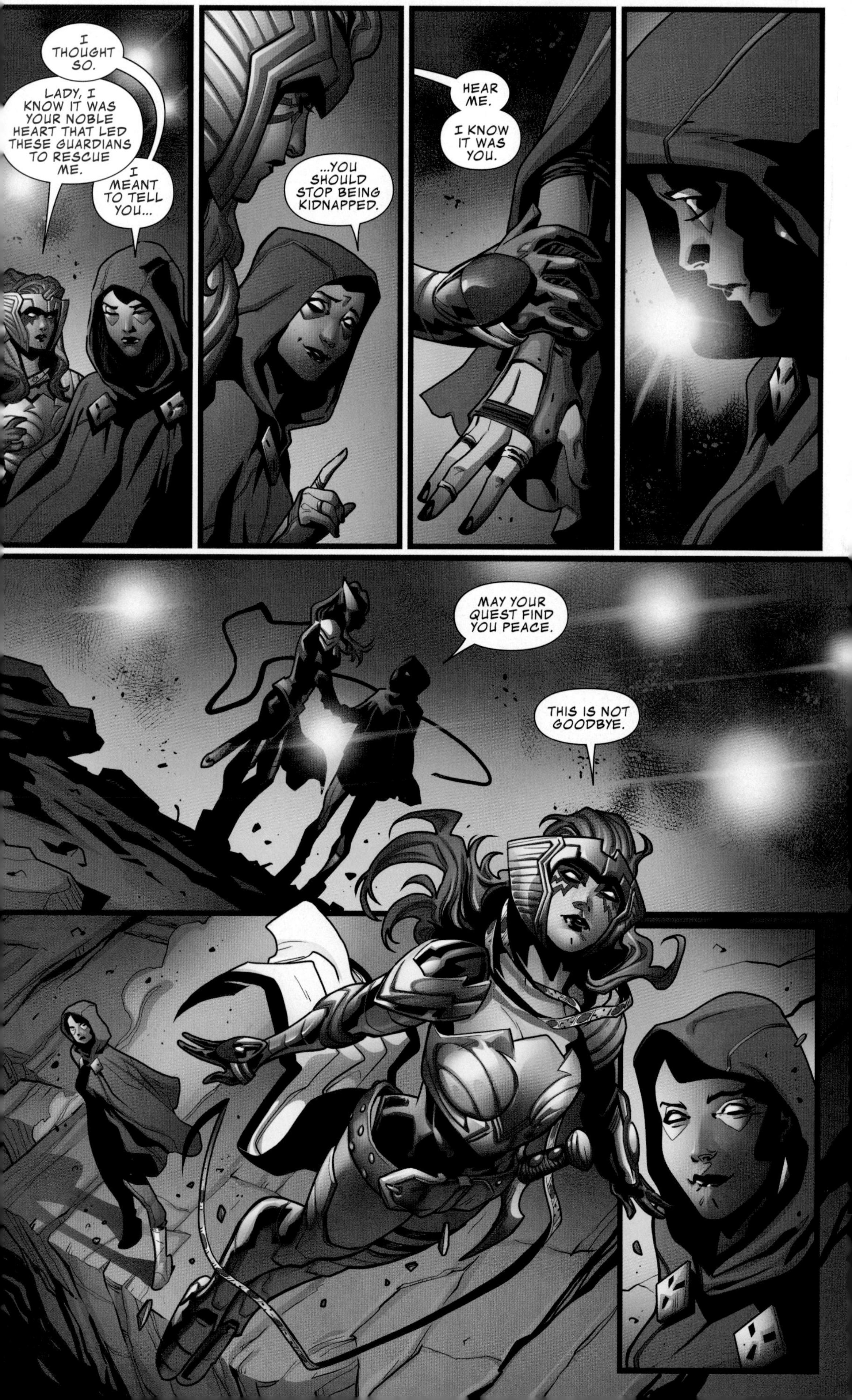
I THOUGHT SO.
LADY, I KNOW IT WAS YOUR NOBLE HEART THAT LED THESE GUARDIANS TO RESCUE ME.
I MEANT TO TELL YOU...
...YOU SHOULD STOP BEING KIDNAPPED.
HEAR ME.
I KNOW IT WAS YOU.
MAY YOUR QUEST FIND YOU PEACE.
THIS IS NOT GOODBYE.

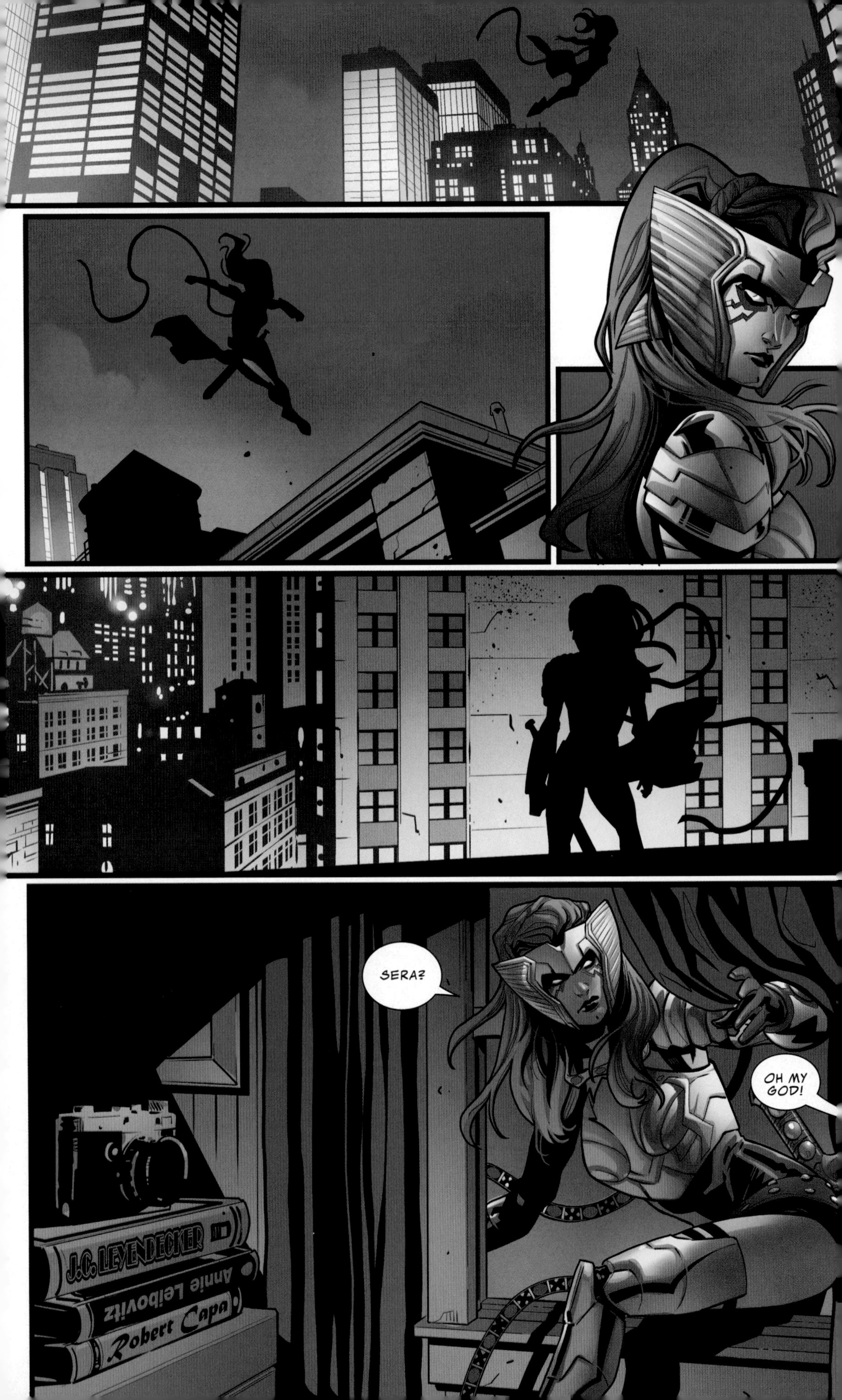
SERA?
OH MY GOD!
J.C. LEYENDECKER
Annie Leibovitz
Robert Capa

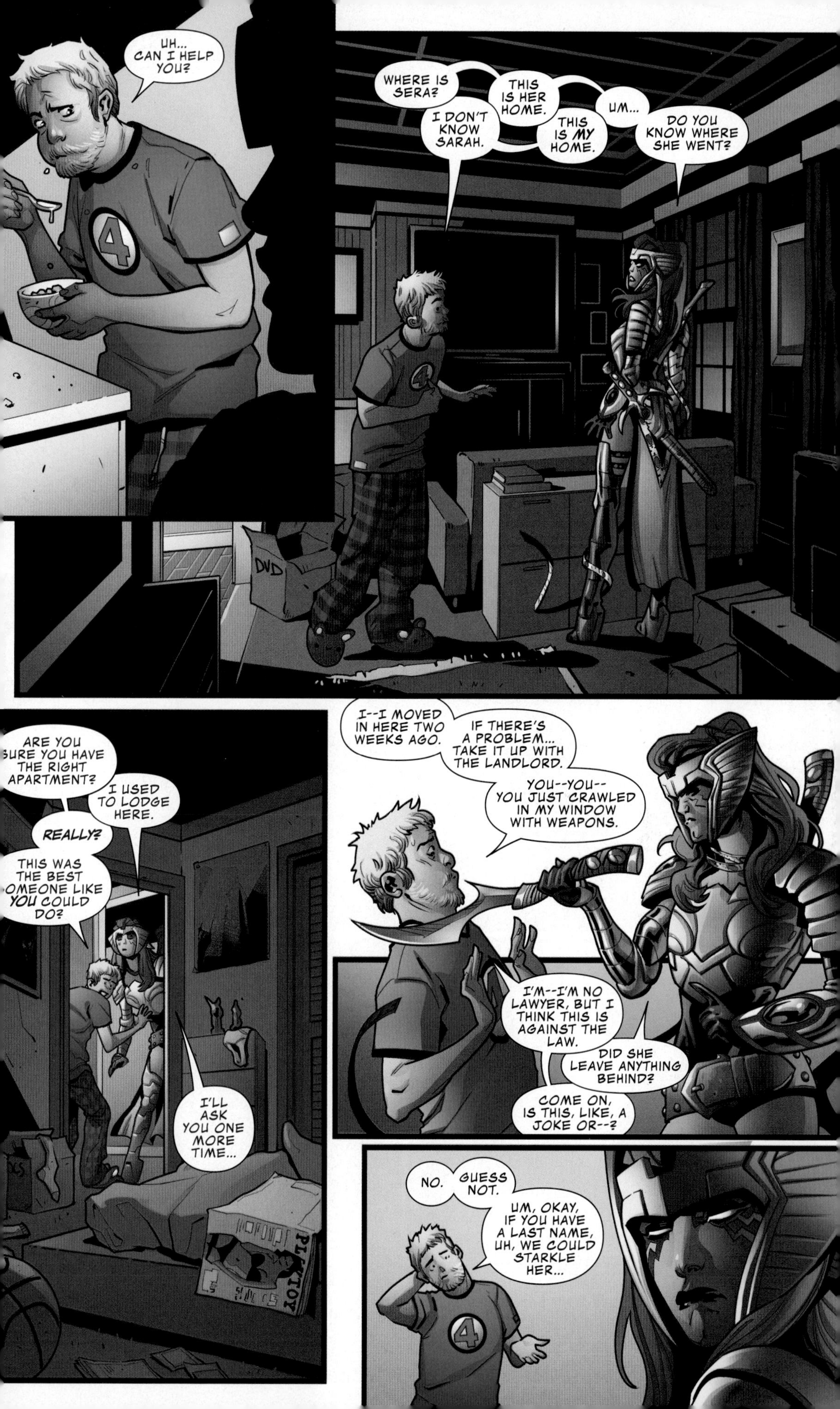
UH... CAN I HELP YOU?
WHERE IS SERA?
I DON'T KNOW SARAH.
THIS IS HER HOME.
THIS IS *MY* HOME.
UM...
DO YOU KNOW WHERE SHE WENT?
DVD
ARE YOU SURE YOU HAVE THE RIGHT APARTMENT?
I USED TO LODGE HERE.
REALLY?
THIS WAS THE BEST SOMEONE LIKE *YOU* COULD DO?
I'LL ASK YOU ONE MORE TIME...
I--I MOVED IN HERE TWO WEEKS AGO.
IF THERE'S A PROBLEM... TAKE IT UP WITH THE LANDLORD.
YOU--YOU-- YOU JUST CRAWLED IN MY WINDOW WITH WEAPONS.
I'M--I'M NO LAWYER, BUT I THINK THIS IS AGAINST THE LAW.
DID SHE LEAVE ANYTHING BEHIND?
COME ON, IS THIS, LIKE, A JOKE OR--?
NO.
GUESS NOT.
UM, OKAY, IF YOU HAVE A LAST NAME, UH, WE COULD STARKLE HER...

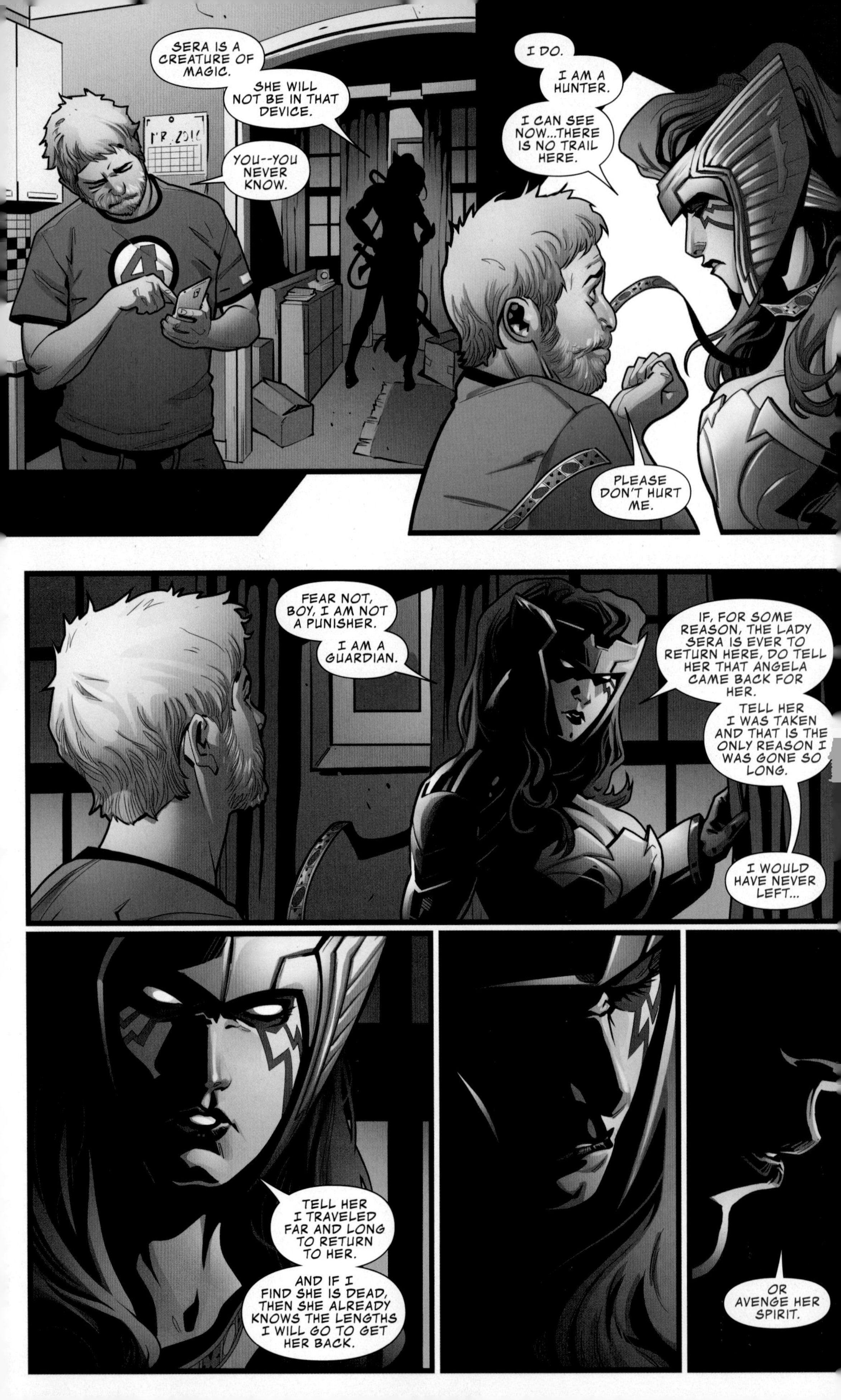
SERA IS A CREATURE OF MAGIC.
SHE WILL NOT BE IN THAT DEVICE.
YOU--YOU NEVER KNOW.
I DO.
I AM A HUNTER.
I CAN SEE NOW...THERE IS NO TRAIL HERE.
PLEASE DON'T HURT ME.
FEAR NOT, BOY, I AM NOT A PUNISHER.
I AM A GUARDIAN.
IF, FOR SOME REASON, THE LADY SERA IS EVER TO RETURN HERE, DO TELL HER THAT ANGELA CAME BACK FOR HER.
TELL HER I WAS TAKEN AND THAT IS THE ONLY REASON I WAS GONE SO LONG.
I WOULD HAVE NEVER LEFT...
TELL HER I TRAVELED FAR AND LONG TO RETURN TO HER.
AND IF I FIND SHE IS DEAD, THEN SHE ALREADY KNOWS THE LENGTHS I WILL GO TO GET HER BACK.
OR AVENGE HER SPIRIT.

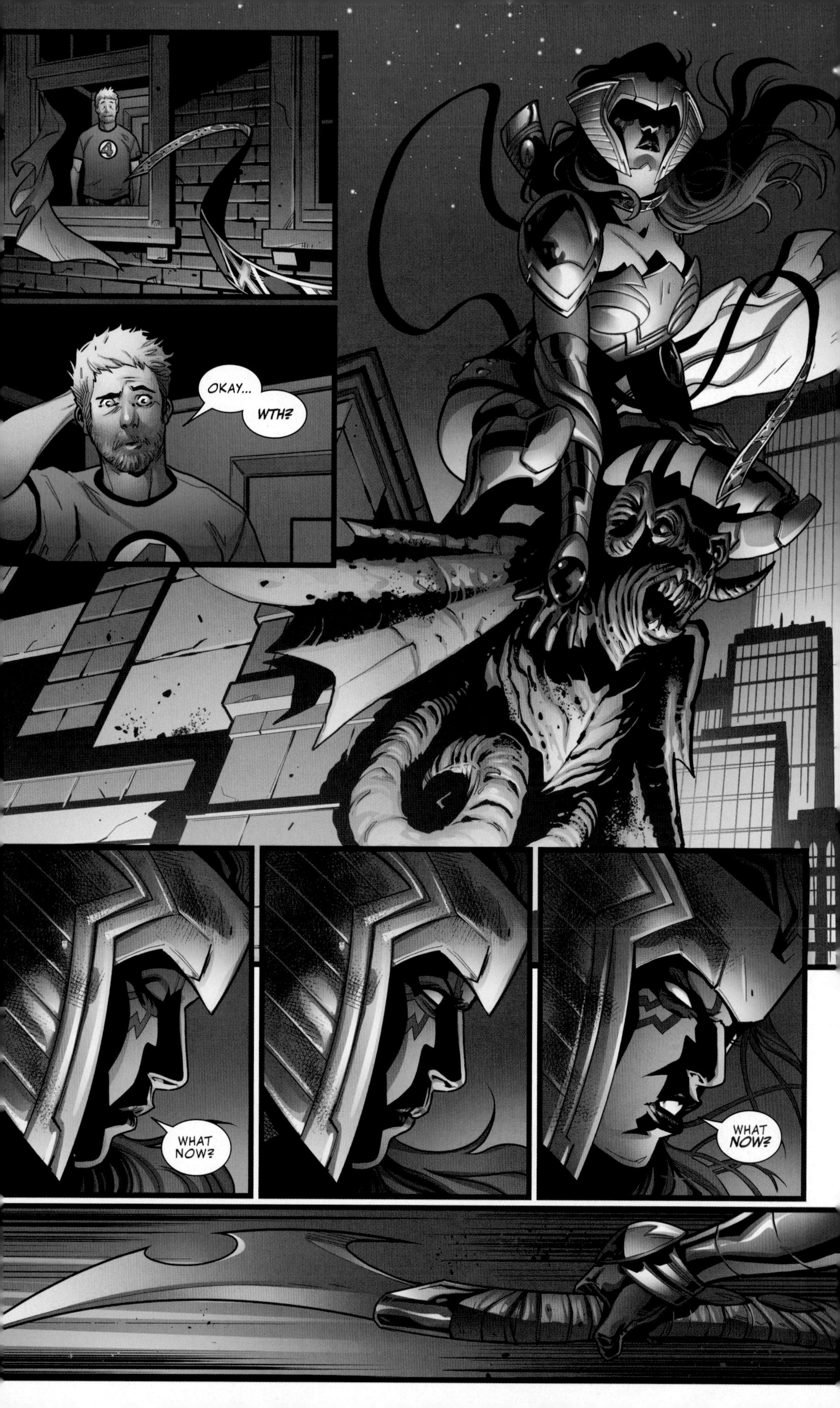
OKAY...
WTH?
WHAT NOW?
WHAT NOW?

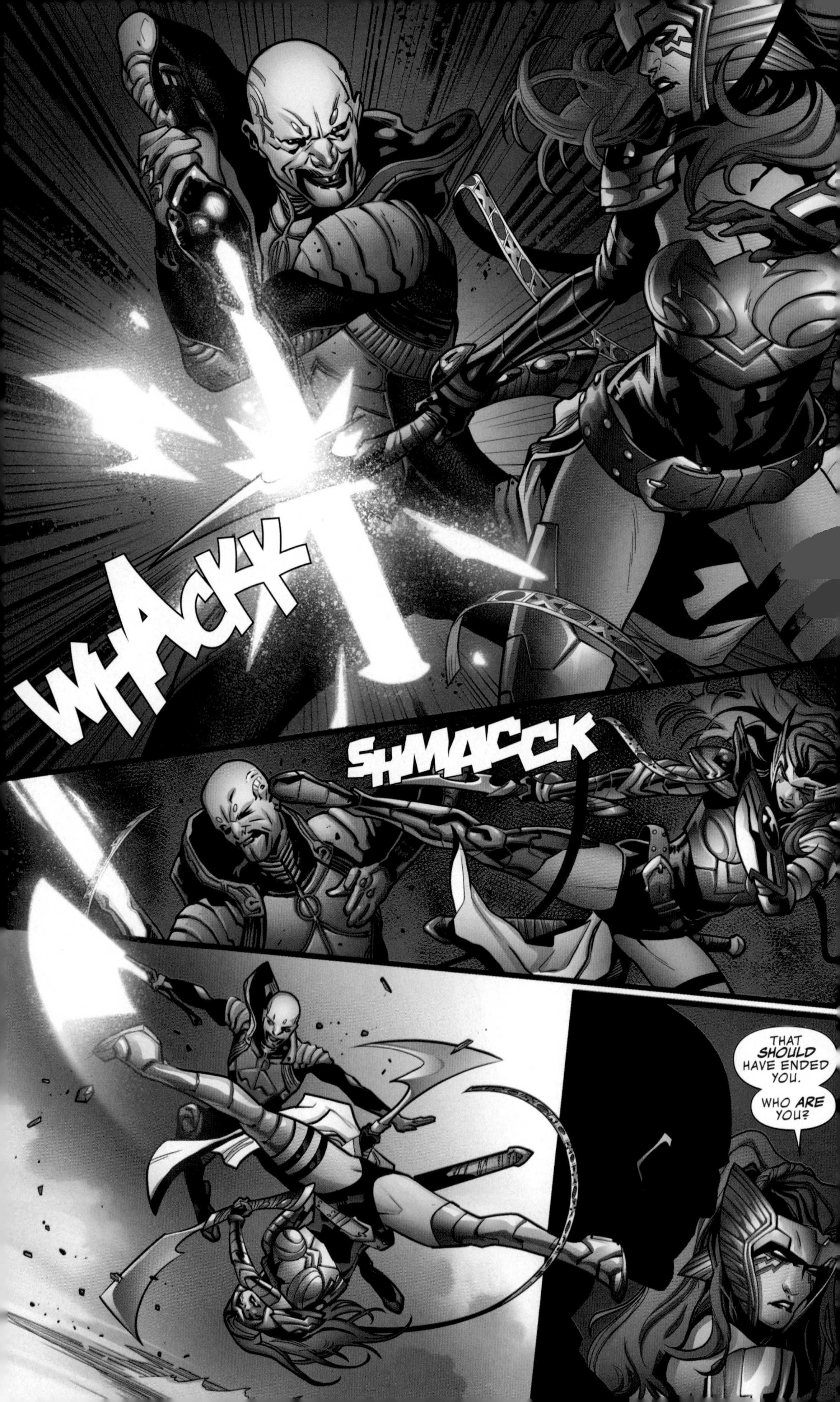
WHACK
SHMACCK
THAT SHOULD HAVE ENDED YOU.
WHO ARE YOU?

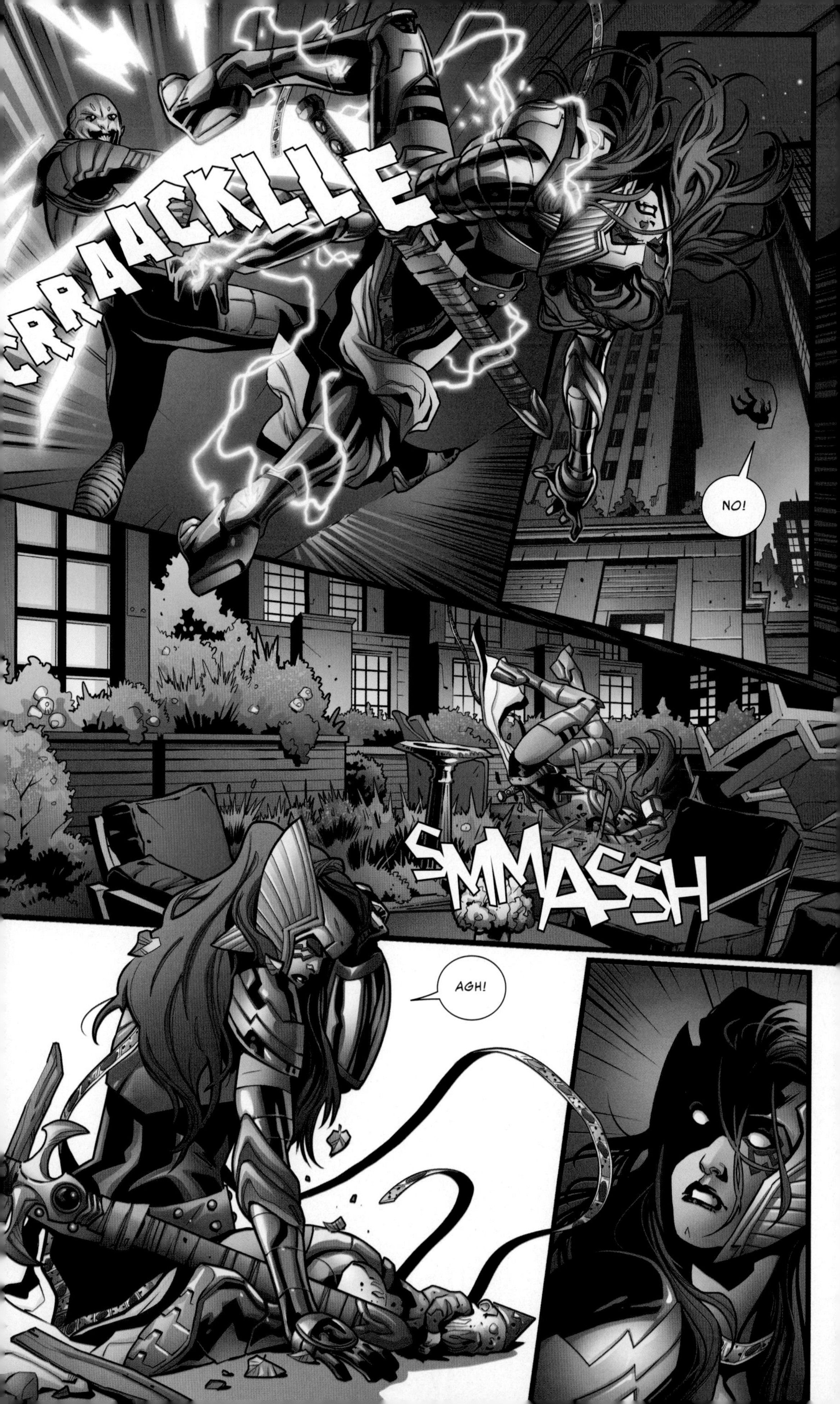
CRRAACKLLE
NO!
SMMASSH
AGH!

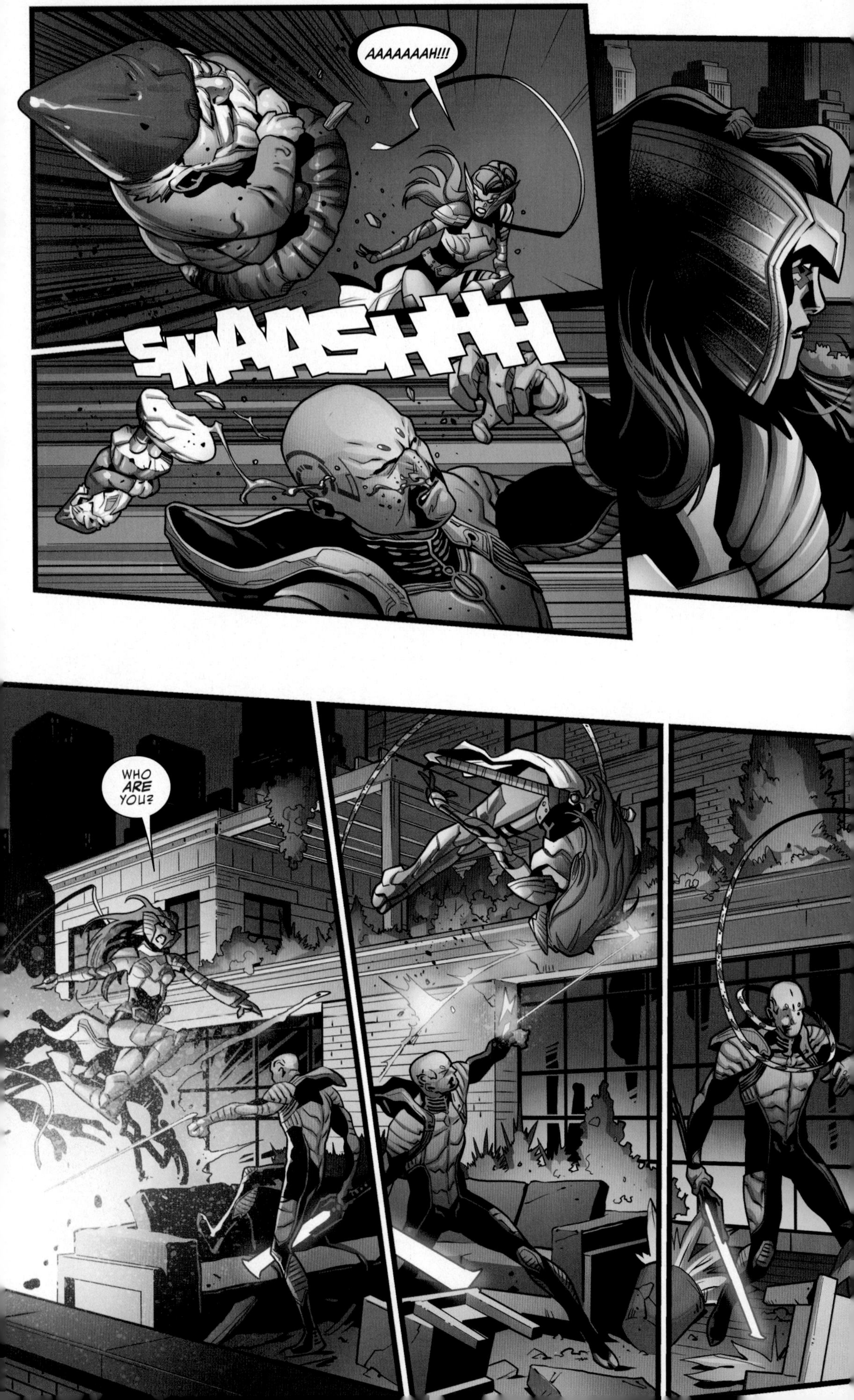
AAAAAAAH!!!
SMAASHHH
WHO ARE YOU?

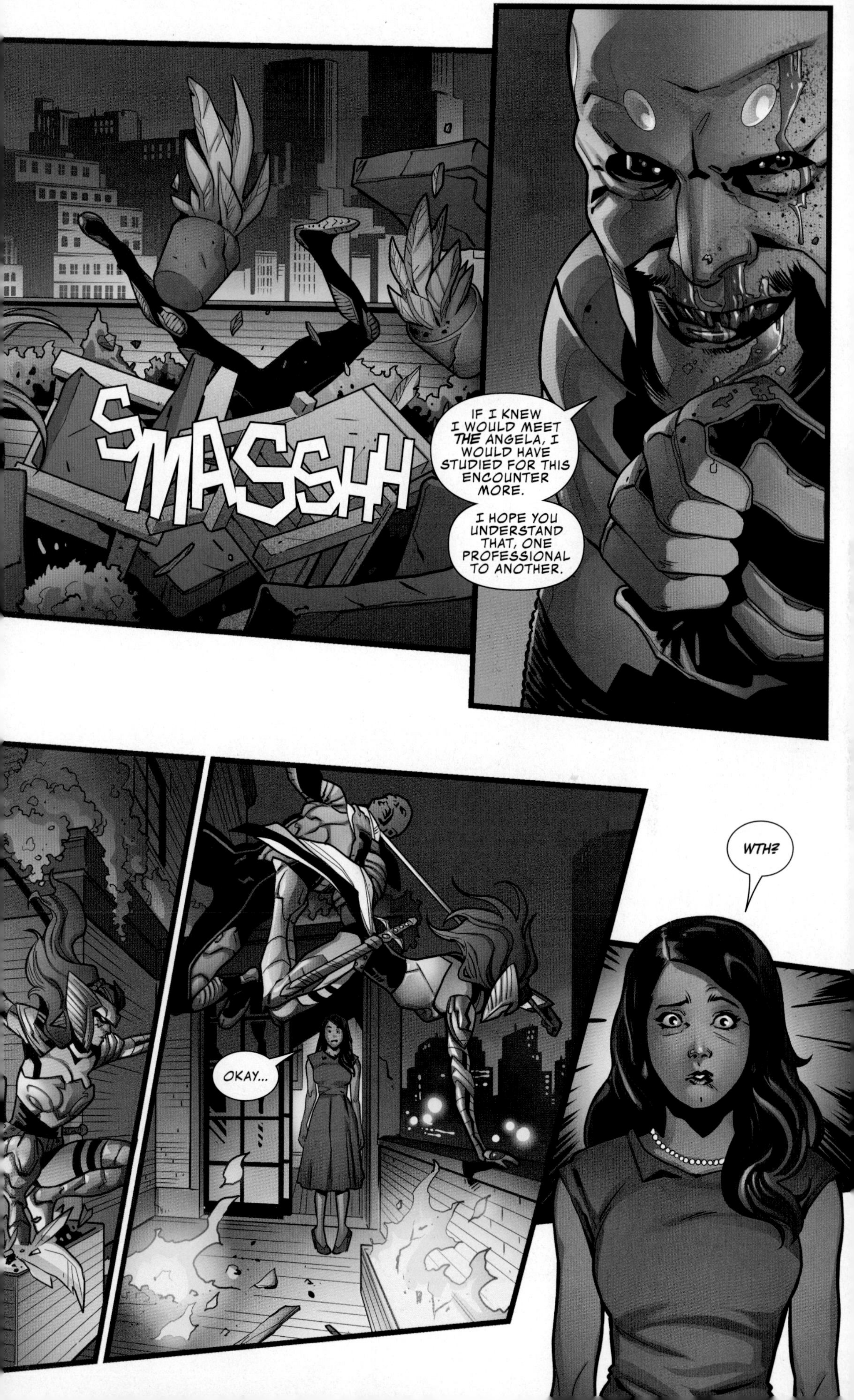
SMASSHH
IF I KNEW I WOULD MEET THE ANGELA, I WOULD HAVE STUDIED FOR THIS ENCOUNTER MORE.
I HOPE YOU UNDERSTAND THAT, ONE PROFESSIONAL TO ANOTHER.
OKAY...
WTH?

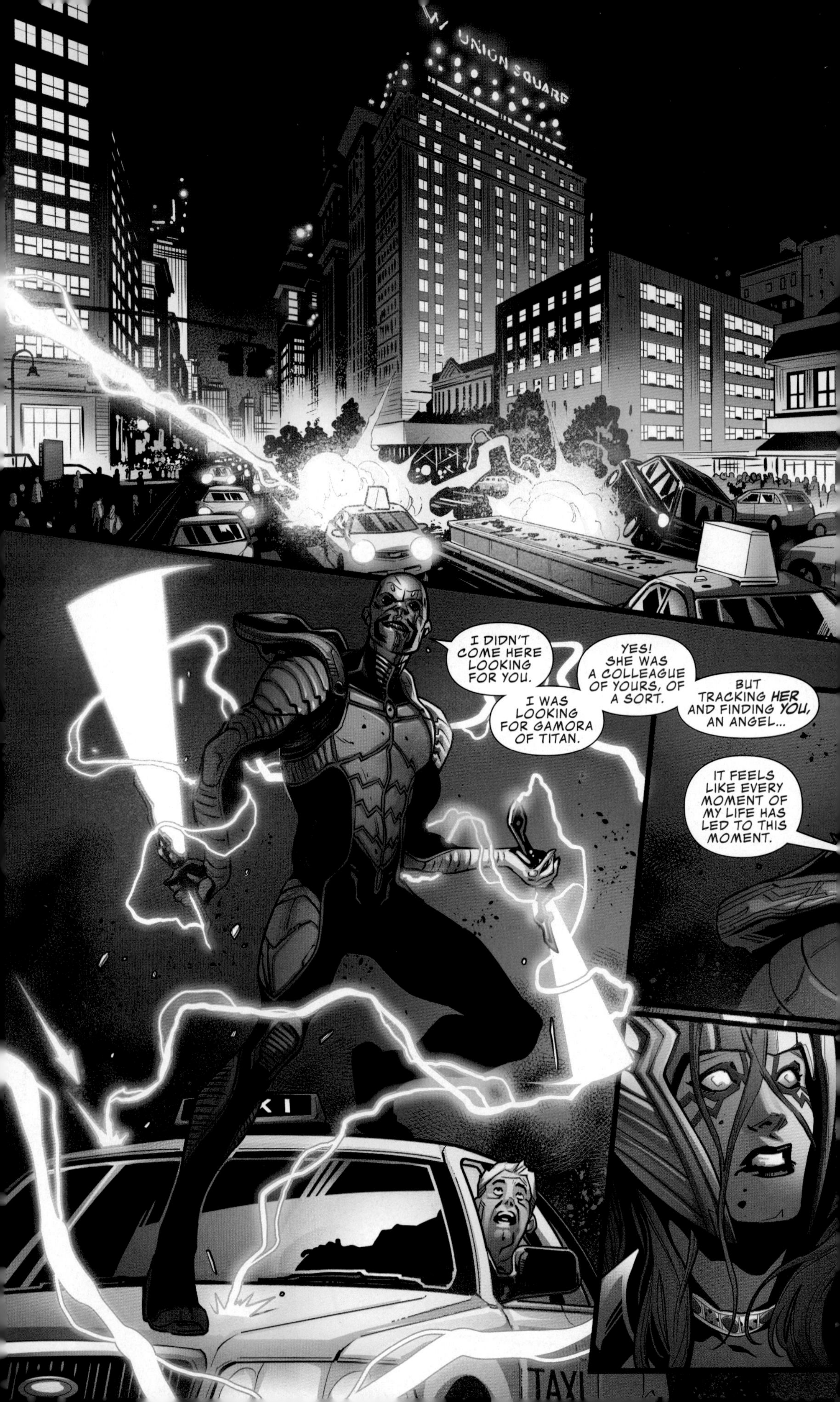
UNION SQUARE
I DIDN'T COME HERE LOOKING FOR YOU.
I WAS LOOKING FOR GAMORA OF TITAN.
YES! SHE WAS A COLLEAGUE OF YOURS, OF A SORT.
BUT TRACKING HER AND FINDING YOU, AN ANGEL...
IT FEELS LIKE EVERY MOMENT OF MY LIFE HAS LED TO THIS MOMENT.
TAXI

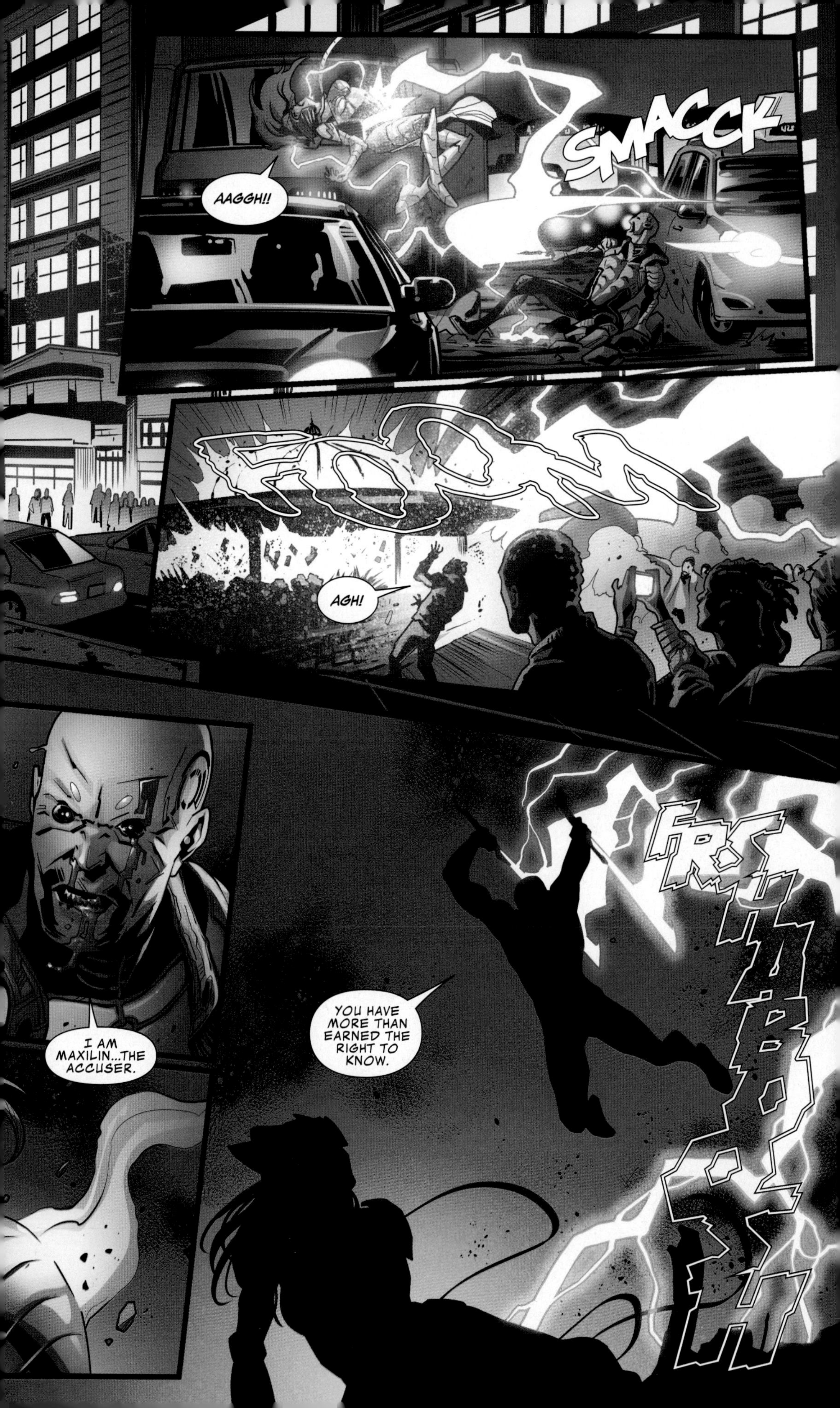
AAGGH!!
SMACCK
AGH!
I AM MAXILIN...THE ACCUSER.
YOU HAVE MORE THAN EARNED THE RIGHT TO KNOW.

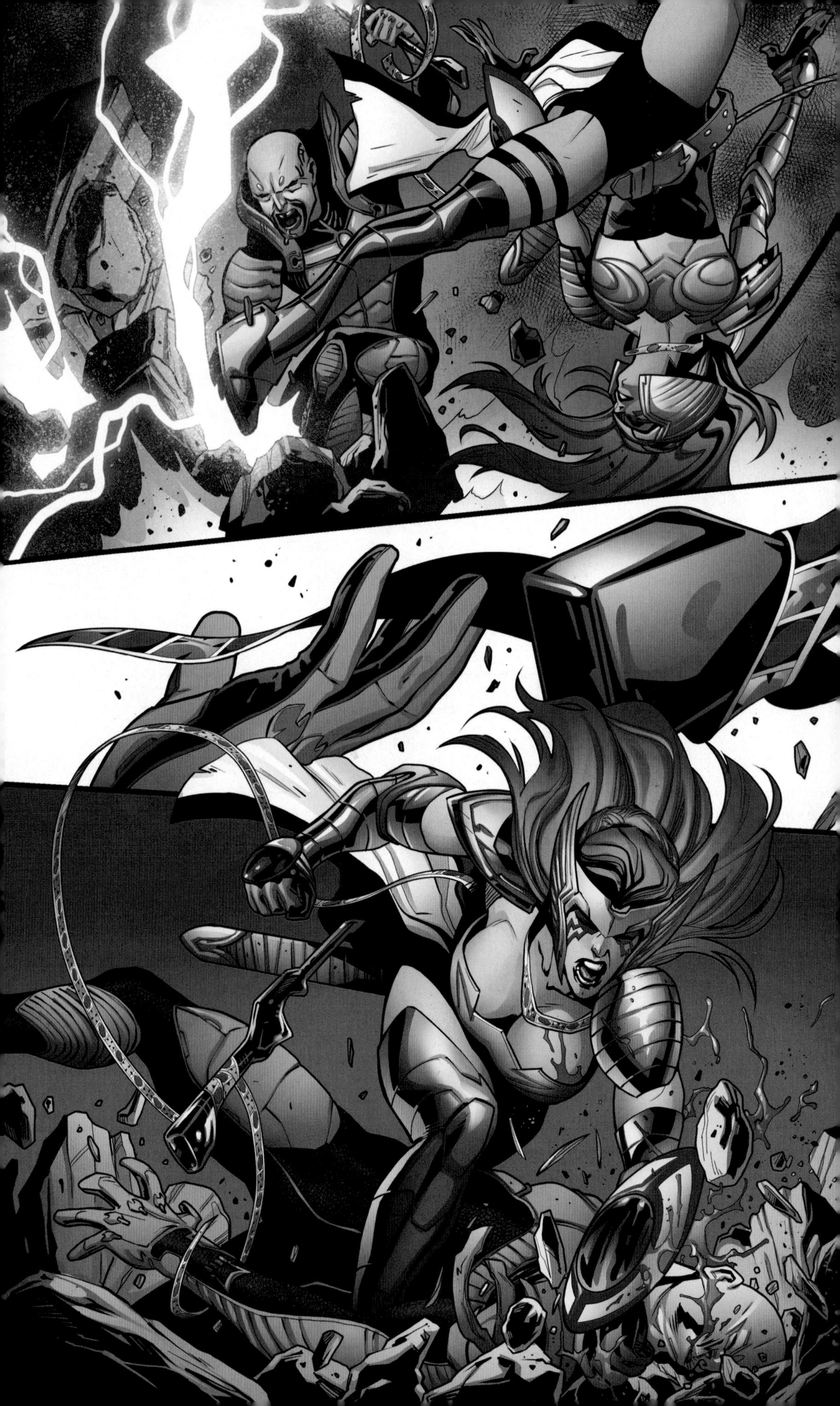

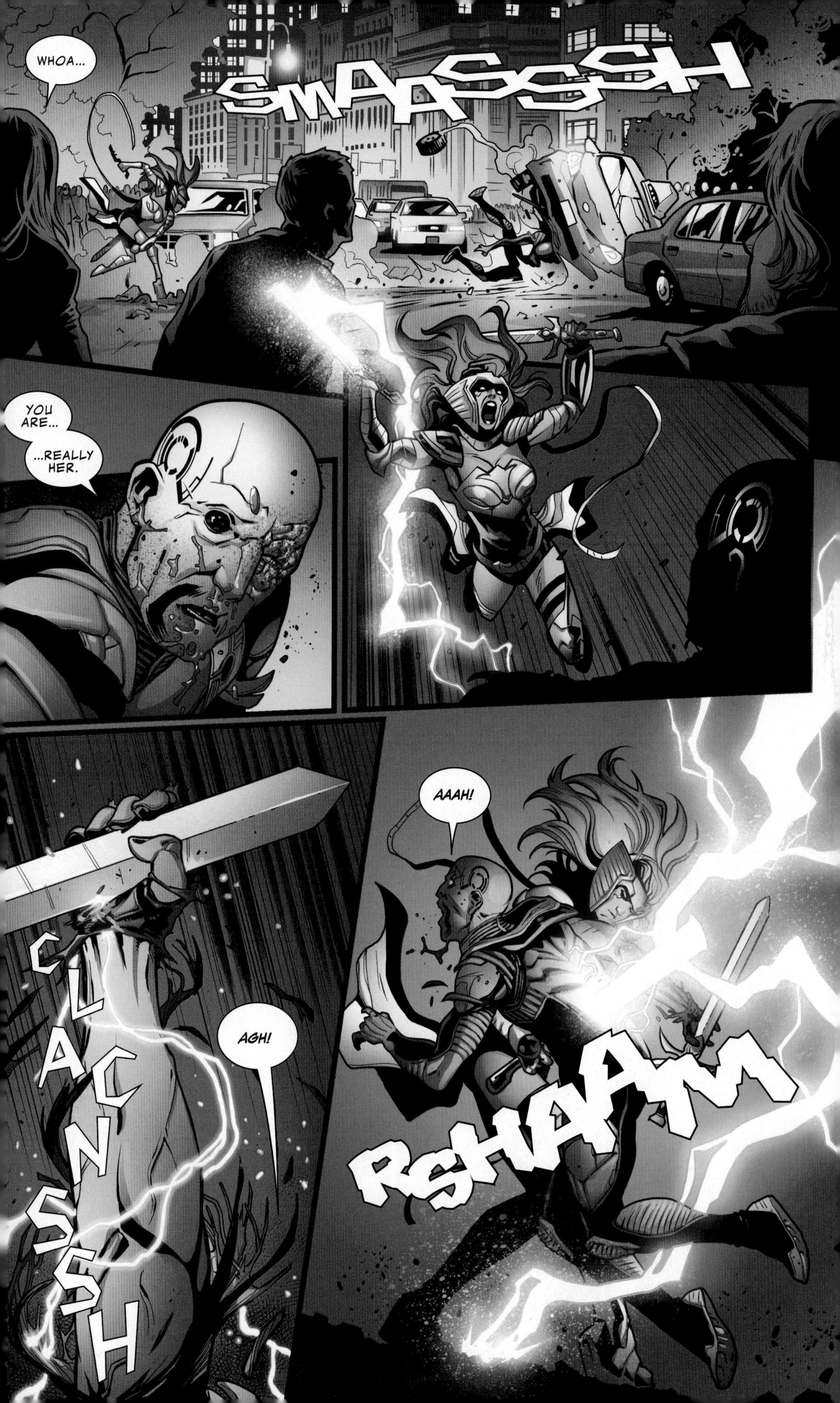
WHOA...
SMAASSSH
YOU ARE...
...REALLY HER.
CLLAANSSSH
AGH!
AAAH!
RSHAAM

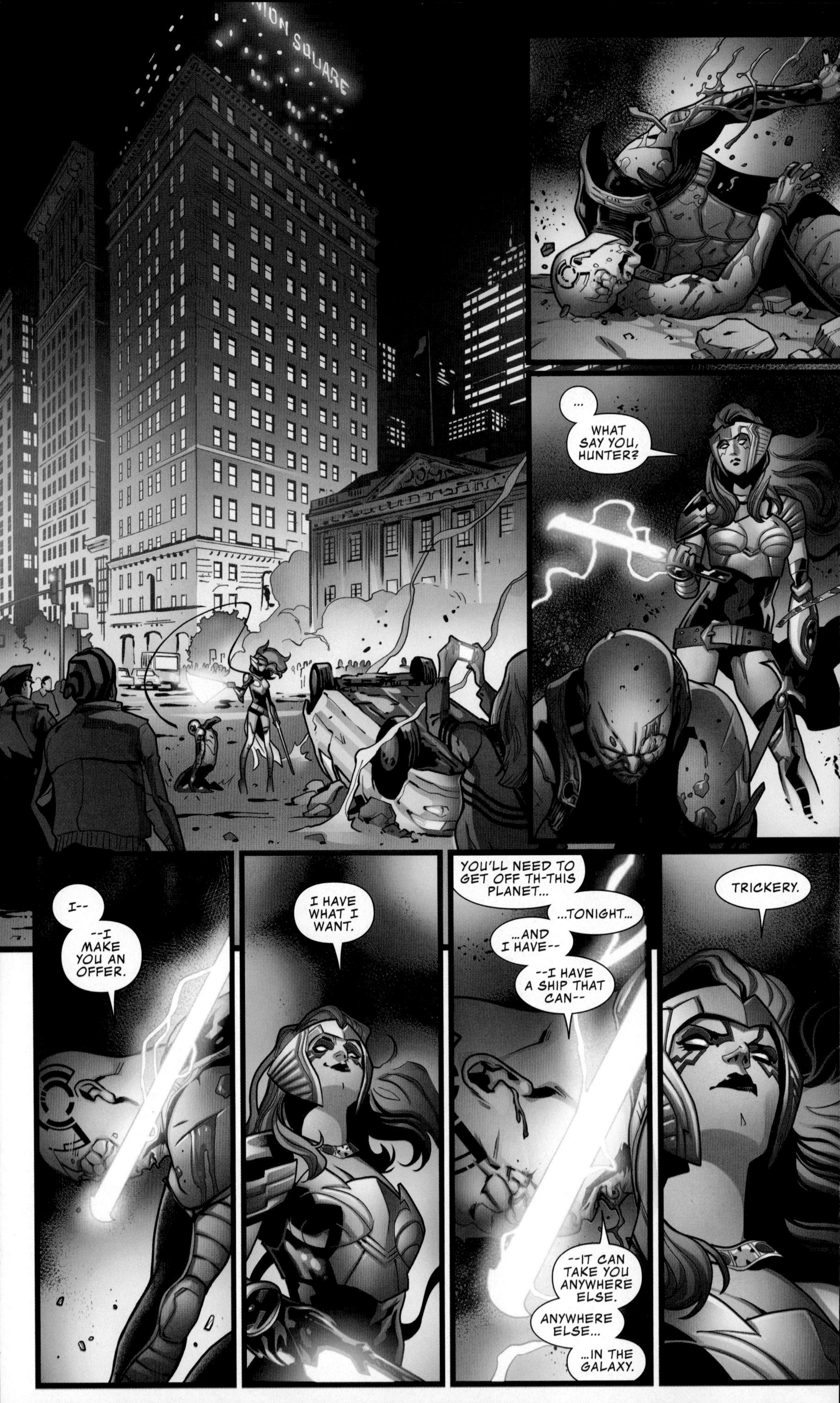
UNION SQUARE
...
WHAT SAY YOU, HUNTER?
I--
--I MAKE YOU AN OFFER.
I HAVE WHAT I WANT.
YOU'LL NEED TO GET OFF TH-THIS PLANET...
...TONIGHT...
...AND I HAVE--
--I HAVE A SHIP THAT CAN--
--IT CAN TAKE YOU ANYWHERE ELSE.
ANYWHERE ELSE...
...IN THE GALAXY.
TRICKERY.

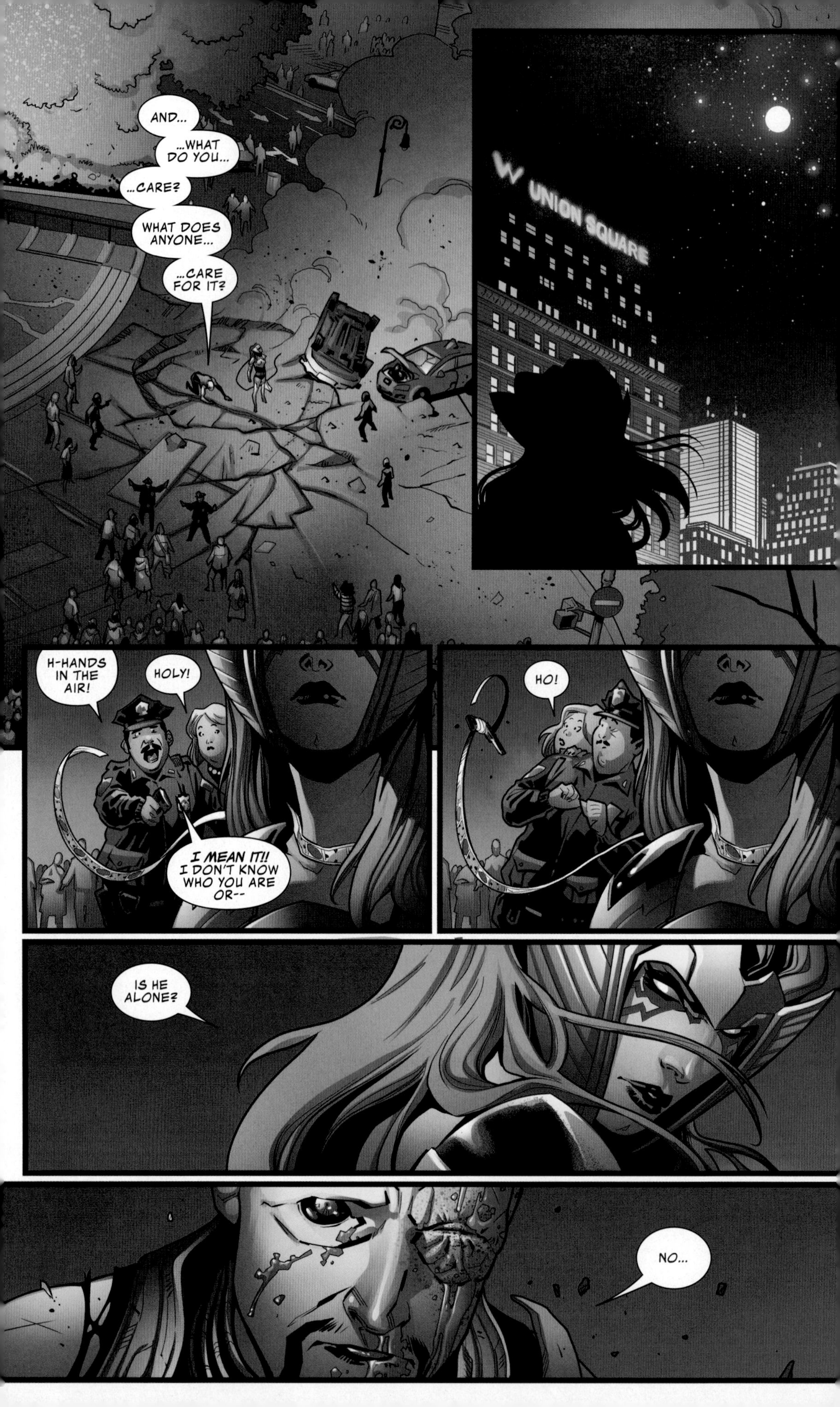

AND...
...WHAT DO YOU...
...CARE?
WHAT DOES ANYONE...
...CARE FOR IT?
W UNION SQUARE
H-HANDS IN THE AIR!
HOLY!
I MEAN IT!! I DON'T KNOW WHO YOU ARE OR--
HO!
IS HE ALONE?
NO...

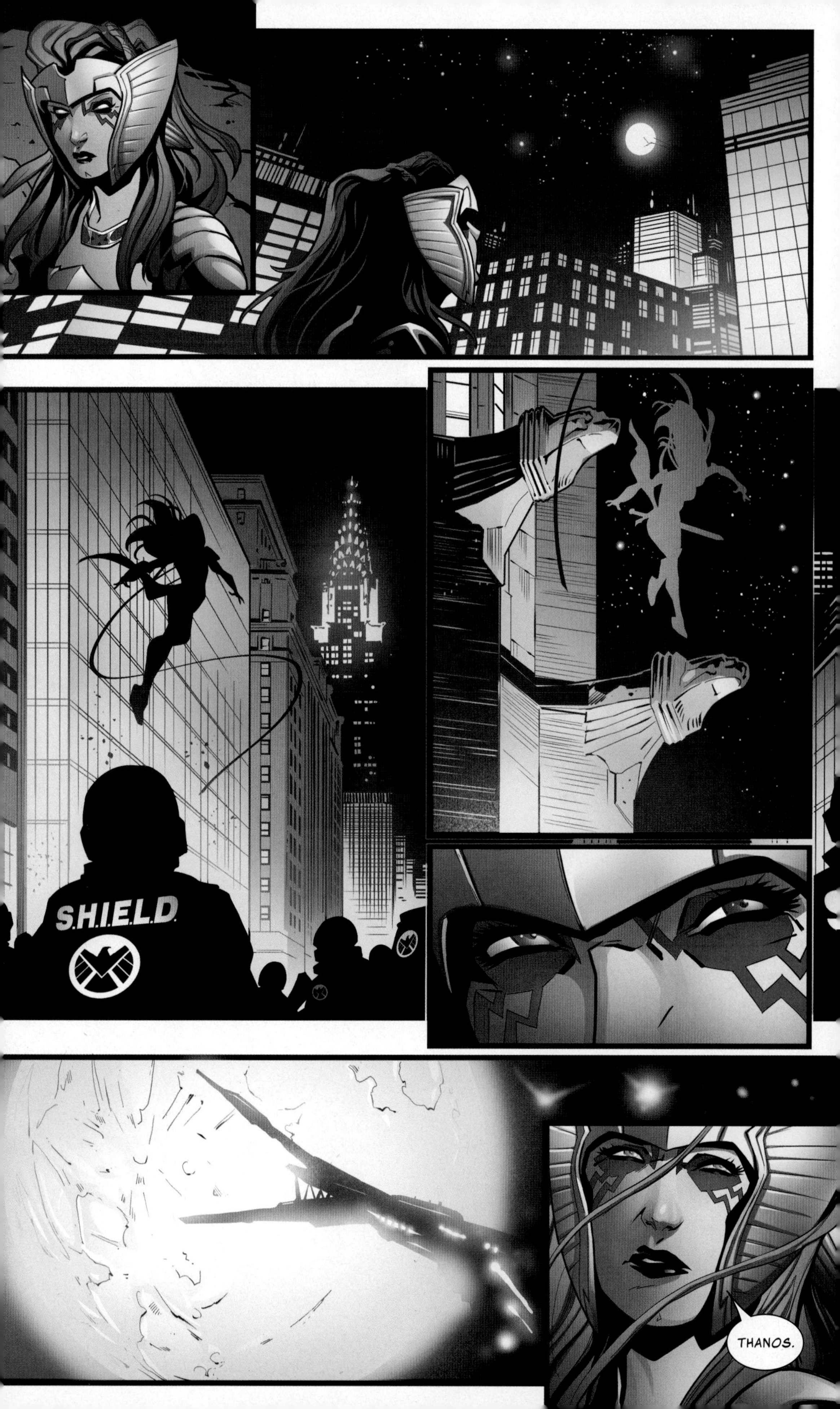
S.H.I.E.L.D.
THANOS.

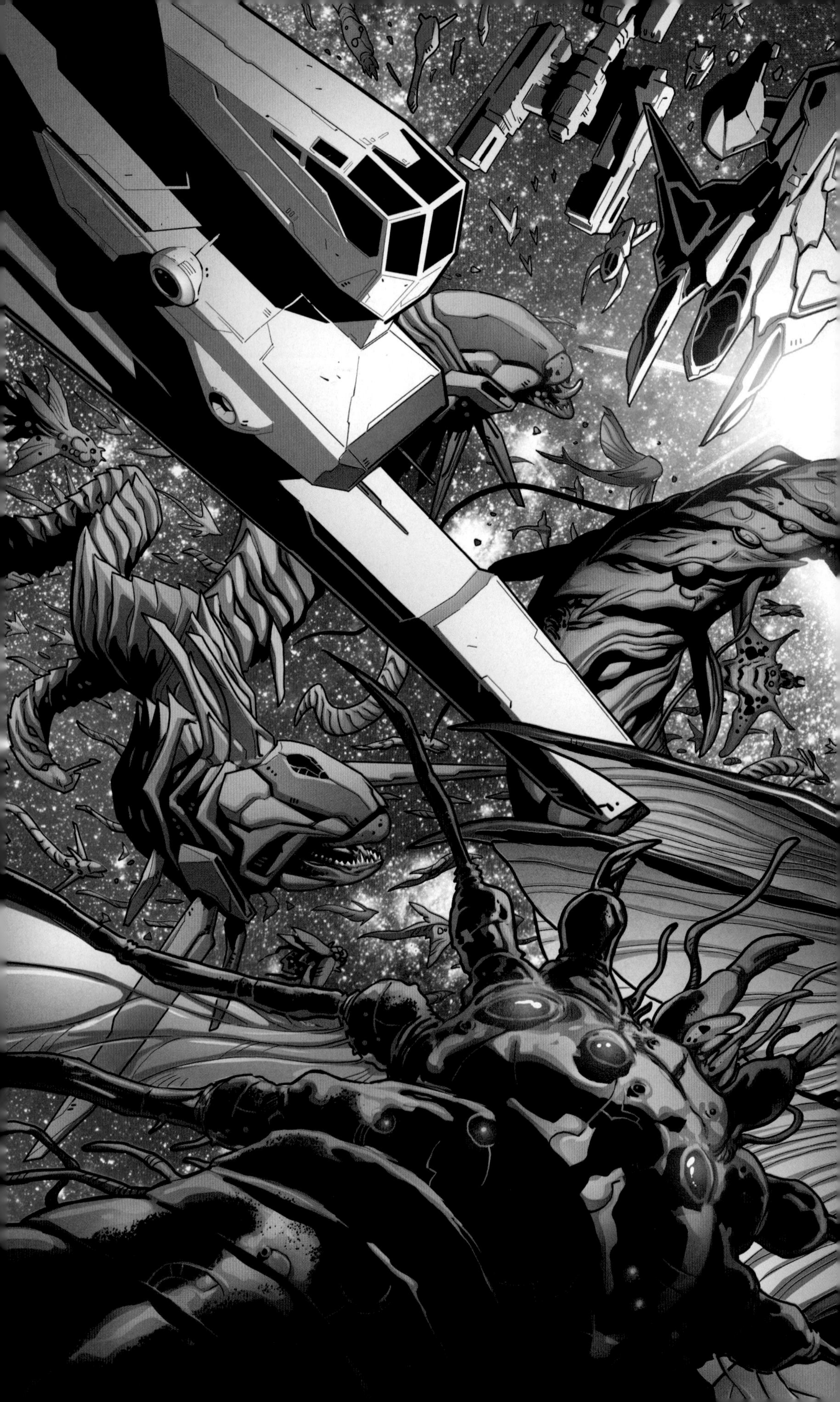

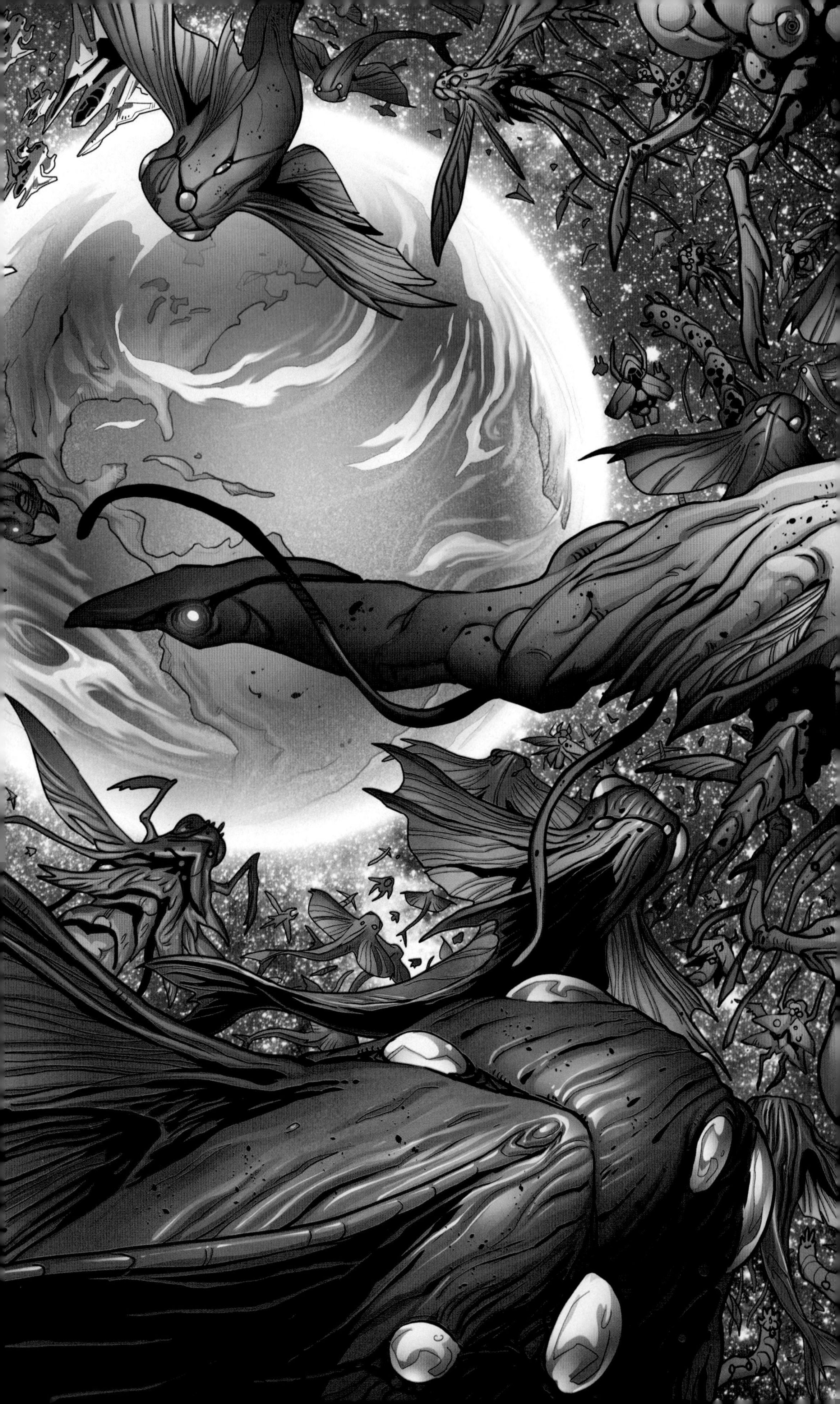

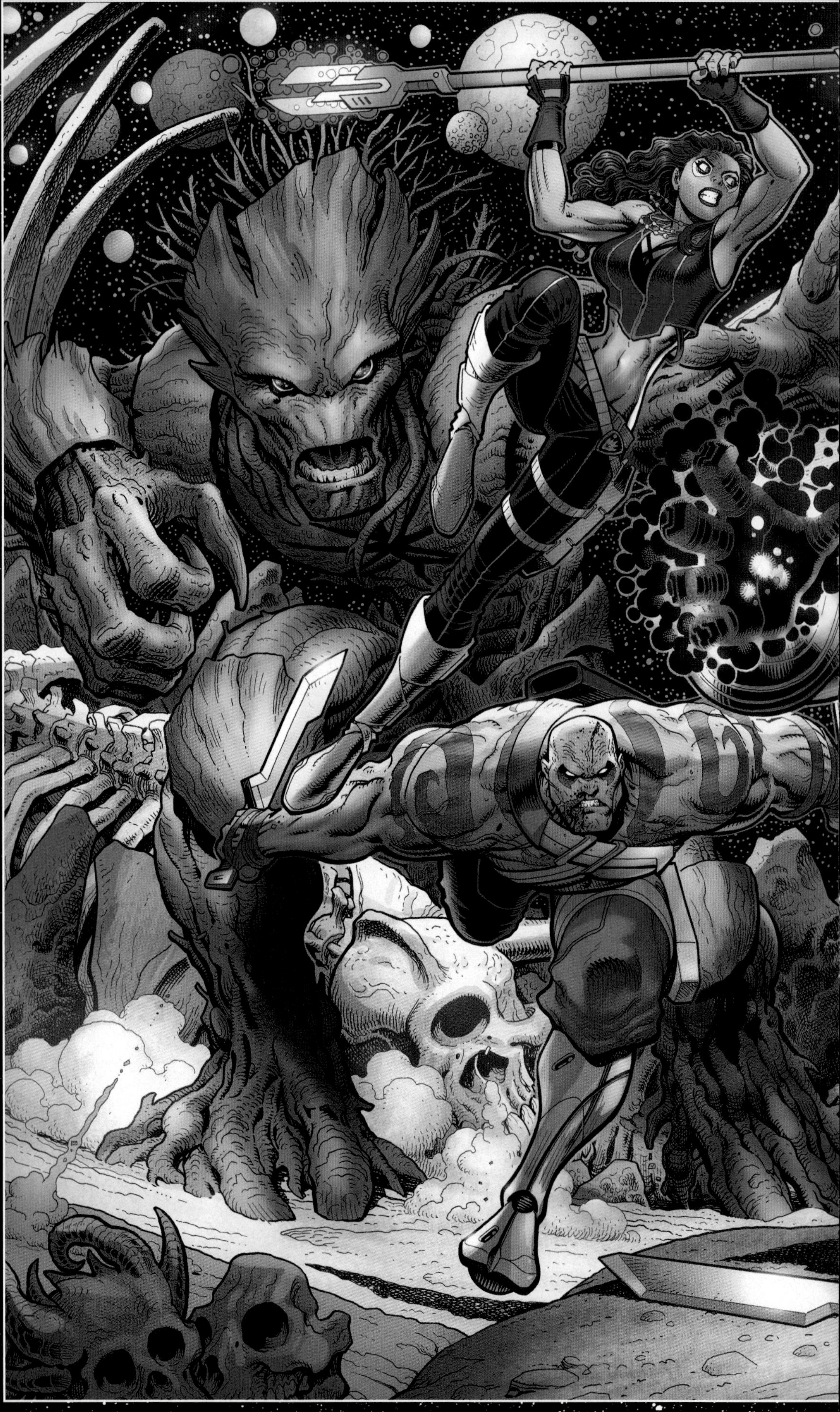

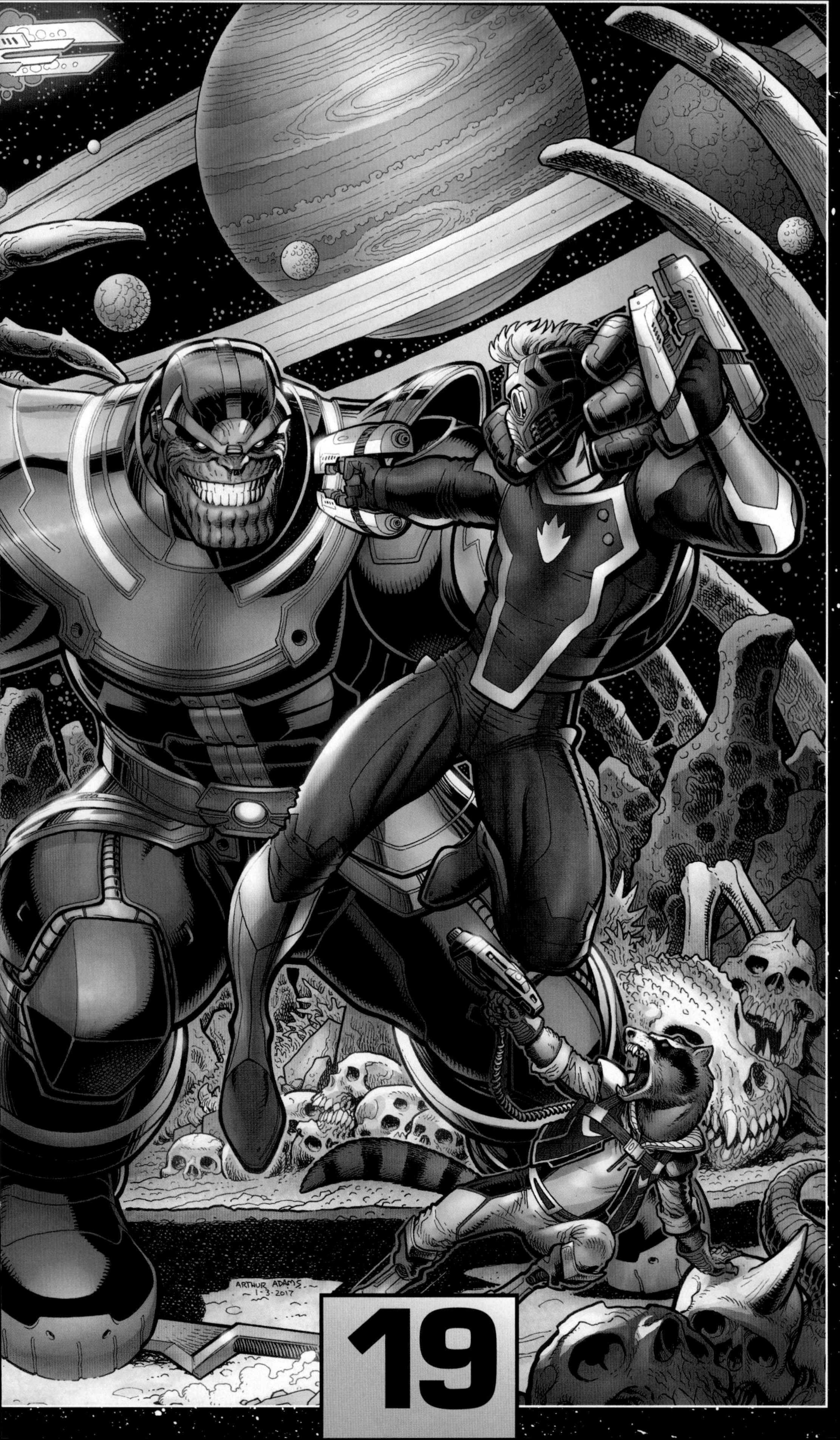
ARTHUR ADAMS
1-3-2017
19

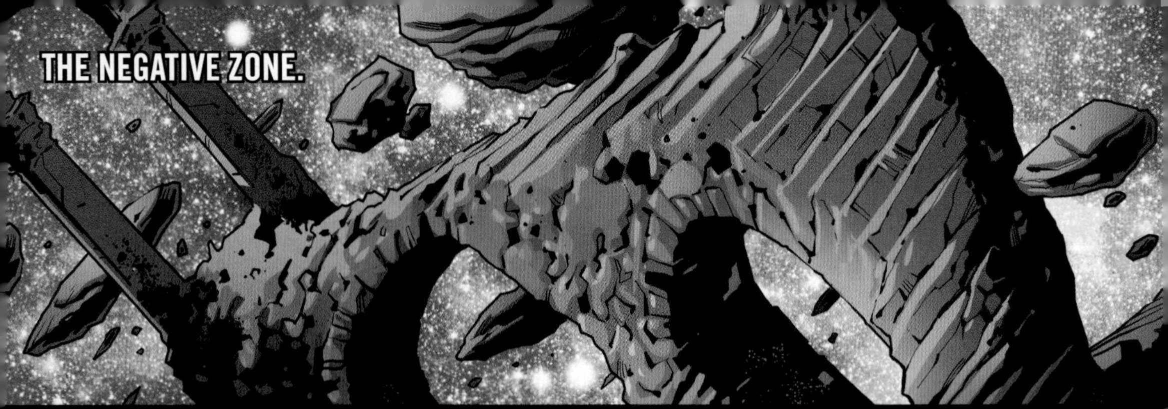
THE NEGATIVE ZONE.

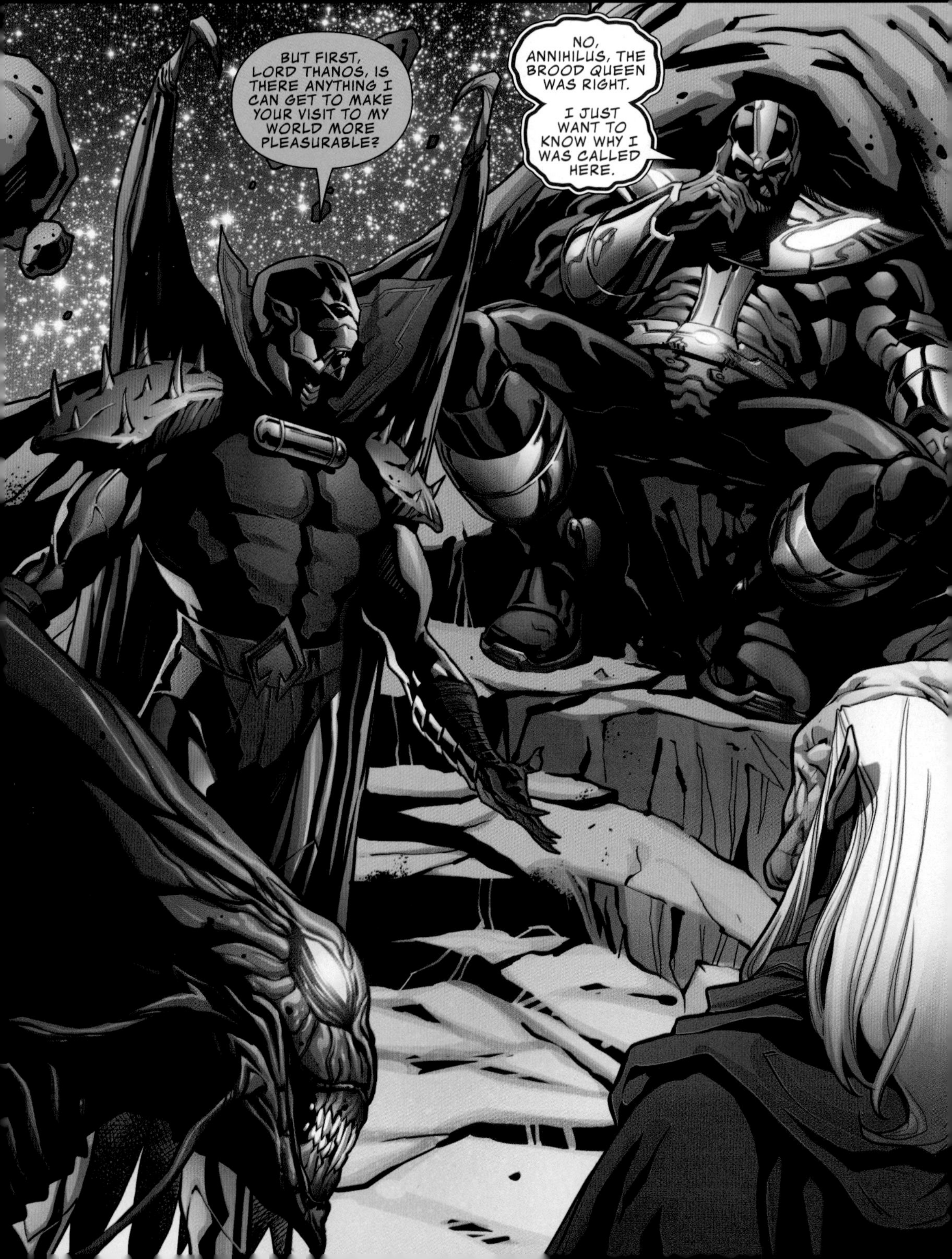
BUT FIRST, LORD THANOS, IS THERE ANYTHING I CAN GET TO MAKE YOUR VISIT TO MY WORLD MORE PLEASURABLE?
NO, ANNIHILUS, THE BROOD QUEEN WAS RIGHT.
I JUST WANT TO KNOW WHY I WAS CALLED HERE.

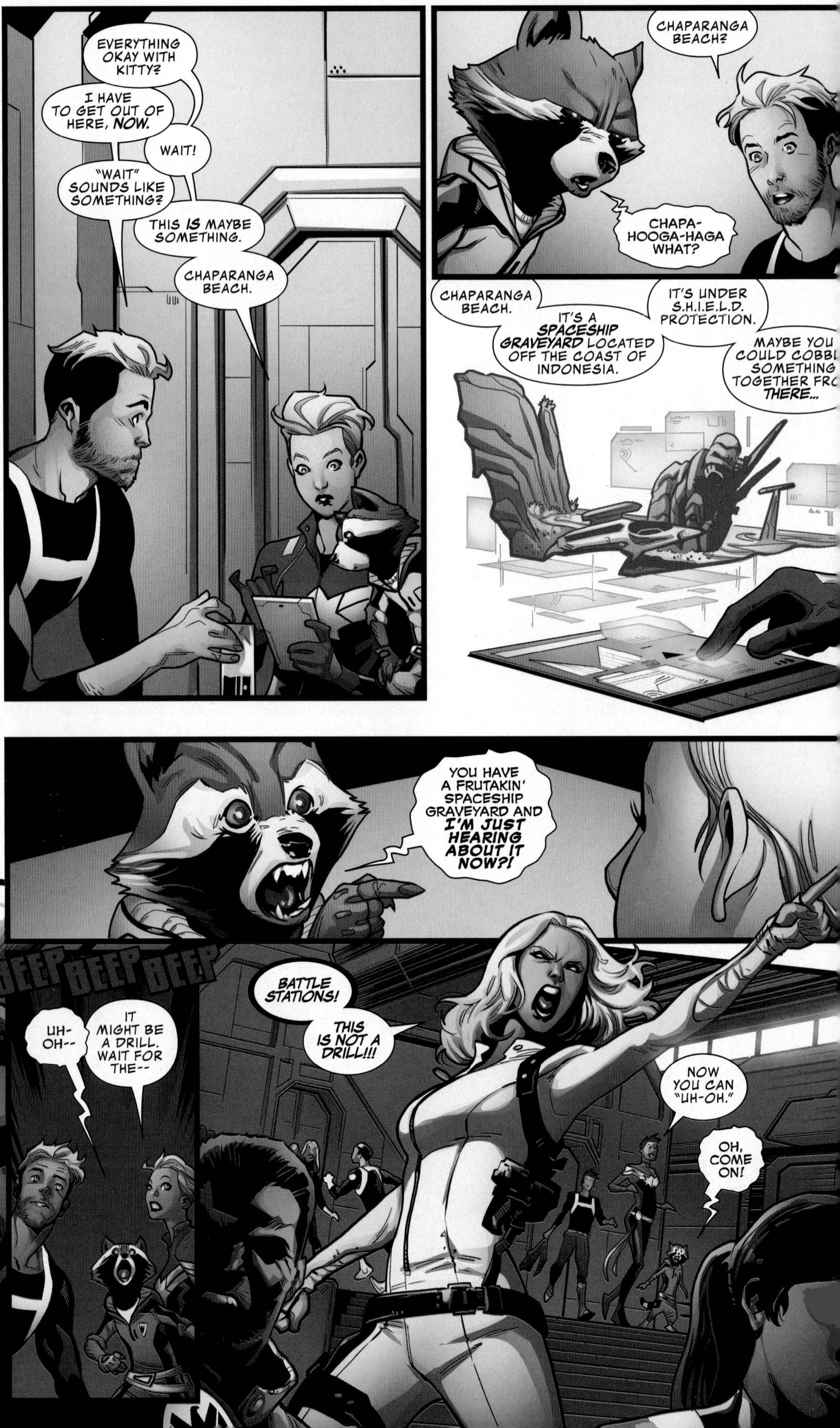
EVERYTHING OKAY WITH KITTY?
I HAVE TO GET OUT OF HERE, NOW.
WAIT!
"WAIT" SOUNDS LIKE SOMETHING?
THIS IS MAYBE SOMETHING.
CHAPARANGA BEACH.
CHAPARANGA BEACH?
CHAPA-HOOGA-HAGA WHAT?
CHAPARANGA BEACH.
IT'S A SPACESHIP GRAVEYARD LOCATED OFF THE COAST OF INDONESIA.
IT'S UNDER S.H.I.E.L.D. PROTECTION.
MAYBE YOU COULD COBB SOMETHING TOGETHER FR THERE...
YOU HAVE A FRUTAKIN' SPACESHIP GRAVEYARD AND I'M JUST HEARING ABOUT IT NOW?!
BEEP BEEP BEEP
UH-OH--
IT MIGHT BE A DRILL. WAIT FOR THE--
BATTLE STATIONS!
THIS IS NOT A DRILL!!!
NOW YOU CAN "UH-OH."
OH, COME ON!

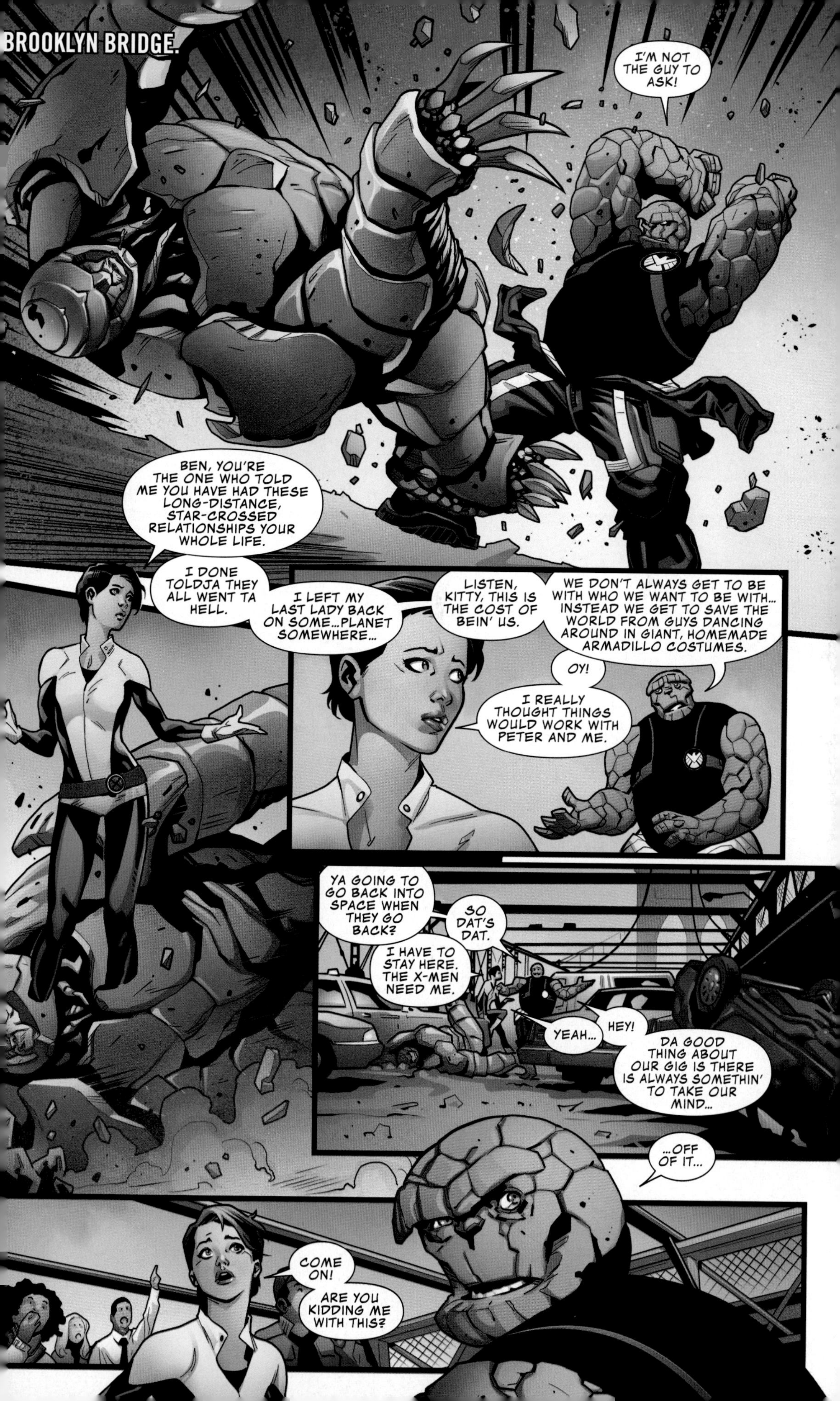
BROOKLYN BRIDGE.
I'M NOT THE GUY TO ASK!
BEN, YOU'RE THE ONE WHO TOLD ME YOU HAVE HAD THESE LONG-DISTANCE, STAR-CROSSED RELATIONSHIPS YOUR WHOLE LIFE.
I DONE TOLDJA THEY ALL WENT TA HELL.
I LEFT MY LAST LADY BACK ON SOME...PLANET SOMEWHERE...
LISTEN, KITTY, THIS IS THE COST OF BEIN' US.
WE DON'T ALWAYS GET TO BE WITH WHO WE WANT TO BE WITH... INSTEAD WE GET TO SAVE THE WORLD FROM GUYS DANCING AROUND IN GIANT, HOMEMADE ARMADILLO COSTUMES.
OY!
I REALLY THOUGHT THINGS WOULD WORK WITH PETER AND ME.
YA GOING TO GO BACK INTO SPACE WHEN THEY GO BACK?
SO DAT'S DAT.
I HAVE TO STAY HERE. THE X-MEN NEED ME.
YEAH...
HEY!
DA GOOD THING ABOUT OUR GIG IS THERE IS ALWAYS SOMETHIN' TO TAKE OUR MIND...
...OFF OF IT...
COME ON!
ARE YOU KIDDING ME WITH THIS?

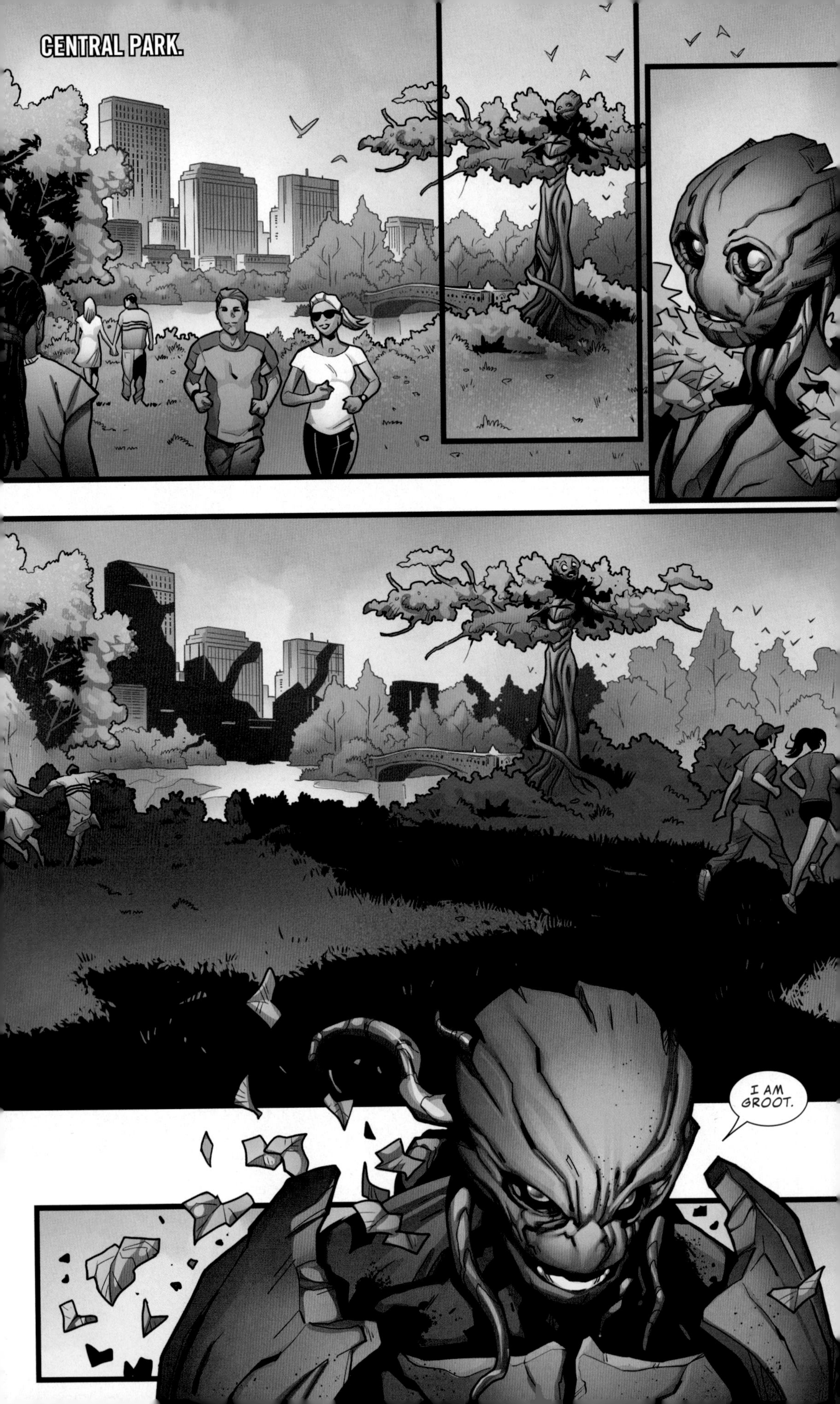
CENTRAL PARK.
I AM GROOT.

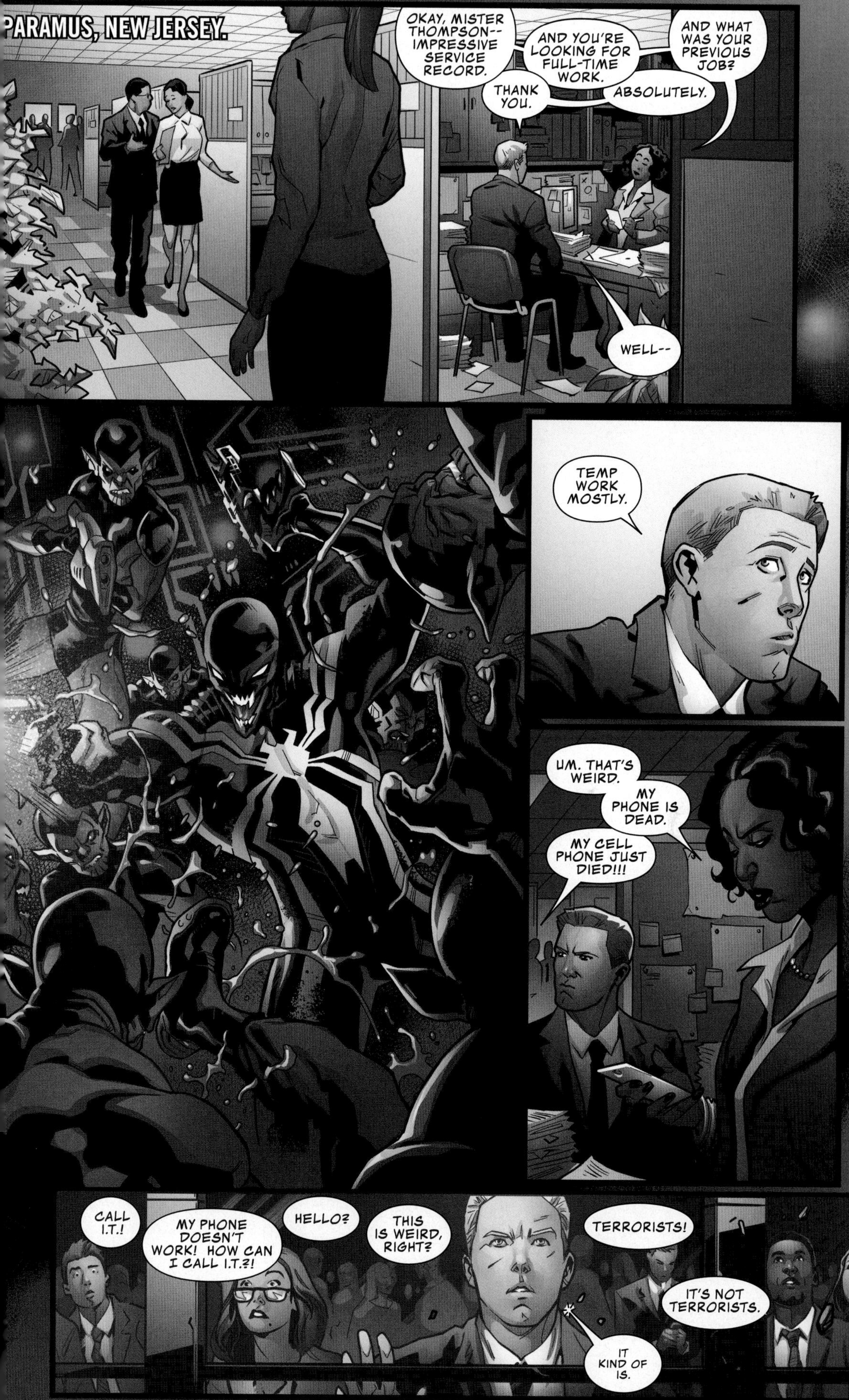
PARAMUS, NEW JERSEY.
OKAY, MISTER THOMPSON-- IMPRESSIVE SERVICE RECORD.
THANK YOU.
AND YOU'RE LOOKING FOR FULL-TIME WORK.
ABSOLUTELY.
AND WHAT WAS YOUR PREVIOUS JOB?
WELL--
TEMP WORK MOSTLY.
UM. THAT'S WEIRD.
MY PHONE IS DEAD.
MY CELL PHONE JUST DIED!!!
CALL I.T.!
MY PHONE DOESN'T WORK! HOW CAN I CALL I.T.?!
HELLO?
THIS IS WEIRD, RIGHT?
TERRORISTS!
IT'S NOT TERRORISTS.
IT KIND OF IS.

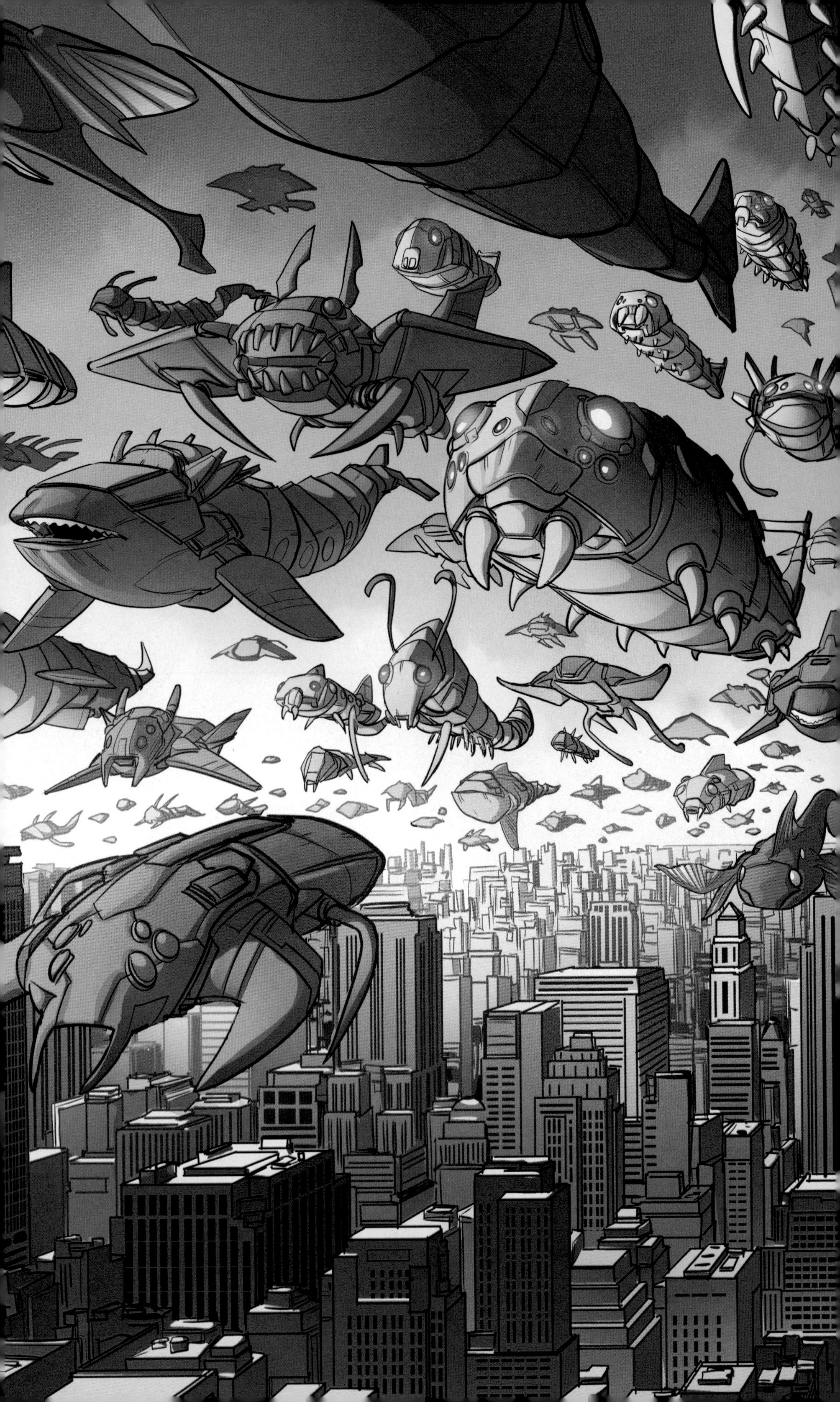

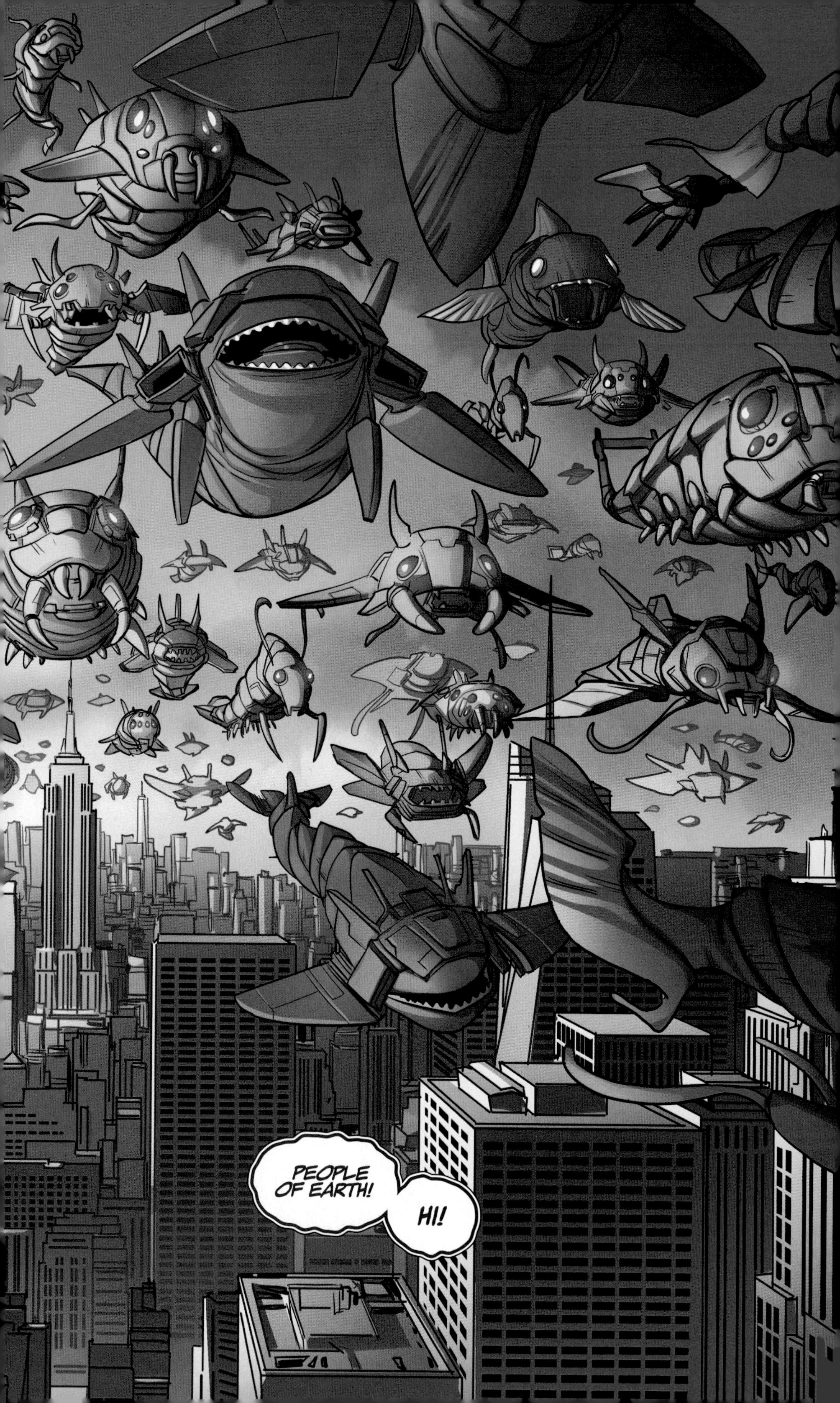
PEOPLE OF EARTH!
HI!

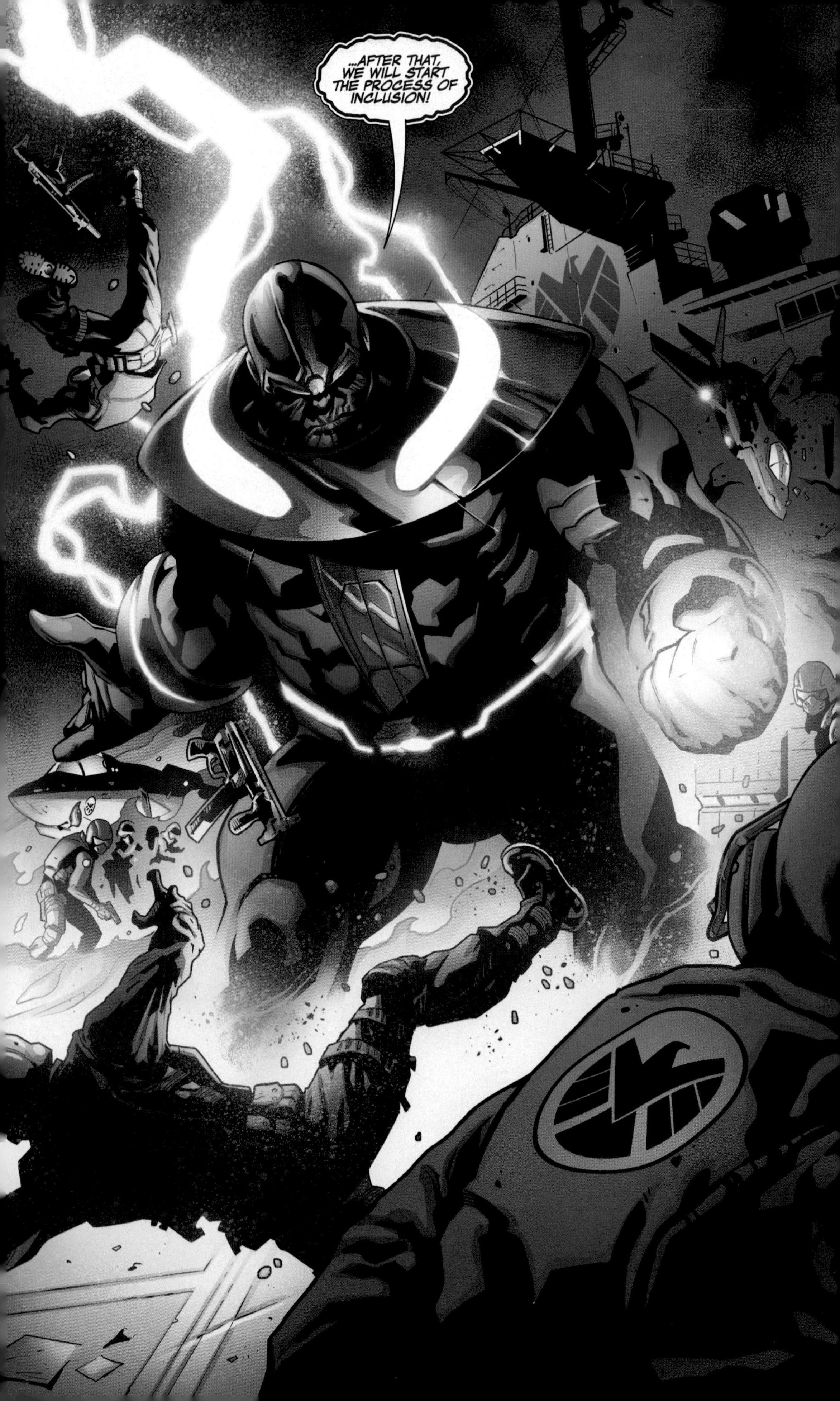
...AFTER THAT, WE WILL START THE PROCESS OF INCLUSION!

THANOS IS HERE.

I HEARD.

AS IN "RIGHT HERE."

WE KNEW SOMETHING LIKE THIS MIGHT--

WOW. ARE YOU OKAY?

I'M REALLY NOT IN THE MOOD FOR THIS TODAY!

CAN YOU GET IT TOGETHER?

NO.

NO?

I MEAN, WHY START NOW?

THIS MIGHT SOUND A LITTLE CRAZY COMING FROM ME, BUT I THINK, MAYBE, AND I COULD BE NUTS, BUT I THINK THANOS MIGHT BE *LYING* ABOUT THIS *NOT* BEING AN INVASION. THIS OBVIOUSLY *IS* A FULL-SCALE, MULTI-SPECIES INVASION, AND HE IS USING *US* AS A DECOY, A DISTRACTION, A DEFLECTION, IF YOU WILL, TO ENGAGE US ALL IN A GAME OF CHASING OUR OWN TAILS WHILE HIS PARTNERS IN THOSE OTHER SHIPS START THE *REAL* INVASION PLAN. MEANWHILE, AND FOLLOW ME HERE, IF HE GETS TO KILL ONE OR TWO OF US WHILE HIS PLAN REVEALS ITSELF, HE IS A VERY HAPPY THANOS, BUT IF HE DOESN'T, IF WE *WIN*, HIS NEW PARTNERS UP THERE WILL JUST STEP OVER HIS DEAD BODY TO GET TO THE REST OF US AND WE'LL BE *SEVERELY* OUTGUNNED AND JUST GENUINELY EXHAUSTED FROM FIGHTING THANOS IN THE FIRST PLACE, AND THEY WILL TAKE THE PLANET AND YOU CAN SAY GOODBYE TO IN-N-OUT BURGER AND VOODOO DOUGHNUTS!

IDIOTS!

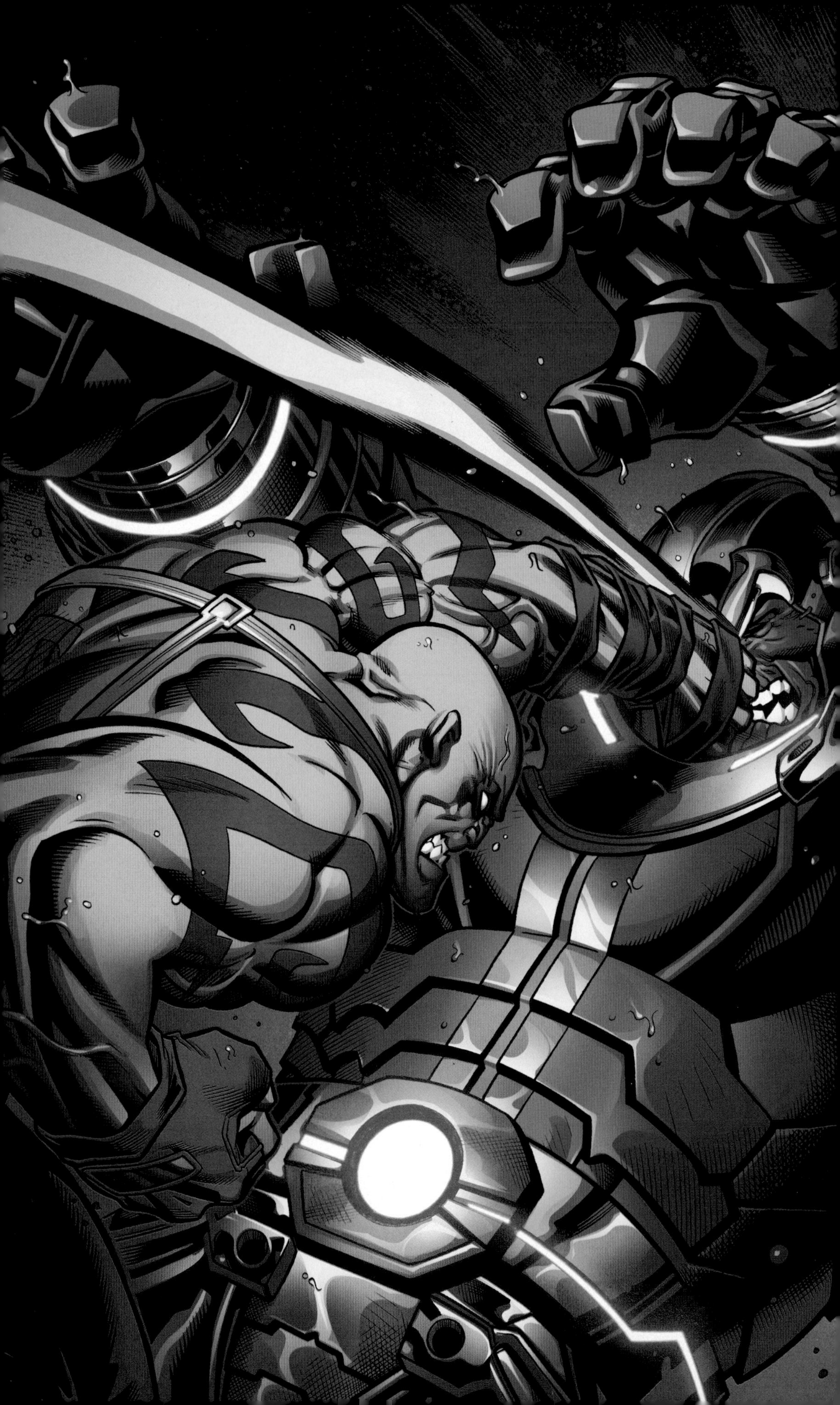

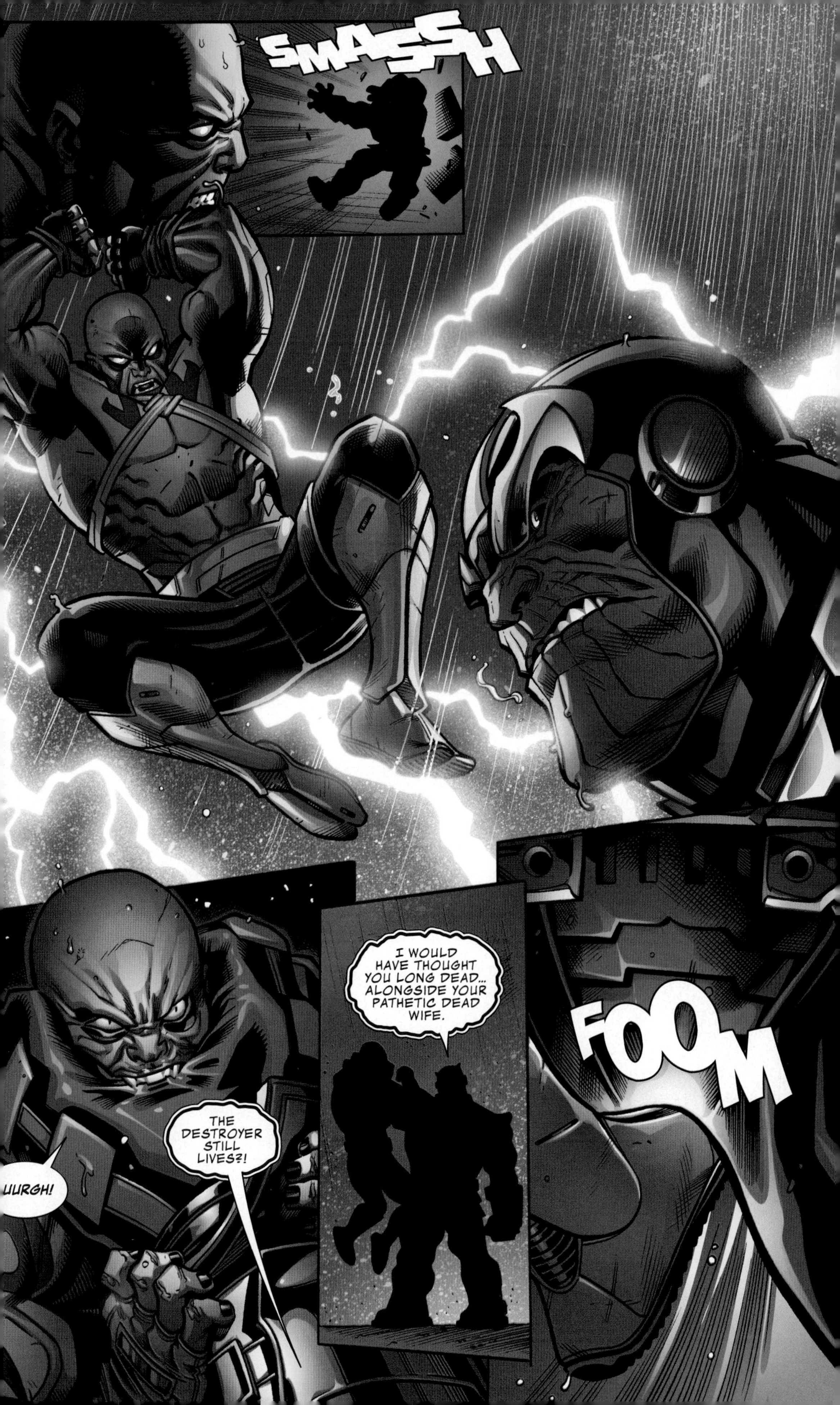

SMASSH
I WOULD HAVE THOUGHT YOU LONG DEAD... ALONGSIDE YOUR PATHETIC DEAD WIFE.
FOOM
UURGH!
THE DESTROYER STILL LIVES?!

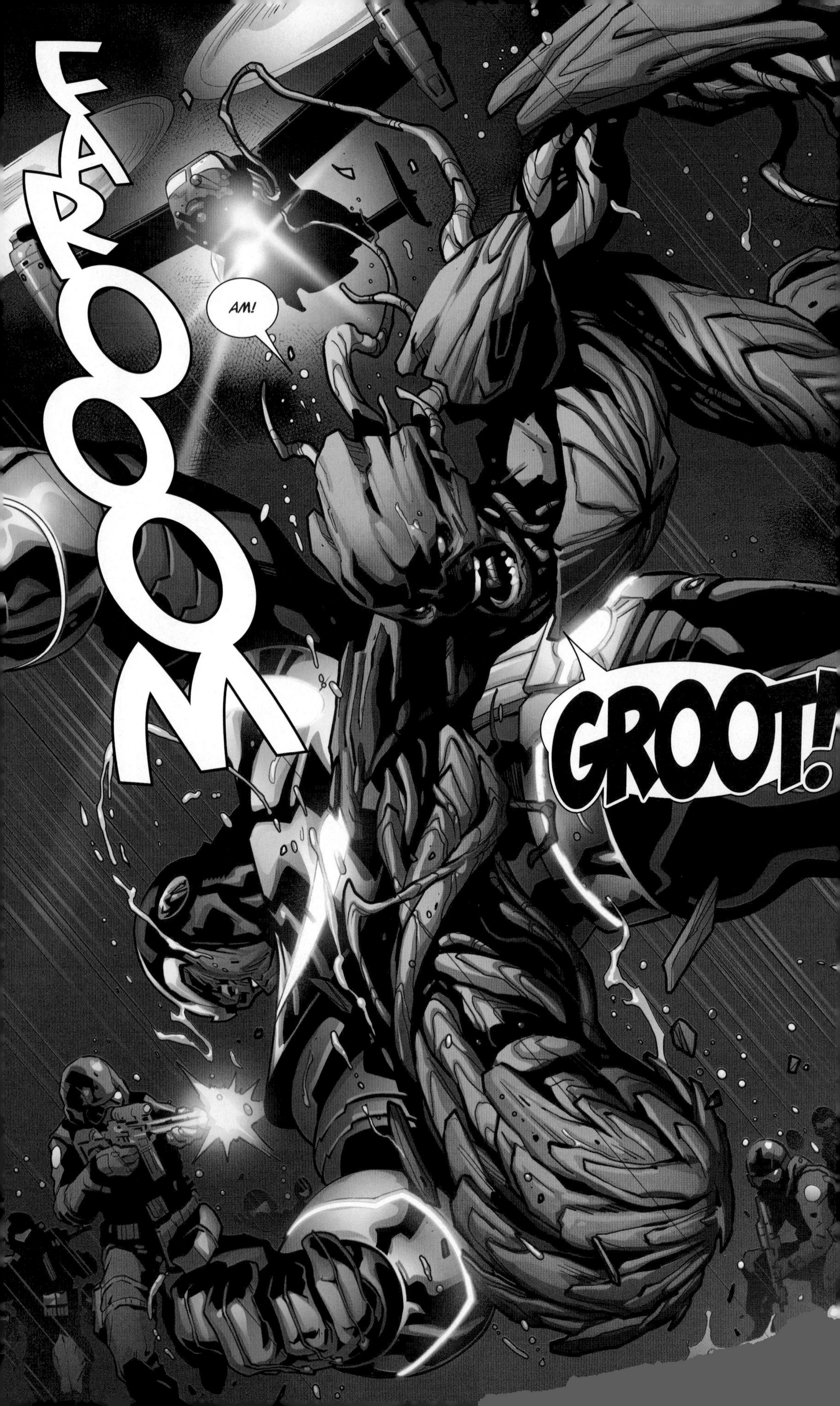

CARROOOM
AM!
GROOT!

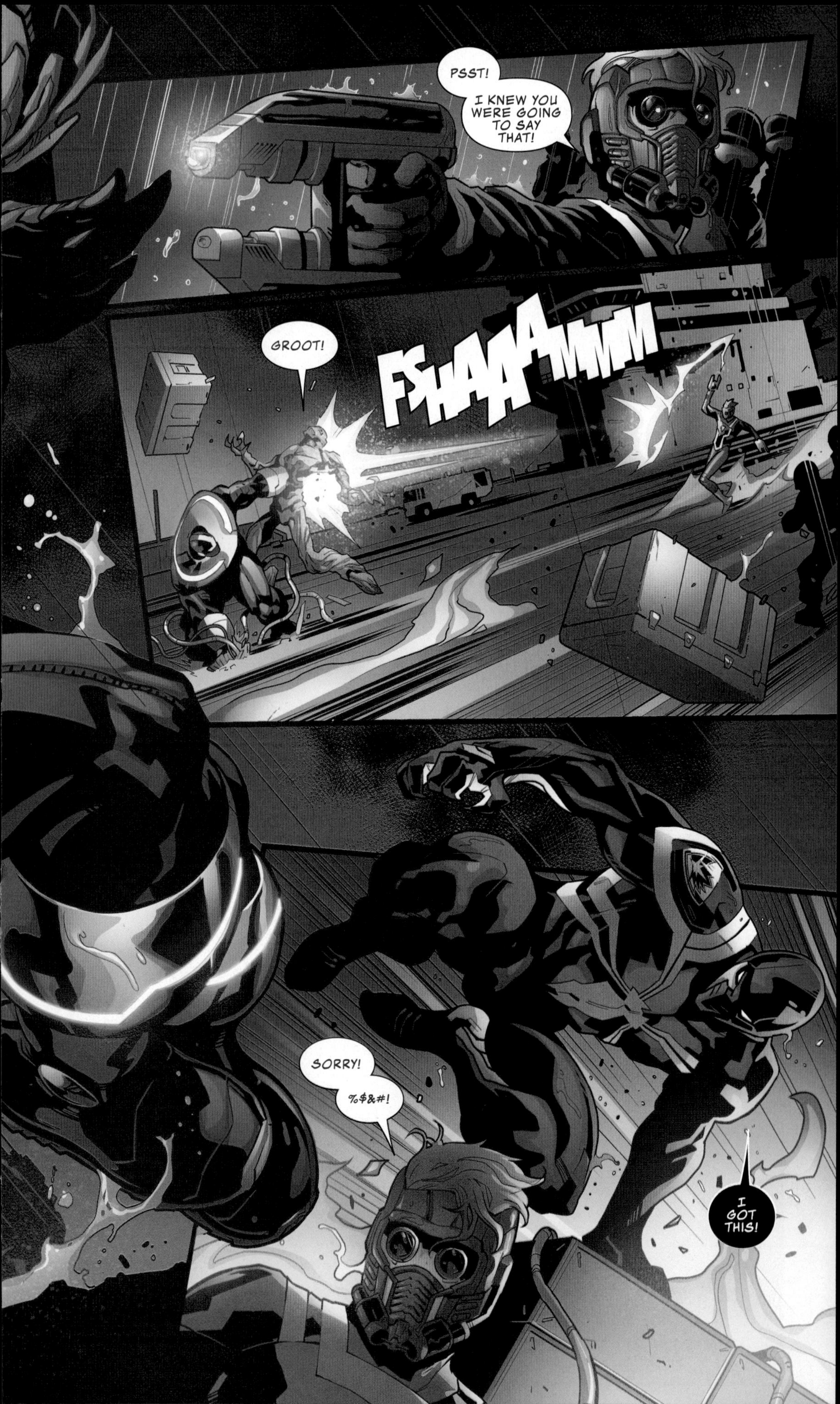
PSST!
I KNEW YOU WERE GOING TO SAY THAT!
GROOT!
FSHAAAMMM
SORRY!
%$&#!
I GOT THIS!

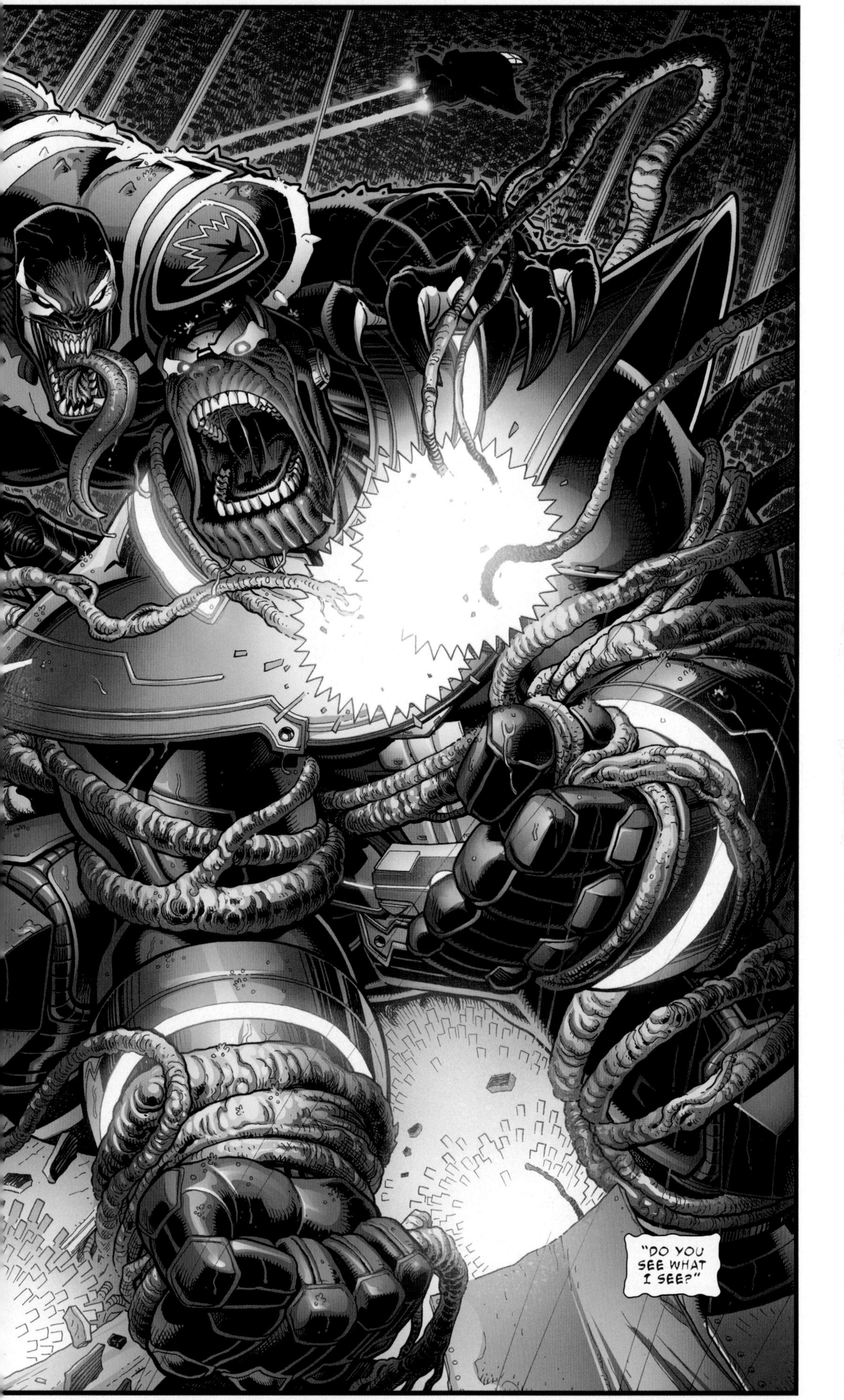
"DO YOU SEE WHAT I SEE?"

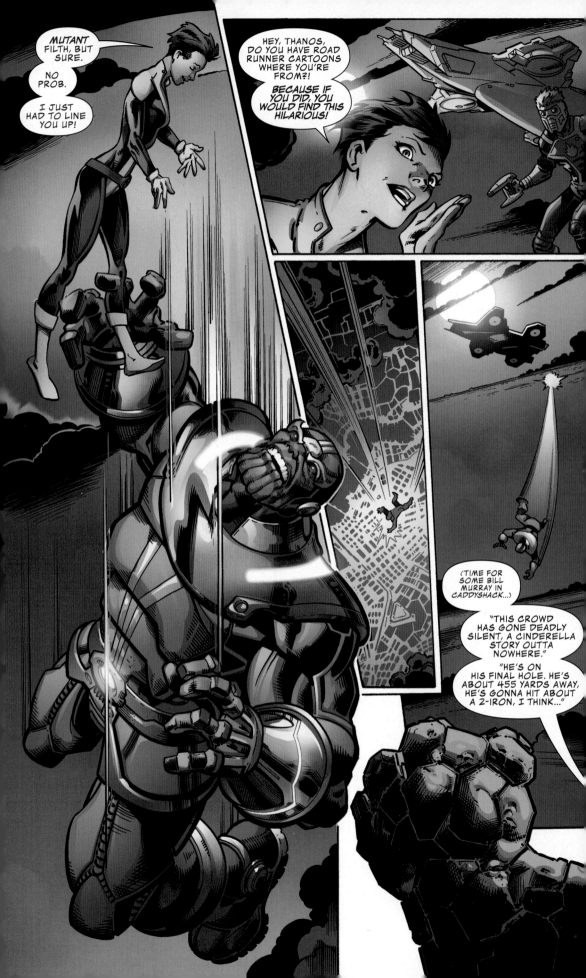

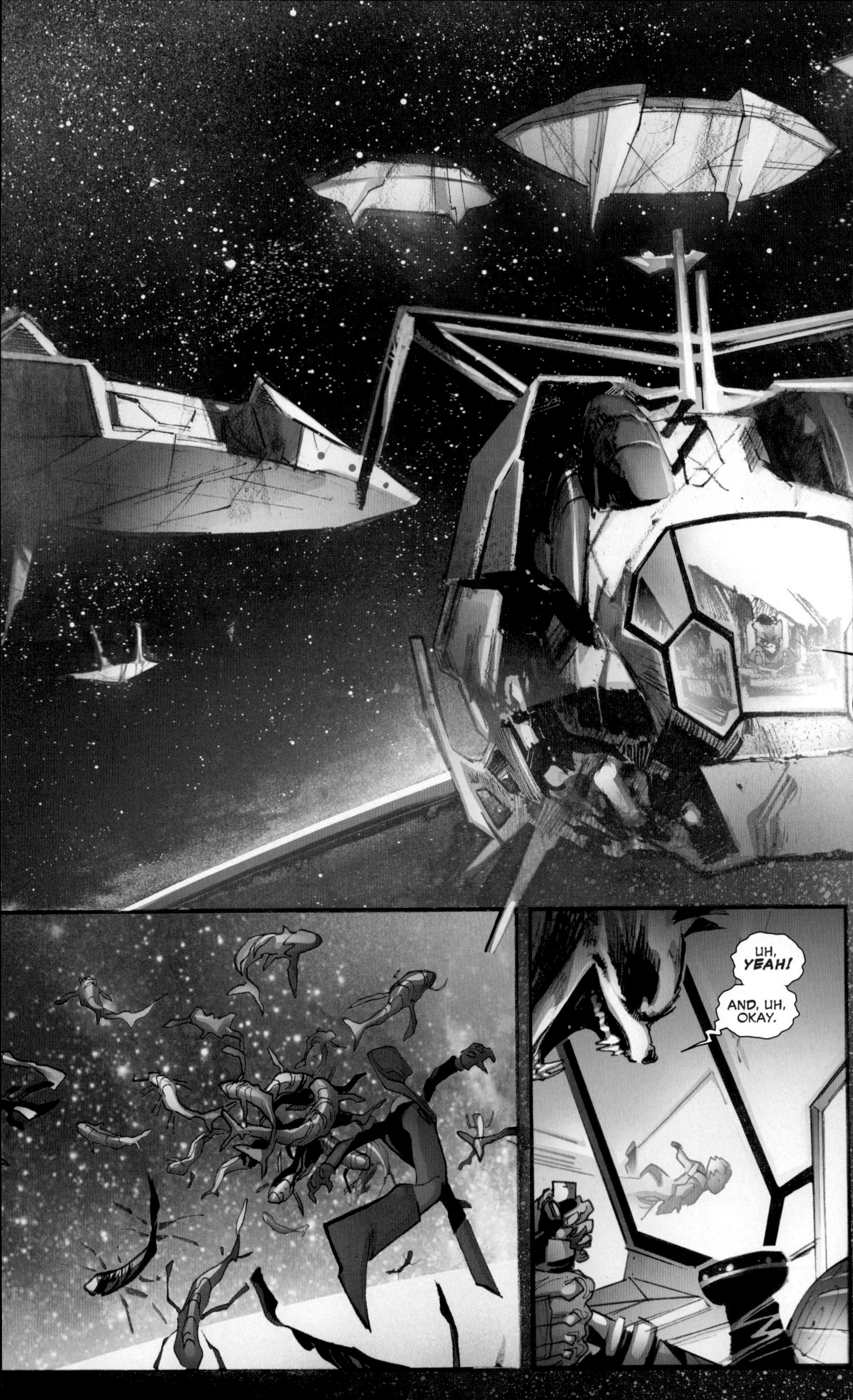
UH, YEAH!
AND, UH, OKAY.

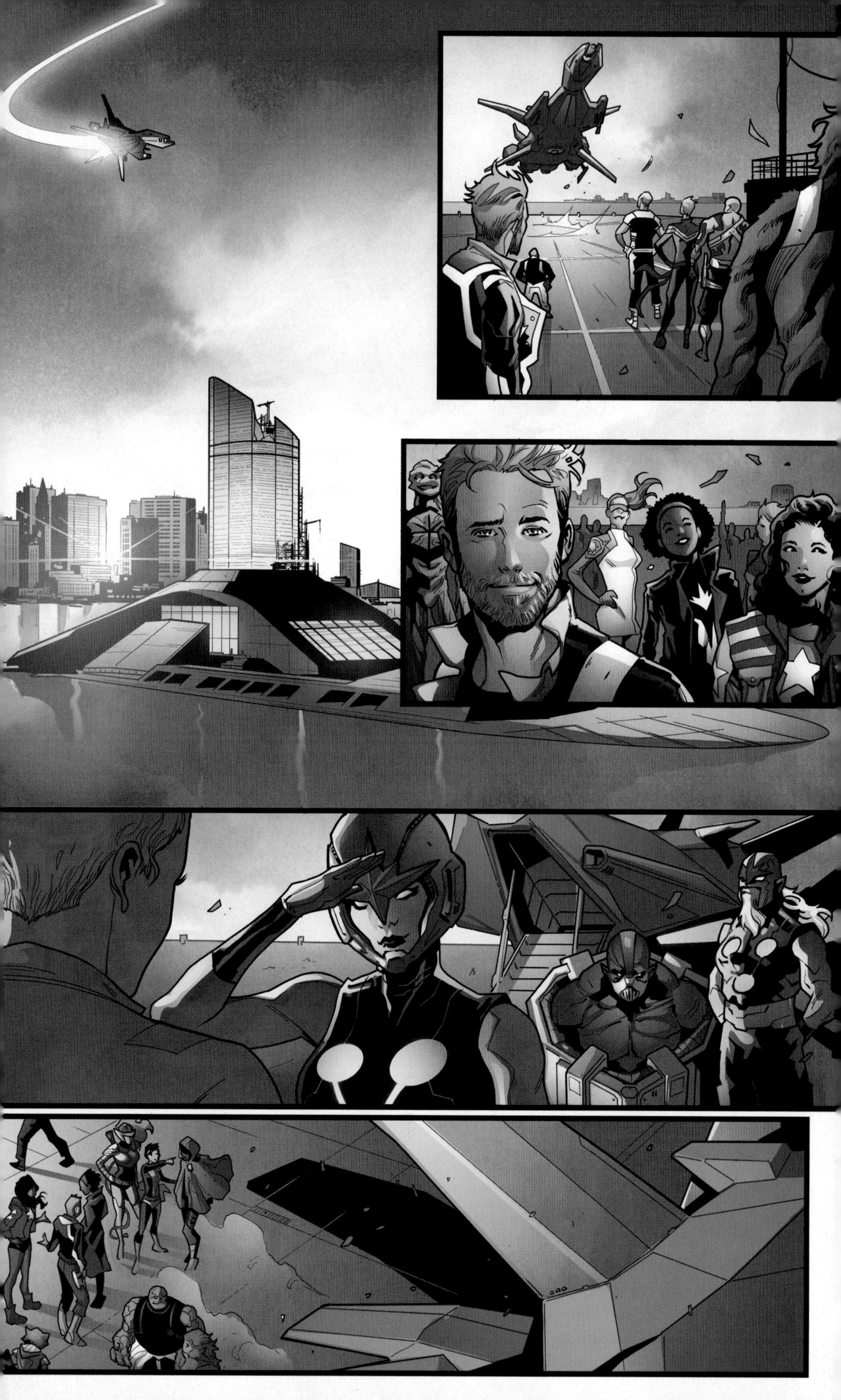

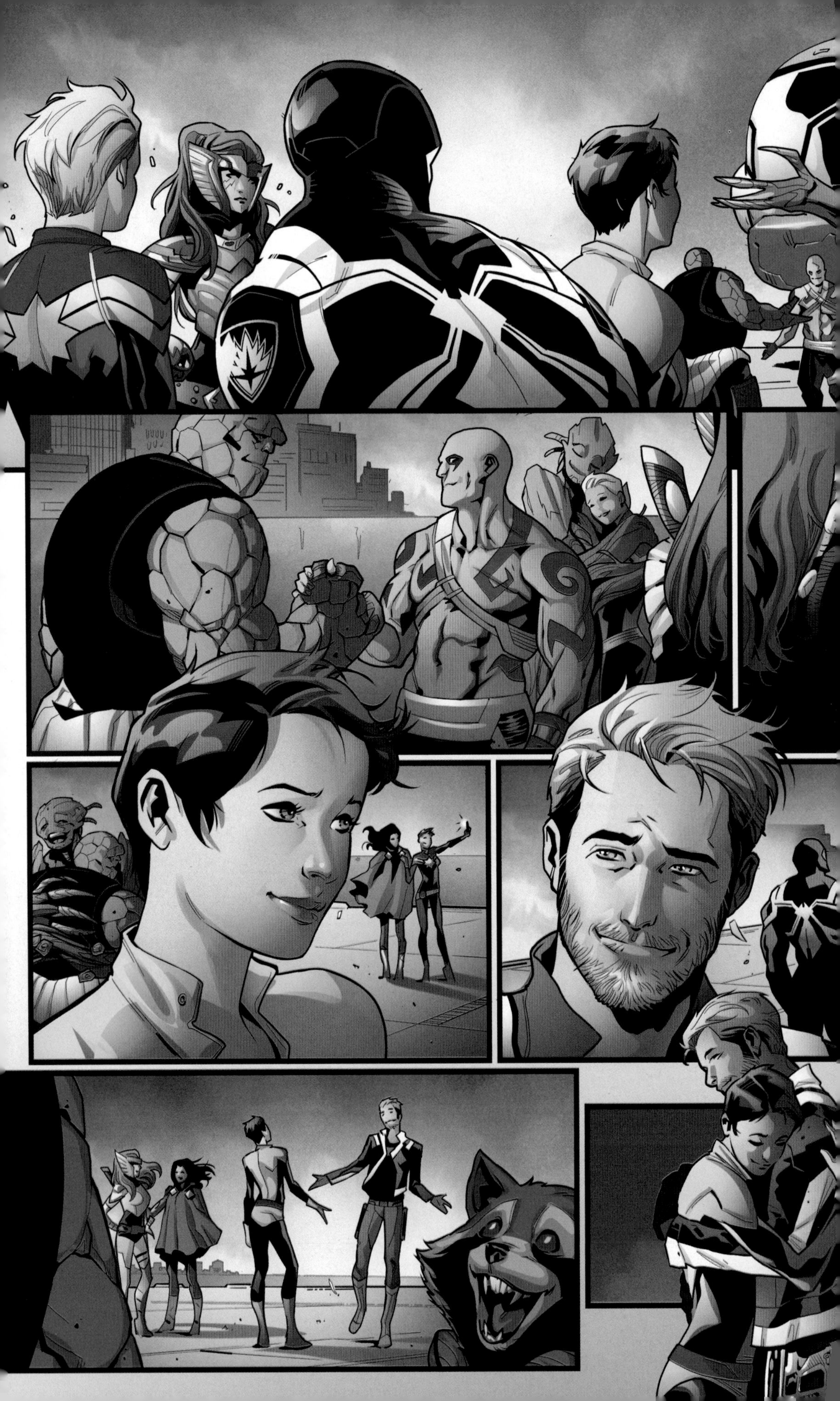

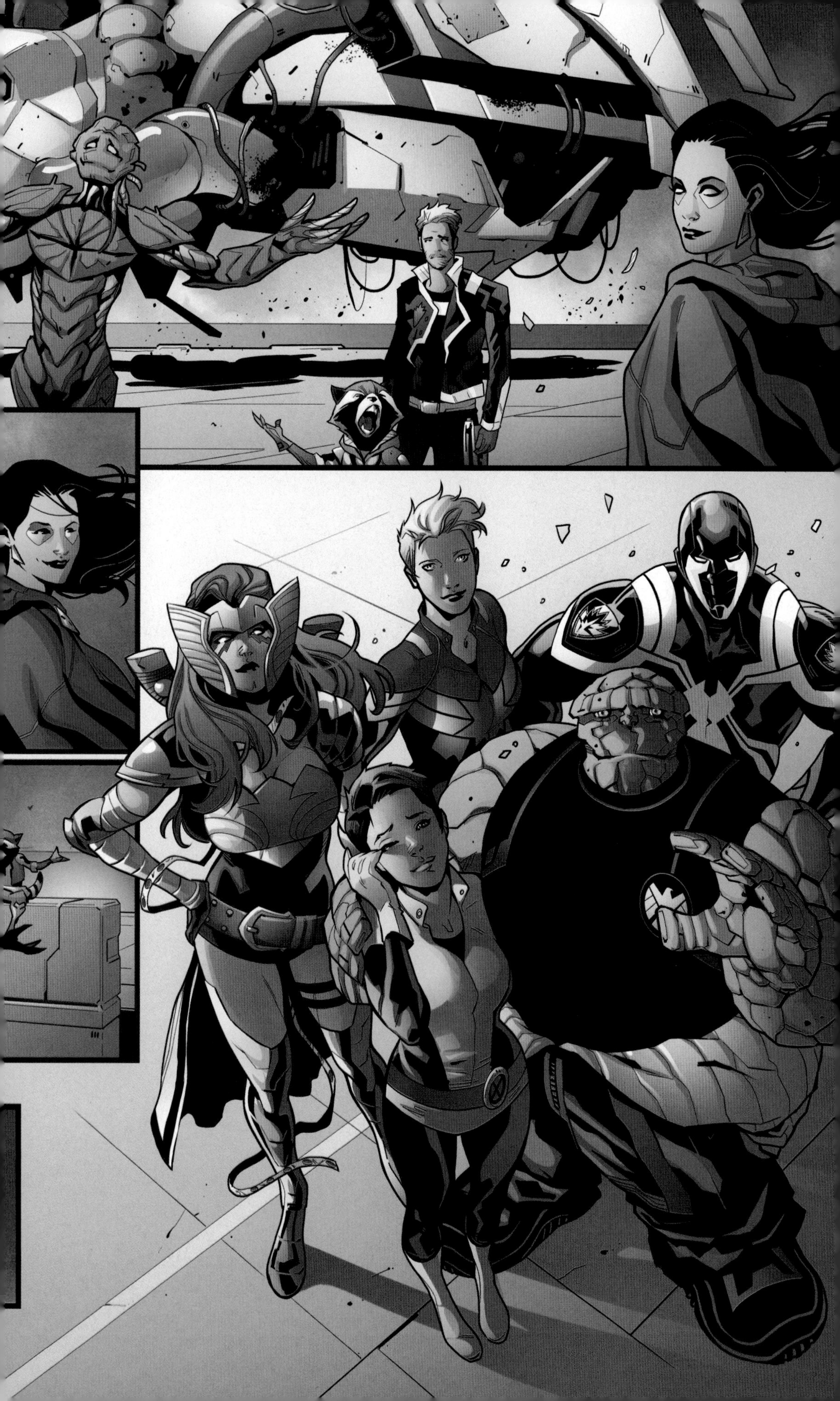

FAREWELL TO THE GUARDIANS OF THE GALAXY ...FOR NOW

By the time you read this I will have already written my final issue months ago. I have some perspective and, good Lord, I do miss GUARDIANS.

It was never a book I ever thought I would write. First of all, I broke into comics as a crime fiction writer and artist. I got whatever success I have off of creations like Jessica Jones. I wasn't the "space" guy. And I certainly wasn't the "talking-raccoon-alien space" guy, I was the "face down in the gutter" guy.

I got the job in an unusual way. Years ago, for quite a few years, the only people who had ever heard of the Guardians of the Galaxy was us deep-level, hard-core, not-messin'-around, always-ahead-of-the-pop-culture-curve-and-never-ever-getting-any-credit-for-it Marvel zombies. We Marvel zombies know what's coming before everyone else.

Abnett and Lanning knew.

Everybody else was stuck watching the trailer for the remake of *The Day the Earth Stood Still*. (It starts off well...)

It was around this time that I was part of Marvel's Cinematic Universe Creative Committee—a group of executives and creators brought together to consult on the bigger choices being made in what is now the most successful film studio in history. Once the hits really started rolling, Kevin Feige and the group started taking a hard look at what the next wave of movies could and should be. They even had writers working on drafts to see what would come out—to see what would rise up.

Because of this I read the early draft of Nicole Perlman's "Guardians of the Galaxy" script. It was she—and she doesn't get enough credit for this, in my opinion—who, with her writing, proved to the studio that the Abnett and Lanning GUARDIANS was a franchise of *Star Wars* potential. It was reading those outlines and drafts that sent me back to the earlier classic source material. I had read almost all of it as a fan but never as someone considering the true potential of these characters on a worldwide basis.

Going back and rereading the '70s origin of Peter Quill and all of the early Starlin material put me in a bit of a creative craze. I said it when we were first promoting this series and I'll say it now: Quill's original origin is as strong as Spider-Man's or Superman's. It's just not as well known.

I was so over-the-top excited about the potential of the Guardians, I guess I never shut up about it. And I guess some of my co-workers were so surprised to see me so passionate about a genre I had shown so little interest in creatively, that when Marvel decided to bring back the comic book, Marvel President Dan Buckley recommended me.

The crime fiction guy accidentally talked his way into a book about talking raccoons and ray guns. (I know that's not what it's really about, shh!)

I actually wasn't sure how long I would write the book for. A year? I had so many projects I wanted to do. And then, as often happens to me, once I start writing I can't stop. The characters start pitching stories themselves. They interact with each other without consulting me as I'm writing them. The entire Marvel galaxy started to take shape in my head. All these ideas. New characters. And, oh my God! I'm also the writer of X-MEN! I love when the X-Men go into outer space. The X-Men have to go to outer space and team up with the Guardians. Like that cool Alpha Flight/X-Men series from years ago that—oh no! Kitty and Peter just fell in love! Neil Gaiman (What? Yes!) just gave Angela to Marvel! Sam Humphries just told me about his idea for "Black Vortex." Oh good, the movie was a hit and now everybody knows who the Guardians are. And they like them!

And all this time the book was so much fun to make. The best artists in comics love to draw the Guardians.

And as if I weren't having a creatively awesome time, as if I weren't working with great artists, there's the fact that every single child that I, as a father of four, come in contact with stares at me as if I'm David Bowie when they hear I work on the GUARDIANS OF THE GALAXY.

I have worked on so many major franchises, braggy time, that have been turned into movies, including co-creating JESSICA JONES with Michael Gaydos, but the most awestruck looks I've ever gotten from strangers and friends are when they hear I work on GUARDIANS OF THE GALAXY!

Just today, I'm waiting outside for my son and daughters to get off the school bus and my 4-year-old son is carrying the brand-new GUARDIANS Treasury Edition that Marvel put out. And from the look of it he's been dragging it around all day, and it's about the same size as him. I asked him why he took it to school. He said, "I can't wait to learn to read because I've been staring at this all day thinking reading it would be a lot of fun. Which words did you write, Dad?"

So, writing GUARDIANS has been creatively rewarding and fun (and comics should be fun once in a while), and I am honored to have worked with every single artist, colorist, letterer, editor, intern, production assistant, proofreader, and designer who worked on this book.

The artist names you know. I can tell you that every single one of them, from the ship-launching Steve McNiven to Valerio Schiti, in whose magnificent hands the book finally settled, there hasn't been one bad-looking page on this book since we began. Every single page was world-class, top-to-bottom gorgeous. Everyone was a pleasure to work with.

Take this issue as an example of everything I love about working with Marvel Comics. Jordan, who leads the outstanding editing team of Kathleen and Darren for all these galactic books and *Star Wars* and all kinds of other projects, really went out of his way to make sure that my last issue had the pages and the talent for a special send-off. He lined up some of my all-time favorite artists for the big jam fight. (And if you think coordinating that is easy, nuh-uh.)

It all just shows the kind of love and dedication that goes on behind the scenes. Jordan leads a team of editors and craftsmen who work tirelessly and, on Fridays, sometimes until the wee hours of the morning...making sure that your books go to press on time and that the stories are well told.

It's a thankless job. Except right here. If you enjoyed anything that has gone on in this book over the years, take a look at the names of the editors and thank them for the job well done.

To all the original creators of the original incarnations of the characters, to the creators on the DnA books that came before us, to the filmmakers and animators who helped craft everyone's shared love of these characters on a global scale, thank you for allowing me to be part of the team.

I'm not leaving the book because I'm sick of it. I'm leaving it because it's time and I've been DYING to do this DEFENDERS book for years! I'm telling you this because for what comics cost I would think you'd like to know that every single issue of this book was made with love and passion.

What will I miss most of all? Making up alien swear words and getting away with it.

If you're looking for me, I'll be over at IRON MAN, SPIDER-MAN, and THE DEFENDERS (please buy it, it's so gorgeous), and I always have a couple of surprises coming.

As for readers of this book, stay right where you are because I know what Gerry and the gang have planned. I will be reading right along with you. Well, not right along next to you but, you know, spiritually.

But for now, may the Force be—no, that's not right. What was the thing for this one? There was nothing for this one, right? Oh, it's classic rock. We can't do classic rock in the letter column!! Flarknard!!

Bendis!
Milky Way Galaxy, 2017

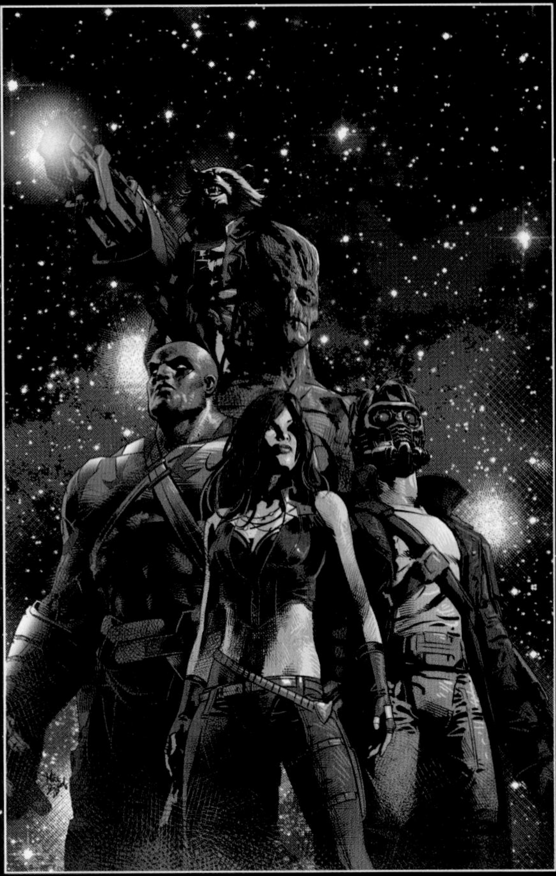

#19 VARIANT BY
MIKE DEODATO JR. & RAIN BEREDO

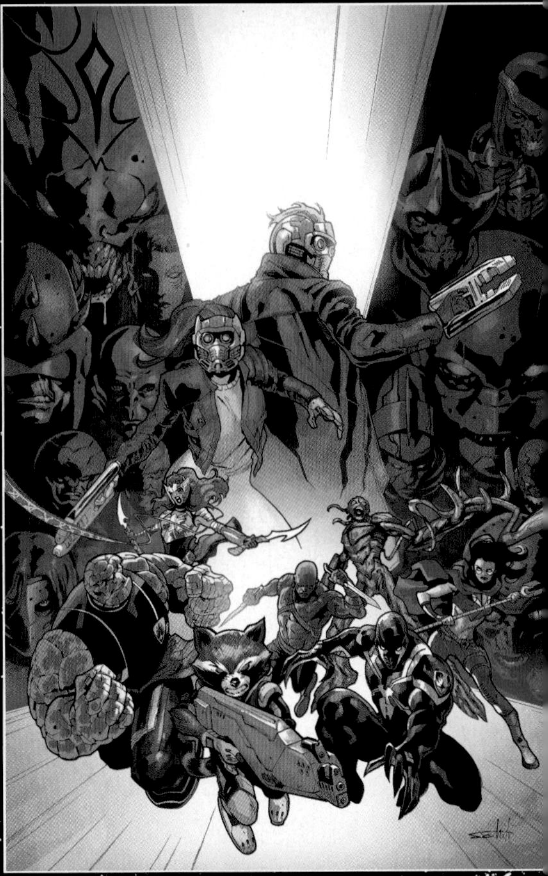

#19 VARIANT BY
VALERO SCHITI & RAIN BEREDO

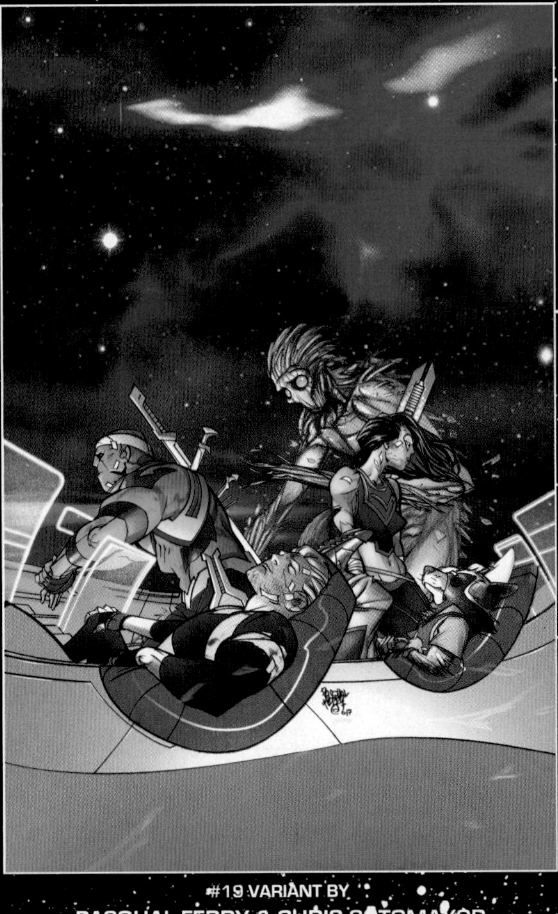

#19 VARIANT BY
PASQUAL FERRY & CHRIS SOTOMAYOR

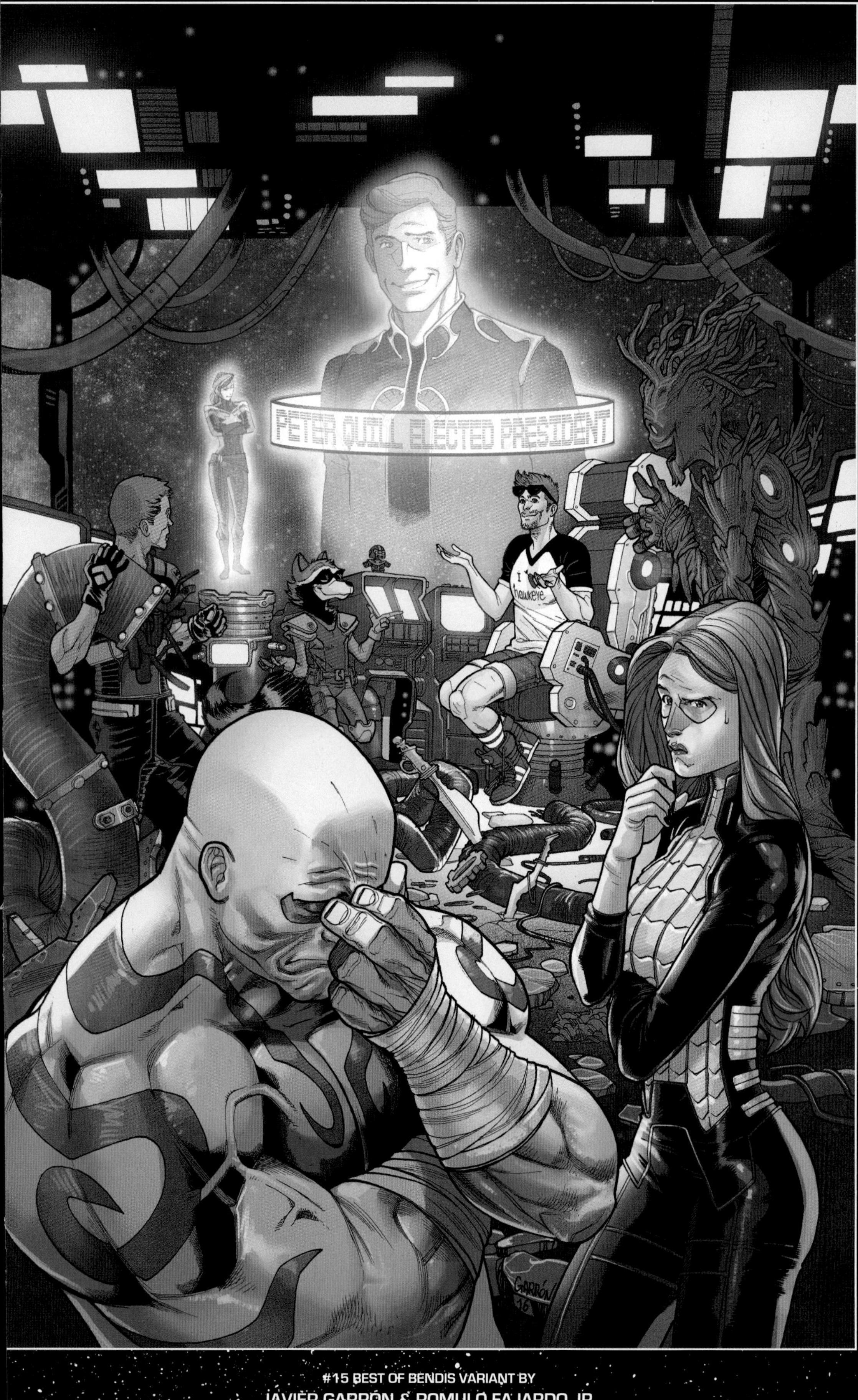
PETER QUILL ELECTED PRESIDENT
I hawkeye
GARRÓN 16

#15 BEST OF BENDIS VARIANT BY
JAVIER GARRÓN & ROMULO FAJARDO JR.

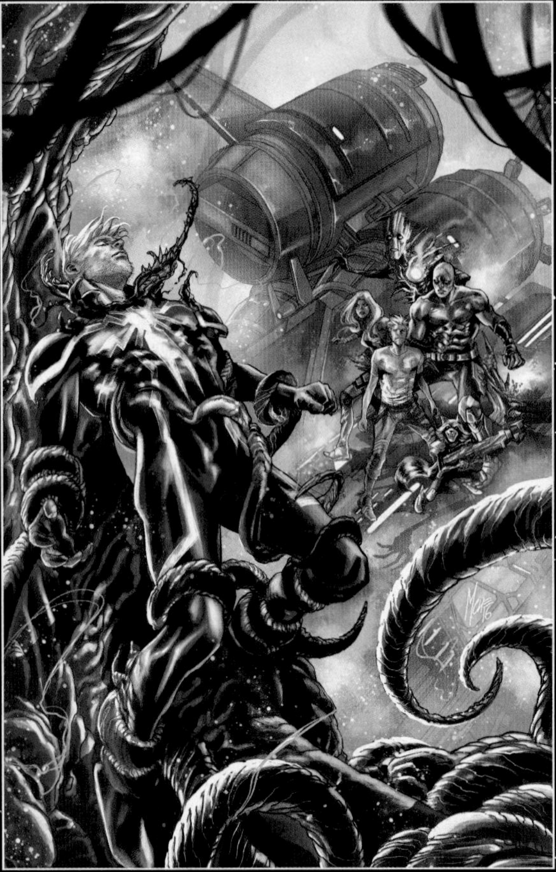

#16 BEST OF BENDIS VARIANT BY
MARCO CHECCHETTO

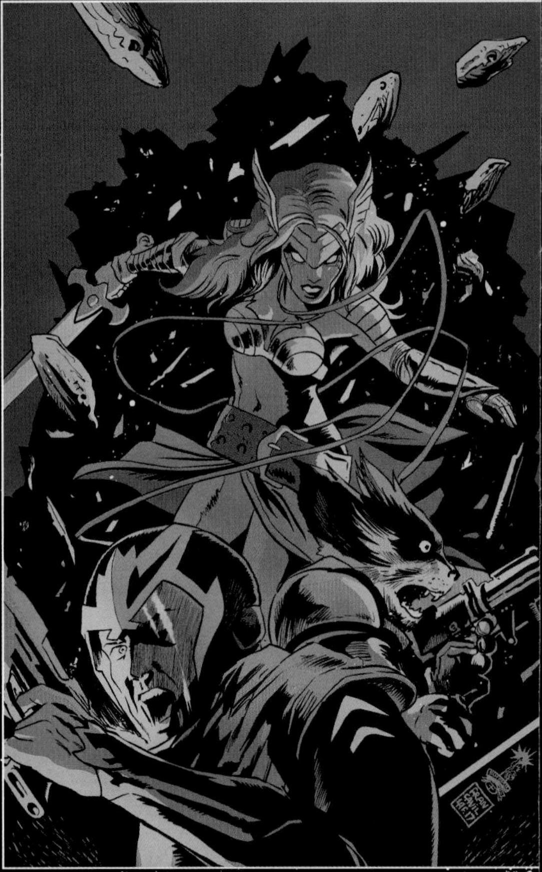

#17 BEST OF BENDIS VARIANT BY
FRANCESCO FRANCAVILLA

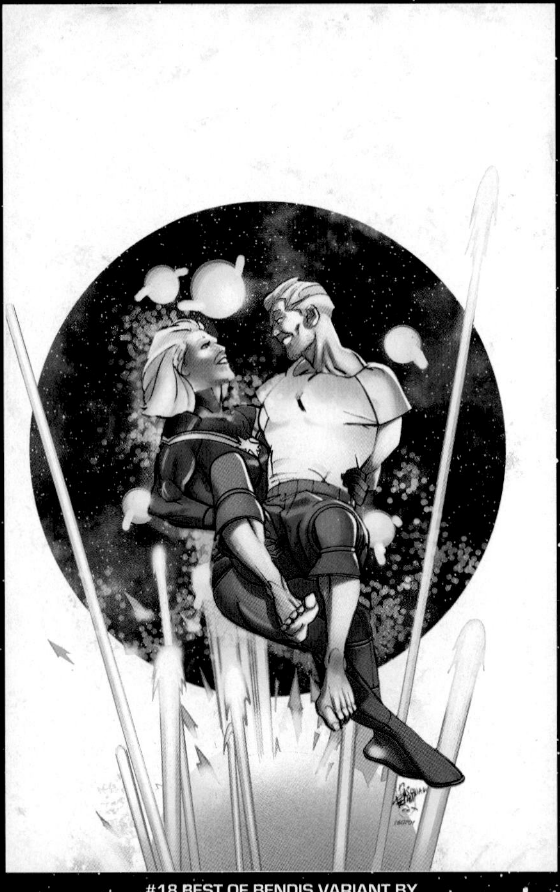

#18 BEST OF BENDIS VARIANT BY
PASQUAL FERRY & CHRIS SOTOMAYOR

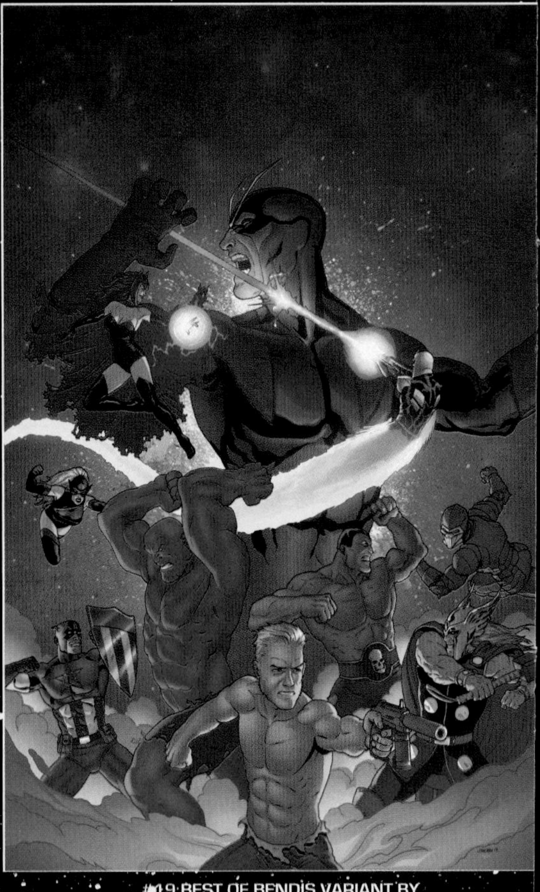

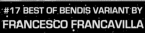

#19 BEST OF BENDIS VARIANT BY
JACEN BURROWS & ANDY TROY